WHIT

WHITE RIOT

The Violent Story of Combat 18

Nick Lowles

MILO BOOKS

First published in November 2001 by Milo Books

ISBN 1 903854 00 8

Printed and bound in Great Britain by
Guernsey Press Co Ltd, Guernsey

MILO BOOKS
P.O.Box 153
Bury
BL0 9FX
info@milobooks.com

About the Author

Nick Lowles has investigated far-right extremists for many years and is co-editor of *Searchlight* magazine. He has worked for *World in Action*, *Panorama* and Channel Four and his work has also appeared in newspapers including the *News of the World*, the *Sunday Telegraph* and *The Mirror*. He is the previous author (with Graeme McLagen) of *Mr Evil*, about the London nailbomber David Copeland, and co-editor of the book *White Noise*, about the international skinhead music scene.

Publisher's Note

The terms Nazi and National Socialist (with capital initial letters) are generally used to define members of the original National Socialist German Workers' Party. The terms nazi and national socialist (with lower case initial letters) are used to define adherents or advocates of policies characteristic of this party.

Contents

Prologue

ON THE MORNING of Saturday, May 26, 2001, a six-feet tall, shaven-headed man walked into The Lark public house in Oldham. David Tickle cut a menacing figure. A pub doorman based twenty miles away in Wigan, he was a veteran of dozens of brawls. Accompanying him was a local hooligan who knew the area well. The two men checked out the bar: it was almost deserted. Good. They bought drinks and waited for their friends to arrive.

The Lark had been chosen for its out-of-the-way location. Small, poorly lit and unpretentious, it lies two miles from the centre of the former east Lancashire mill town and draws its clientele from several surrounding council estates. Almost all its customers are white. Though it sits on a road connecting two of the main arteries out of Oldham, there is little passing trade. Today would be an exception.

The pub was to be the meeting place for some of the most hardened racist streetfighters in Britain. They had chosen it to avoid the scrutiny of the police and of Anti-Nazi League protestors who were gathering in the town centre. More importantly, the route into town would take them through Coppice, a predominantly Asian housing estate. Oldham had become a focus for racial violence in the preceding few weeks; now these men planned to make it much, much worse. Central to that planning was a hardcore nazi gang known as Combat 18 (C18). Formed less than a decade earlier, it took its name from the first and eighth letters of the alphabet – A and H – the initials of Adolf Hitler. It was committed to racial terror.

Tickle and his friend were soon joined by the London

contingent of Mark Atkinson, Darren Wells and two others. Atkinson and Wells had been key members of C18 for years. "If you don't come on Saturday then you can forget about being involved in Combat ever again," Atkinson had growled into the phone in the days leading up to the Oldham mobilisation. "This is what we always wanted. This is what we've talked about all these years. This is a race war."

With them was another Oldham man who had also been highly active in the preceding weeks, making calls and visiting other towns to rally support. Martin Fielding had been born and bred in the northern town. He was not a typical C18 supporter. His parents were known locally to be fairly liberal and middle class, while his older brother was studying at Cambridge. Fielding was in his early twenties but already had several years experience in C18 behind him. He was also a leading figure in the Oldham football gang known as the "Fine Young Casuals" and, through his hooligan network, had spread the word. Three weeks before, he had helped to bring "boys" from Stockport, Stoke and Huddersfield to Oldham for a confrontation with the Asians, but the police had thwarted their efforts. This time he was more calculated.

"I know The Lark is out of the way but that is the point," Fielding had said, in exasperation, to one local hooligan who complained about the pub's location. "We can gather up without the police watching." He also knew a walk through Coppice estate would elicit a response from the highly tense Asian community.

While the gang in the pub slowly grew, some of their friends were already about in the town centre. Five right-wing Oldham hooligans walked provocatively into an Anti-Nazi League leafleting session; they had been sent to determine ANL numbers in readiness for a possible attack later in the day. After verbal exchanges, the police swiftly move in, holding the racists against a shop front while taking personal details and photographs.

By 11.30am, thirty-five men had assembled in The Lark. Fielding was having to revise down his expected numbers of over 200 but was still optimistic of putting together 150. Then the police turned up. They parked a van outside the pub, much to the hooligans' annoyance. A few tried to slip out the back into a park behind the pub but were soon rounded up and held by police reinforcements who arrived in a second van. Other officers entered the pub and took everyone's details.

The hooligans decided to split up into small groups and reconvene in another pub down the hill. Fielding was in touch with everyone by phone and quickly disseminated the changing plans. He was also in contact with the "Limeside Boys", a local white gang based on the nearby Limeside estate and known for its racism. Even though it was not yet lunchtime, up to fifty Limesiders were drinking in the pub in the heart of the estate. They had intended to link up with the others and march together through Coppice but with the arrival of the police they decided to sit tight until the uniformed presence declined.

Gradually the hooligan/C18 mob began to move, with some heading to The George while others stopped at the White Hart. The police, however, were never far behind and a van was parked outside each pub. At about 1.30pm, the thugs started to congregate in the Britannia, a few hundred yards down the road from The Lark. Their numbers had now swelled to sixty, with the Limeside Boys still remaining out of sight. They were also joined, briefly, by a highly significant figure: Nick Griffin, leader of the British National Party, Britain's largest far-right political party. Like C18 and the National Front, the BNP was keen to capitalise on the racial tension and had recently announced its intention to contest the two Oldham seats in the forthcoming General Election. The local BNP organiser knew some of the people out that day, including Fielding, and he and Griffin came down to the Britannia to meet them.

The C18 boys – especially Atkinson and Wells – were not pleased to see them. Their gang had originally been formed to protect the BNP at marches and rallies but had long since split from its progenitor, amid much acrimony. After a tense exchange – during which on of the C18 men threatened to "do" him – Griffin thought it prudent to leave.

The sun was shining and the beer was flowing but the problem remained of how to escape the police. There were between seventy and eighty now, mostly from Oldham but with small contingents from the gangs of Manchester United, Stockport and Shrewsbury. The Limeside Boys would push the numbers up to over 100, though this was well down on what Fielding had initially thought. He was particularly annoyed at Shrewsbury and Newcastle for failing to turn up with any real numbers despite earlier promises. After a discussion, they decided to split up again.

It seemed to do the trick: though they lost between twenty and thirty along the way, the police failed to keep track of most of them. A flurry of phone calls saw a fleet of taxis ferry about fifty to the Junction pub on the main Ashton Road, on the edge of the Coppice estate. One of their number had a police scanner and had picked up a report that Asian youths, alerted to their presence earlier in the day, were gathering on the estate. The Junction, tactically situated, had seen fighting between whites and Asians only a few days before. Its windows were boarded up, making the pub appear closed. It was an ideal location for the hooligans. They had no immediate intention to steam into the estate, believing that it would not be long before the Asians were aware of their arrival and would come to them. With the boarded windows acting as a shield, and bottles and glasses at hand – not to mention the optics, which had already been eyed up as potential weapons – the mob sat and waited. The air was thick with tension. The police scanner reported Asians mobbing up on the estate and trouble seemed only minutes away.

Their plans were again interrupted by the arrival of the uniformed officers, who, in large numbers, quickly began blocking the main road from the pub into the estate. "You can drink anywhere in town but you cannot go into this estate," an officer told the hooligans. "Anywhere but in here."

A few harangued him. "I thought there were no no-go areas in Oldham," one drunken hooligan retorted sarcastically.

After a half-hour stand off, the main faces discussed their options around a table in the heart of the Junction. Recognising that there was nothing they could do in Coppice, they decided to regroup in The Star, a pub further into town. They would sit out the evening in the hope that the police would eventually stand down. Then, with darkness as a cover, they would take their chances. Martin Fielding, however, had to leave, heading off for his nightshift at a newspaper plant.

Frustration, drink and anger consumed them all. When a car carrying four Asian youths hurled abuse at some of the C18 supporters during the walk down to The Star, one picked up a roadside sign and threw it at the vehicle. The incident put paid to any doubts that the Asians were aware of their presence. Only thirty had reached The Star when another report came through on the scanner of a white woman being dragged from her car and attacked by Asian youths in Coppice. While that would be the only report of the alleged incident, it was enough to enrage the hardcore racists, none more so than the man who had thrown the road sign minutes before.

About thirty minutes later, two teenage boys – one white, one Asian – had a fight in a corner shop close to the predominantly Pakistani area of Glodwick. The skirmish was the continuation of an incident the previous day, when four boys had returned to a school from which they had been expelled for racism and had hurled abuse, and later stones, at Asian pupils. After the disturbance at the shop, the white boy ran off and took refuge in a nearby house. Someone phoned for help.

A small group of white men arrived in the area. There was a confrontation with some Asian youths in Salford Street, near the shop, and a further incident in nearby Roundthorne Road in which Asian-occupied homes were allegedly attacked. The young Asian men of Glodwick estate reacted with fury. Up to 500 spilled onto the streets. In seven hours of mayhem, they pulled together makeshift barricades and hurled petrol bombs, bricks and firecrackers at police lines. Shots were fired from the crowd and, at times, the bombardments of missiles forced police to withdraw. Fifteen officers and ten civilians were injured, and seven people arrested. It was the most serious race riot in Britain for years. The police described as it as "sheer carnage."

C18 was jubilant. It felt that its presence in the town had

helped to provoke the trouble and its leaders were confident that the riots would soon spread. When major racial disturbances followed over the next few weeks in Bradford, Burnley and Stoke over the next few weeks – and when the BNP won the biggest votes ever for a hard-right party at the June General Election – it seemed they might be right. Oldham appeared to have set a pattern. While the riot in the town was the result of racial tension, social deprivation and, to some extent, inadequate policing, its trigger was the actions of C18 thugs and their football hooligan allies who, over a number of weeks, had been trying to incite violence. It seemed C18 had finally got what it wanted. Race war.

CHAPTER ONE

We Are Everywhere

"WE HAVE GOT your location, where you live, and we will be watching you and we will take you out. It's as simple as that. You're nothing but a Jew slag. You will be taken out by the Ku Klux Klan."

Alison Loughlin shuddered as she played back the message on her telephone answering machine. The proprietor of a guesthouse in rural Norfolk, she was not used to violent threats. Then, in 1992, she donated a weekend at her guesthouse as a prize in a raffle for what she thought was a good cause: the Anti-Apartheid Movement. Soon after, the calls began.

She was in the next time the phone rang.

"Have you ever had anyone from the Anti-Apartheid Movement with you?" a brusque, cockney voice demanded.

"Yes, I have," Alison replied, nervously. "I was happy to receive some people who'd won the raffle. In what connection do you ask?"

"We've heard that you've had these people and we don't like it."

"I'm not sure you've got the right impression about this..." She was unable to finish her sentence.

"Oh yes, we've certainly got the right impression," interrupted to man, in a slightly mocking tone. "We don't like it and we're going to make a very nasty impression on you." Then he shouted a phrase she had never heard before: "Combat 18!"

The line went dead.

Throughout the country, dozens of people began to receive similar calls. Sometimes the callers claimed to be from the Ku Klux Klan, sometimes from Combat 18 and sometimes from

"Redwatch". The latter, it emerged, was a tatty newssheet
distributed at nazi meetings that first appeared in March 1992.
"Right lads, the holy war has begun," it announced. "We expect
every one of you to help in this crusade. NO EXCUSES. At the
very least make one phone call a day to one of the numbers
listed, keep it in awkward hours too if possible, really early or
late. If you are out of work, go down to the library and go
through the lefty papers and get some addresses, watch your
local papers and go through your telephone directory. Let's find
out who they are and make their lives sheer hell."

"They" were left-wingers, trade unionists, gay and lesbian
people, students and even Members of Parliament who had
spoken out against the far-right. They were also people the neo-
nazis identified with ZOG – the Zionist Occupation Government,
an alleged Jewish conspiracy to run the world. *Redwatch* listed
them all: hundreds of names, addresses and phone numbers, all
targets to be dealt with.

> Photocopy this sheet and pass the ammunition to fellow
> brothers, let the bastards know, WE ARE EVERYWHERE.
> Get off your ass and start getting your own lists in your
> area, names, numbers addresses, where they meet, activities
> etc. Remind yourself that the most dangerous adversary is
> the one you cannot see. To this end dress neatly or wear a
> shirt and tie. Blend in and be discreet, what ZOG can't see
> ZOG can't kill. Ours will be a war of insurgency and terror.
> You must be able to hide in the face of hordes of ZOG's
> putrid, mud infested cities. To be able to chat, laughingly
> with a nigger and his white slut over cocktails, but when
> they turn their back, slam a knife into them. To nod and
> smile at the cops and in the next instance draw your gun.
> Work alone or in small groups, bigger isn't necessarily
> better, as that is how traitors get in. You must be many
> things, soldier, spy, actor. This is the new era, the silent
> hunter is the most feared enemy, one it can neither name
> nor can find, UNDERMINE – DEMORALIZE –
> DESTROY."

Redwatch was produced by a young north London soccer casual named Steve Sargent, whose older brother Charlie was emerging as leader of the shadowy gang known as Combat 18. Sargent took the idea for *Redwatch* from an American magazine, *Jew Watch*, published out of Texas, which listed Jews in positions of influence. Aside from being "fun", it was, in C18 eyes, simply doing to the Left what they themselves had been doing to the Right for years through publications like *Searchlight*, a monthly British magazine that exposes fascists. "You'd go into the pub and there was the guy who went round thieving from the lefty bookshops, he used to go in there and steal twenty copies of *Searchlight* or remove the SWP [Socialist Workers Party] paper from the racks," remembers Steve Sargent. "He used to come down the pub and sell them for ten or twenty pence and the money would go to the fighting fund. You'd read in *Searchlight* them gloating over someone getting done, or nicked, or see all the adverts in the SWP paper. You'd get pissed off with it all."

Steve could not have imagined that his *Redwatch* would have such appeal. "I can remember when the first one was handed out in the pub, we were queuing up outside the phone boxes shouting 'fucking cunts' at Reds. You'd see in the paper to 'phone Tracy for details of a lefty meeting' and she gets fifty calls a day, I think Tracy is going to have second thoughts about advertising her name and address again.

"It was a bit of intimidation, a buzz through the beer. I remember once we rang some guy up and started singing Skrewdriver's *White Power* and he started singing the Red Flag back at us. But once it started, it was so surprising; you'd get people turning up in the pub and saying, 'We've got so-and-so's name and address.' You'd ask them how they got it and they'd say that they worked for Telecom or British Gas. It was unbelievable the amount of shit that was coming in on people. People just never thought of doing it before."

Taking their lead from *Redwatch*, C18 supporters unleashed a wave of terror. Five masked men stormed into the Anarchist Bookshop in east London in daylight, smashing up £5000-worth of computer equipment and furniture. A month later they were back, this time attempting to torch the building; only the quick response of the Fire Service prevented widespread damage. Another East End target was the office of the left-wing daily paper the *Morning Star*; this time it was only the alertness of an employee who was staying in the building that contained the fire to the entrance. The headquarters of London Labour Briefing, a left-wing group within the Labour Party, was attacked. The Cable Street memorial, which depicts Oswald Mosley's brown-shirts being routed in east London during the 1930s, was vandalised, causing over £20,000-worth of damage. Leon Greenman, a survivor of the Holocaust and active anti-fascist campaigner, had his front window smashed with a brick. In north London, four Jewish students were attacked on their way to an anti-racist march, while back in the East End C18 followed up a fight between one of its supporters, Nicky Cooper, and two local black men by paying one of the blacks a "visit" at home. Cooper later boasted of a spate of attacks against black and Asian people. "We are attacking them all over the place," he told a fellow C18 activist. In west London, Charlie Sargent led a group of fifty C18 and Chelsea hooligans to Twickenham hoping to confront anti-apartheid demonstrators protesting outside an England versus South Africa rugby match. With a large number of police on hand, the nazis could do little more than shout abuse before retiring to a local pub. When a fellow drinker complained about their nazi songs, he was attacked by Sargent, who would later be fined £300 for the assault.

C18 drew most satisfaction from larger-scale attacks on its left-wing opponents. Soon after it was formed, a small group of its supporters stormed a coach of Anti-Nazi League supporters waiting at Borough Tube station. A few months later, fifteen C18 supporters clashed with political rivals in New Cross, south London, before a concert being headlined by the Blaggers, an anti-fascist band closely aligned to Red Action, a left-wing group renowned for its muscular opposition to nazism. But arguably the most ferocious encounter during this period was a street fight between twenty C18 followers and thirty anti-fascists near Old Street station following an Irish Freedom Movement march in south London. After the march, anti-fascists and Irish Republicans made their way back into the City for a social event that evening; so too did a group of C18, who had been prevented from reaching the march by a heavy cordon of police. Rarely did the Left and Right get close enough for a real tear-up and when it did happen the police usually arrived within seconds. Old Street was different. During the early evening the two groups met and, though outnumbered, the C18 contingent emerged from a pub armed with pool cues, bottles, glasses and chairs and steamed into the anti-fascists, forcing them back down the street. A ten-minute battle was fought with a variety of makeshift weapons in the complete absence of the police. A group of anarchists arrived a short time later but they too were beaten off. One anti-fascist was caught in the Tube station by half a dozen C18 thugs and hit repeatedly with concrete slabs.

The ANL were on the receiving end again in August. Campaigning in east London before a council by-election being contested by the right-wing British National Party (BNP), they were set upon in Brick Lane, the symbolic heart of London's Bengali community. Thirty C18 supporters had been mobilised the day before by phone. Taking up position in the Blade Bone pub in Brick Lane, they waited for their prey to arrive. A young C18 supporter, Will Browning, who had been acting as a scout, returned to the pub in great excitement. "The SWP have turned up," he shouted. The assembled nazis downed their drinks and left the pub *en masse*. On their way down Brick Lane they stopped off in the market, arming themselves with an array of Lucozade and milk bottles, bricks and stones, before continuing to where the ANL had erected pasting tables to display their literature.

"Then we saw them and they saw us," remembers former National Front member Matthew Collins, who was out with C18 that day. "They didn't seem too bothered at first, they seemed to think they were dealing with the usual shouting and slanging match that there is sometimes between us and the Anti-Nazi League, but then it just went. We ploughed into them. We used bottles on them, bricks, we hit everybody we could, turned their stalls over, kicked them senseless really. One particular bloke really took it very bad in the head. Then his girlfriend laid on top of him but that didn't stop it, everyone just kept kicking and used bottles, bricks. The locals couldn't believe it. They've seen a lot of violence but they'd never seen anything like this."

The man on the floor was Paul Williams, a local schoolteacher and committed anti-racist. "It was a very busy day so we didn't realise straight away that they would come to attack us," he later told the ITV programme *World In Action*. "But then we saw them carrying bottles and a metal bar. I was struck over the head with an iron bar and then, as I turned, I was smashed over the head with a bottle. I think I must've momentarily lost consciousness then because the next thing I know I was lying in the middle of the street and there were about five of them kicking me to the head and to the groin and there were two of them on my ankles to prevent me rolling over into a foetal position. I don't know how long they would have continued but I was very fortunate that a woman bystander jumped on top of me to prevent them kicking me, but unfortunately she only received the kicking that was intended for me." (C18 would react with anger when Williams appeared on a *World in Action* investigation into the group. Having discovered the school at which he taught, a couple of its goons paid him a visit on the final day of the school year. Brazenly walking up to Williams as he was taking a lesson, they handed him a picture of Hitler with the words, "Hello Paul, next time you die!" scrawled across it.)

In November 1992, the gang was out on the streets of Eltham, south-east London, to ambush a march organised by the Anti-Racist Alliance in memory of Rohit Dougul, an Asian who had been killed by racists in the area. Joining C18 were supporters of the BNP, skinheads from another fascist clique called Blood and Honour, and older British Movement activists, many of whom lived in the area. Following an initial rally in a park, the marchers made their way through the streets, stopping at the scene of Dougul's murder to lay wreaths. As the march continued to a crossroads, it was met by dozens of nazi-saluting racists, including many children. "Six million lies," the nazis chanted – a reference to the number of Jews killed in the Holocaust – as the police made a human line across the street to keep the groups apart. Around the whole area were teams of C18 and local hooligans, all seeking an opportunity to hit the marchers. Most of the thugs had gathered in a churchyard just across the road from a British Legion Club which contained dozens more nazis. Members of the rival Anti-Fascist Action were prepared to take them on but, at the very moment they began organising, the police sent in horses to disperse the nazis. Not that they all left the area: some later ambushed and smashed up a minibus used to convoy people from the march.

Excited by developments in the capital, right-wingers across the country would begin adopting the Combat 18 name for their own activities. The attacks spread into the regions, though they tended to be isolated and cowardly in nature: in any larger-scale confrontations, the nazis generally came off worst. This later led Steve Sargent to rue the day his organisation developed beyond a London base. "In London we were invincible, we never lost a big fight. Yet when C18 expanded outside London, fights were lost and that undermined our credibility. We should have remained a London mob."

For now, though, the thrill of victory was intoxicating. Combat 18 had hit the streets of England like a malevolent whirlwind.

*　*　*　*

IN MANY WAYS C18 was a logical conclusion to what had been occurring for several years, as the political Left and Right clashed with increasing regularity in the capital. This came against a backdrop of rising racial violence, much of it fuelled by tabloid hysteria over a rise in foreigners seeking asylum in Britain and government policy that dumped the responsibility on the taxpayers of a few London boroughs. Among the most disenchanted at this was a circle of young men who would form the core of the gang. "It was a small clique of people who had known each other for years," reflects Steve Sargent. "There was trust between us. It wasn't so much a political thing but more like mates out on the piss together. It was always there, maybe not in name, but if you go back to the late Eighties it was the same people doing the same things."

The emergence of C18 was also a by-product of the rising militancy of the British National Party, which by 1990 had replaced the National Front as the main fascist group in Britain. Its founder, John Tyndall, was a tall, chinless figure with a slightly disengaged air: a poor man's Colonel Blimp. He was, however, a fiery speaker who would work himself and his audience into frenzy in the manner of his hero, Oswald Mosley. He had first joined a nazi organisation in 1959 and went on to be a leading member of the White Defence League, the National Socialist Movement and the Greater Britain Movement. He also acquired several convictions, including possession of a gun and organising a paramilitary group. In 1967, he joined the recently launched National Front and within a short time became its chairman. Yet while the NF was to become the most successful British post-war fascist group, reaching a membership of 17,500, Tyndall was constantly attacked for his authoritarian leadership style. By 1980, the NF was in decline. Tyndall left, claiming that the party had been taken over by gays and skinheads. He formed the New National Front and then, two years later, the BNP.

Joining Tyndall in the move from the NF was Richard Edmonds, a former teacher who was to become the BNP's national organiser. A tall, gangly man, Edmonds was a committed national socialist, being instrumental in ensuring the production of a second edition of *Holocaust News*, a publication which denounced the Holocaust as a Jewish and American lie. Edmonds was also popular among the rank and file. While Tyndall rarely ventured out from his Sussex base, Edmonds attended virtually every BNP activity possible. His long-time ambition was for a party headquarters and bookshop; for him this represented respectability and progress. His dream was fulfilled when he accepted redundancy from his employers, Cable and Wireless, and used his payoff to purchase a shop and flat in Welling, Kent, thus providing the BNP with a base.

Under Tyndall and Edmonds, the BNP courted controversy

through a series of highly provocative marches and rallies in areas with large ethnic minority populations. In 1989, a static BNP rally in the West Yorkshire town of Dewsbury attracted several hundred local white youths who went on to run riot, attacking Asian shops and passers-by. In 1991, the party marched through Thamesmead in south-east London, passing within yards of the spot where the black teenager Rolan Adams had been killed only weeks before. Unsurprisingly, this confrontational stance attracted recruits to its cause: not only many disillusioned NF and British Movement supporters but also the skinheads of Blood and Honour and football hooligans who had previously been unaligned to any political group.

Much of the BNP activity during this time was concentrated on east London where, in 1990, it launched its "Rights for Whites" campaign, hoping to capitalise on the perceived injustices felt by many local white people. The stabbing of a fifteen-year-old white boy in a Tower Hamlets school was used for maximum political advantage: the BNP galvanised support with a 400-strong march and rally addressed by the dead boy's step-father. In an area of high unemployment, bad housing and under-funded public amenities, BNP propaganda pinned the blame, regardless of the true causes, on the shoulders of ethnic minority communities and, more generally, on "Britain's multi-racial experiment". The BNP rallied the disenchanted and within two months its policy was paying dividends; it obtained 9.7 per cent of the vote in one local election. This was to be the beginning of two years of rolling success for the party.

It was following a violent clash in early 1991 at a BNP by-election rally at Weavers Field school – where they had to fight off a concerted anti-fascist onslaught – that a group of younger activists began to form themselves into a small mob. They called themselves the "East End Barmy Army". The gang consisted of a dozen or so younger members in their late teens and early twenties, banded together by right-wing politics and a love of fighting and primarily concerned with defending party events from anti-fascists or other opposition. Many of them were soccer hooligans, some with the "Yids" of Tottenham (named,

ironically, for their club's perceived Jewish links), others with the
Millwall "F-Troop". A couple were followers of the "Inter-City
Firm" at West Ham, while they were later joined by a few older
members of the Charlton Athletic "B-Mob". As with their football
loyalties, their first job was protecting "their manor", but it
wasn't long before they went on the offensive. In the year
following the Weavers Field meeting, the Barmy Army became
increasingly active. At first their targets were "Red mobs" but
they also made random attacks on blacks and Asians in the area.

Much of the violence was initiated, or at least approved of, by
the BNP leadership. When residents of Welling held a meeting
to discuss the opening of the party's headquarters there, the
party responded by breaking up the meeting with iron bars,
chains and chairs. Leading the forty-strong attack squad was
Richard Edmonds and London BNP organiser Tony Lecomber,
who in the mid-Eighties had been sent to prison for trying to
blow up the offices of a left-wing organisation. The party later
boasted in its paper of how they had "hospitalised 13 Reds". In
1991, the violence intensified. April saw the BNP attack a public
meeting being addressed by the Reverend Al Sharpton, the
controversial American black rights leader, who had arrived in
Britain for a "crusade of social justice". In words echoing the
calling cards of the soccer gangs, the following issue of the BNP
paper *British Nationalist* boasted "his meeting had just been
visited by the British National Party!"

The Left fought back. In late May, a west London meeting of
the secretive and influential League of Saint George, due to be
addressed by representatives of most of Britain's nazi groups,
was aborted after 200 anti-fascists took over the hall before the
meeting had begun. Humiliatingly, the event's security team was
taken out by a small group of anti-fascists posing as nazis, who
arrived early carrying forged entrance tickets. They locked the
security men in a downstairs room, then gave a warm welcome
to delegates arriving for the meeting: in a scene reminiscent of a
warzone, the street outside the venue, Kensington Library, was
littered with the bodies of unconscious skinheads. It was to be
the Right's most comprehensive street defeat for years and

outraged nazi supporters, especially the younger elements who gathered in east London pubs every Sunday. It was here at the Sunday drink-up, a nazi tradition dating from the British Movement (BM) days of the late-Seventies, that talk of revenge grew.

An opportunity to avenge Kensington came in late August when the National Black Caucus, a group campaigning for the advancement of black rights, declared its intention to march through Bermondsey, an area hotly contested by the BNP and the NF. The Caucus march was foolhardy from the beginning, with the route going through a predominantly white area, allowing its opponents to portray it as an "anti-white" event. Even more foolishly, the march was organised only hours before Millwall Football Club – with its notorious following – was due to play at home. Both the NF and the BNP mobilised for the day, beginning with paper sales in Bermondsey's Blue Market. While there was a sense of competition between the two groups, the BNP took control because of its vastly superior numbers.

"By the time the march went past, the BNP demo was in a real frenzy," remembers Matthew Collins, a former NF official who switched allegiances to the BNP during this period. "Coins and bottles were being thrown at the police. When the march disappeared from sight, the Millwall fans kicked down the barriers and charged into Rotherhithe Road. There were hundreds of them with bricks and bottles, screaming things like, 'Get the niggers.'"

What little co-ordination there was rapidly disappeared as the riotous mob swelled in numbers. "By the time we were on the busy main road, the first confrontation with the police occurred," says Collins. "One van of police tried to stop us from getting to the park, but they were well outnumbered and were being pelted from close range with heavy bricks and the obligatory Lucozade bottles. In the park there was a scramble for wood, sticks and bricks. There was one final charge on the blacks. By now, however, the police finally seemed to have a grip on things; they put the Caucus behind their lines and refused them a rally. There were more emotive speeches on the megaphones from the

BNP leaders; all seemed to be breaking the law. The police took the Caucus back out onto the march route and left the BNP supporters, believing that we would finally disperse. However, we didn't. We charged back onto the street, through an unpoliced alley."

The few hundred on the march fled in panic as dozens of nazis were joined by hundreds of local youths and Millwall hooligans. "We had no police escort and so we were able to rain stones down on the police and members of the Caucus. The police were forced to retreat. A constant battle with the police went on for about ten minutes before they were able to seal off all the exits. As Millwall fans hate the police, a massive charge of their lines followed. Eventually they gave way and we poured further into Bermondsey. This was home territory for the Millwall boys and they knew all the back streets, in and out of the estates. Once more the police came into the area, but five motorcycle cops were pelted and chased, as was a photographer who was singled out as a 'Paki'. He was beaten badly.

"By now the numbers were no less than two hundred. We ran through an estate and onto another road which the police had cordoned off. This was the first charge by the riot police, but everyone was on a high and we even fought them. At the time we thought we were invincible. Eventually the police drove us into a shopping centre where many of the shops were Asian-owned. Two cars were smashed up and another was turned over with two black people inside. An Indian guy was busy trying to lock up his shop when his windows were smashed. He was assaulted and his shop looted. Boots was left alone, but Wimpy had its shutters smashed out of their hinges before the windows too got done. The police were just slowly walking about a hundred yards behind, trying to snatch people. In the next road off, which was through another estate, there were more riot police, but they were just pelted with beer cans and bottles. In a little side street more cars were smashed. One of the cars had a black driver; he had a dustbin thrown through his windscreen."

The BNP leadership were ecstatic after Bermondsey, believing that local white people would flock to their cause as a result.

However, publicly at least, they were quick to deny blame. "The BNP continues to advocate that lawful political action is the correct method for opposing the evils of the multi-racial society that the rulers of Britain have created," its newspaper reported, "but as long as those rulers do not respond to the people's wishes by bringing their hideous experiment to an end the kind of street warfare we saw in Bermondsey on this day is inevitable." Privately they celebrated. "This is brilliant," *British Nationalist* editor John Morse told one party supporter that night. "This is the beginning, we must keep this going, we could have this every time we have an activity."

The rising confidence of the BNP was reflected in its annual rally held in mid-October. The success of Bermondsey, coupled with the disintegration of the NF, provided the perfect backdrop for 500 supporters who gathered in an east London hall in what was to be its largest-ever rally. Loyalist paramilitary banners draped the hall, bookstalls displayed nazi imagery and Holocaust denial propaganda and the mood was euphoric. "Welcome to Nuremberg, Bethnal Green-style," said Richard Edmonds as he greeted newcomers. The party's north-west organiser countered claims that the BNP was responsible for desecrating Jewish graves by saying, to loud applause, "The Jews have desecrated this country for years." Tony Lecomber declared Bermondsey "the great white victory". And every time Edmonds mentioned the Jews, who he blamed for the world's problems, the audience responded with boos and hisses.

Finally John Tyndall took the dais. At first the crowd listened in silence but as he went on, building to his customary histrionics, he was repeatedly interrupted by shouts of "Fuhrer". At the climax of his speech, he declared that all the race traitors would be in need of protection when – not if – he came to power. The audience was in a state of frenzy and gave their leader a three-minute standing ovation while the Blood and Honour skinhead contingent stood at one side giving straight-arm salutes.

The following day saw another flashpoint as Anti-Fascist Action mobilised against the weekly BNP paper sale in Brick Lane. Edmonds told close supporters in the party bookshop that he wanted to meet their challenge head-on. He speculated that a Bermondsey-style riot could be repeated, thus galvanising the physical support of white youths against the Reds and the Asian community. It never materialised, as police kept 300 nazis away from a similar number of anti-fascists. However, Edmonds was caught later that day by AFA supporters near Kings Cross station and given a beating.

With the 1992 General Election looming, the BNP was well aware that its run-up campaign would attract concerted opposition from anti-racist and anti-fascist organisations. To combat this, it decided to re-organise its stewards' group, until then a collection of the toughest-looking individuals available for selection on any given day. Chief steward Derek Beackon believed that something more streamlined was required: a tightly-knit group drawn from among the fittest and most violent of the party's supporters. To this end, he organised a meeting in the large City of Paris pub in east London in early 1992. While Beackon was nominally in charge, it was Eddie Butler, the party's election officer and architect of the Rights for Whites campaign, who pulled the strings at the meeting, distributing information sheets about roles and responsibilities for each steward.

Butler believed that the best form of defence was offence, citing as evidence an incident just before the stewards' meeting: when the newly-reformed Anti-Nazi League had announced its first major activity in east London, the BNP had gone on the attack. A BNP officer, Tim Hepple, was among those present. "This had been organised at least a week in advance," he later told *World In Action*. "There were in fact two plans. I was involved in one and people like Eddie Butler had planned another. We knew where they (the ANL) were going to meet because they'd put their posters up all around this area, they were going to do a mass leaflet. We walked out of the pub and the group that I was with was a skinhead group, about fifteen of us, and then we saw the leafleters. As we approached them there was a skip full of bricks and bottles and we armed ourselves. They didn't know we were going to hit them until the last minute."

By then, it was too late. "We trailed them at a discreet distance, but once they were on the estate, we ran at them. There was no shouting or threats; a whole gang of nazi skins just poured down on the Anti-Nazi League, who were nearly all youngsters, including women. The wave of skinheads just swept over them kicking, punching and, as if prearranged, driving them in the direction of two narrow exits from the flats. One anti-fascist youngster had a camera and attempted to photograph the attack. He was stabbed in the arm with a broken bottle."

Teacher Ian Gregory was out leafleting that day and was lucky to leave the area alive. He was one of the first struck by the skinheads. "I think they caught me before I actually made the floor and there was quite a few around me. When I eventually fell I saw this lump of concrete that was being held in two hands coming down towards my face. I immediately turned away and tried to bury my head. Unfortunately it hit me in the back of the head and split it open."

Hepple saw the ensuing events from a slight distance but there was nothing he could do to save the ANL activist – even if he had wanted to. "His head was all open, blood coming out of the back of it, it was disgusting. He was sort of whimpering. If the police hadn't turned up he might have been kicked so badly unconscious he might never have woken up."

For those who managed to escape the first wave of skinheads, another group was waiting nearby. The only available exits for the Anti-Nazi League supporters were concrete subways connecting the estate to the nearby roads. Here, hidden in the shadows, were dozens of other nazis, this time not skinheads or bootboys but older, more hardened extremists. As the left-wing activists fled in terror, they were met with baseball bats, iron bars, heavy spanners and bottles.

"The mood in the pub afterwards was complete elation," recalled Hepple. "It was like Christmas come early, everybody was patting themselves on the back, they thought it was marvellous. The leadership of the British National Party, John Morse, Richard Edmonds, they loved it. They thought it was really funny and the most sickening thing about the whole incident was they didn't even have to get their hands dirty because they had their cannon fodder to do it for them." However, the leadership had been present, with Edmonds ferrying people around in the party minibus and Hepple having to help Eddie Butler clean other people's blood off his clothes. "Without a doubt," reflected Hepple, "we had set the pattern that day for future actions. The failure on the part of the police to follow up the attackers gave the BNP and emergent Combat 18 a lot more confidence for the future."

This was exactly the kind of robust action that Eddie Butler wanted to encourage. Yet even as he outlined the virtues of an elite stewards' group to the faces in the City of Paris pub, others had their own ideas about how it would work. Huddled around a table in the far corner of the cavernous boozer were the inner circle of the East End Barmy Army. "This is it," grinned Charlie Sargent, as he sipped from his pint, enjoying the stories of the attack on the ANL the previous week. A short, rotund man with a balding pate, Sargent liked to see himself as the leader of his little firm. He wasn't inclined to take orders from anybody.

Beside him, sweeping aside long dark hair from his face, Alan Thompson was equally sceptical about being under total BNP control. He didn't particularly like the skins and was not going to be bossed by them, though he had grudging admiration for what they had accomplished against the ANL. The solidly-built Gary Hitchcock, possessed of a short temper and a long track record, was in agreement. Steve Martin joined them at the table after a tour of the pub selling Loyalist literature: he had done a good trade, the mood of solidarity at the meeting persuading more people than usual to part with their cash. Steve Sargent, Charlie's younger and quieter brother, was also there, listening intently.

The corner-table group exuded danger. They had little respect for Butler, with his "posh" accent and educated background. Their cliquey discussions were punctuated with sly winks and nods of the head in the direction of others entering the pub. They didn't have a problem with the BNP forming a bodyguard; if anything, they wondered why it had taken so long. However, they agreed that such a force would be hobbled if kept under

BNP control. The Barmy Army had shown how effective a tight
mob could be. A lot could be accomplished if only they could
run the show themselves.

"What about the name Combat 18?" suggested Hitchcock.

★　★　★　★

COMBAT 18 WAS born at that session in the City of Paris pub, and
at a follow-up meeting of some of the same men a few days later
at Steve Martin's north London flat. A logo was even devised: a
"death's head" skull-and-crossbones similar to that worn by a
particularly evil division of Hitler's Waffen-SS. Yet C18 could
hardly be described as organised in the few months following its
formation. There was no membership, no clear leader and no
plan of action. Many of its early activities were sporadic and
disorganised, reflecting the natures of the men involved. "You'd
go to the pub and have a beer," says Steve Sargent. "Obviously
it would be centred around something, if the BNP where doing
something or the Reds were doing something, you'd pick a pub
in the area and just take it from there. We never had spotters, the
Reds did but we didn't. We always lagged behind in things like
intelligence. The Reds always were better at that sort of thing.
More to the point, no-one wanted to be out of the pub. Who
wants to stand around on a street corner looking for the Reds
when you could be beering it up?"

It was the thrill of the brawl that drew them together. Steve
Sargent vividly remembers one clash with AFA at the Enkel
Arms pub on Seven Sisters Road, following a Troops Out march
in north London. "That one was memorable because it wasn't
planned, we went up there to photograph the march but when
we was in the pub there were some squaddies in there, so we
started talking to them. They said they were up for it. We were
all really pissed up. When the march came we came out of the
pub, giving it to them and few of them tried to get over but the
Old Bill got in the middle. Then a group of NF turned up and a
mob of Chelsea. No-one knew it was going to happen. There
were about fifty of us. The geezer who was taking photos, well

he was going home but returned saying, 'They're all around the corner in the Enkel Arms.' There was a market there. We ran out of things to throw and there was this bloke selling potatoes, so we got hold of them and began throwing them at the Paddies. There was no actual fisticuffs, it was all glasses and bottles. A few of the soldiers tried to get into the pub, kicking the door and trying to whack them with pool cues, so it was nearly all just throwing bottles."

Those inside the pub included some of AFA's top fighters; they, and more particularly the combatants of Red Action, were viewed with some trepidation by many on the Right. While C18 were not able to take the pub, or even get close enough to exchange punches, their football mentality of "taking liberties" in their opponents' manor saw the day remembered as a great victory. AFA saw the day differently as, heavily outnumbered, they held the pub in the face of the onslaught. Even Steve Sargent admired their defiance. "You knew with Red Action, with Gary O'Shea and O'Farrell, that they would have a tear-up. I remember that Gary O'Shea just standing there in the pub doorway throwing pool balls. Give him his dues, game geezer."

Where C18 differed from previous strong-arm groups of the British Right was that it ran itself; even the bootboys of the British Movement (BM) had a political leadership. C18 may have started as a BNP offshoot but its own organisers naturally emerged as it grew as a rank-and-file street force. Some came to the fore through their unwavering commitment, their willingness to turn up week after week and stand at the front; others because of their ability to talk a good fight and their past reputations.

For Gary Hitchcock, who came up with the name Combat 18, it was certainly the latter. A veteran nazi, he had joined the NF in' the Seventies before switching to the more hardline BM, where he was to become involved in its Leader Guard. He became a prominent figure in the world of skinhead music as it underwent a revival in 1979. As manager of the 4-Skins, a leading band in the raucous post-punk style known as Oi!, Hitchcock hosted gigs, arranged album deals and oversaw security. In 1980, his band hit the headlines when a planned gig in predominantly-

Asian Southall, south London, ignited local anger and led to a riot in which the venue was burnt down. Hitchcock's far-right views were exposed in the national press and the incident did much to marginalise Oi! music as the domain of racist thugs. Shunned by promoters and record labels, the 4-Skins folded.

Hitchcock remained on the fringes of the far-right, attending anti-IRA demonstrations. In the late Eighties he drifted over to the BNP, turning up at events in east London, often in the company of Charlie Sargent, who he had known since his days in the BM. Hitchcock was present at the punch-up at Weavers Field school at which the East End Barmy Army was formed. He also became a regular at the Sunday drink-up, where his reputation in the worlds of football hooliganism and far-right music earned him the respect of his peers. His large, muscular frame added to the demeanour of a man who meant business. Yet Hitchcock was rarely seen to be involved in violence.

Far keener for "trouble" was the man who would become one of the two most important figures in C18. Paul David Sargent was born in July 1960, one of five children, and was brought up in New Barnet, north London. From an early age he adopted the name Charlie; quite why remains a mystery that even his brother Steve cannot answer: "Because he always has been," he says when asked. Charlie adopted the skinhead image at an early age and by 1975, at the age of fifteen, was already involved in the BM, following in the footsteps of his brother William, or Bill, nine years his senior. Their father was a strong supporter of the Loyalist cause in Northern Ireland.

Despite being only five feet seven inches tall, Charlie soon earned a reputation for violence, mostly with a knife. Gary Bushell, latterly TV critic of *The Sun* but then a punk writer for *Sounds* magazine, described him as a "particularly obnoxious nazi" in a letter to *Searchlight* in the early 1980s. "A real nasty piece of work," he wrote, going on to claim that Sargent "prides himself in being something of a 'blade merchant'." Among the early attacks Sargent is known to have initiated was the stabbing of Oi! musician Si Spanner for the crime of being Jewish. After an ill-tempered relationship with his father, Sargent left home at sixteen and moved in with nazi friends in Barnet. At eighteen, he received his first convictions as an adult, for possession of an offensive weapon, threatening behaviour and violent disorder. Three years later, he was jailed for eighteen months for attempting to import drugs into Sweden from Amsterdam. A year after that, and shortly after his release, he was again caught in possession of drugs, this time entering Britain at the port of Harwich.

Like Hitchcock, Sargent played an influential role in the skinhead scene of the early Eighties, organising security for, among others, Combat 84, a band led by Chris "Chubby" Henderson, a prominent member of the "Chelsea Headhunters" soccer gang. The two men were to become good friends, despite Charlie supporting Arsenal. In the mid-Eighties, he lodged at the Camberwell flat Henderson shared with his girlfriend, Maxine Durrant. Henderson was arrested and charged following an undercover investigation into the Headhunters known as Operation Own Goal. After the trial collapsed due to inconsistencies in police note keeping, he received compensation and left for Thailand, where he opened a bar. Sargent switched beds and moved in with Durrant. Together they had two children, both girls, to add to the boy she already had with Chubby.

With the demise of the British Movement in 1983, Sargent had swopped allegiances to the National Action Party, launched by Yorkshire nazi Eddie Morrison and former BNP organiser and League of Saint George council member Kevin Randall. But Sargent quickly returned to the NF milieu, attending their anti-Irish counter-protests and annual Remembrance Sunday march. By the late Eighties, with Chubby in Thailand and another close friend, Skrewdriver singer Ian Stuart Donaldson, leaving the capital for the East Midlands, Sargent gravitated towards the BNP, which had emerged as a more hardline successor to the NF. He was never formally a member but he attended meetings, occasionally bringing his brother Bill, who now lived in East Anglia and had achieved national notoriety after secretly being filmed participating in an illegal cockfight by the RSPCA. Also at BNP meetings was Charlie's younger brother Steve who, out of the three boys, was by far the most political and well-read. While Charlie's contacts and experience propelled him to the fore of C18, Steve became the group's principle propagandist.

Five years Charlie's junior, Steve Sargent can remember little before nazi politics. Though a skinhead from the age of eleven, he strongly denies he was influenced by his brothers. "How could I be?" he says. "Bill was never around and Charlie left home when he was sixteen. It was just the thing at the time, being a skinhead. Everyone I grew up with was the same." He says his parents did not complain, but even if they had there was little they could do. "Every kid in my street was a skinhead, it was quite normal."

Steve's world evolved around drinking, fighting and football. He fought against the local rockers, neighbouring gangs, punks at music venues and rival fans at matches. "You know how it is, you go four down and you just want to punch someone in the face," he says with a smile. At the age of thirteen, he went on his first political rally, a BM march, though he associated himself with the Young National Front during his teens. Within a couple of years he was going down to east London for the right-wing drink-up, first to the Panther public house, where Charlie would be boozing with his BM friends, and later to the Weavers, where Chubby Henderson and his Headhunter gang would travel in from west London. Most of his fighting was done locally in Barnet, either at football or around local pubs. "Being a skinhead you always stand out, people always wanted to have a pop at you or take the piss. In your local areas, where there are only a few of you, people would often say 'you skinhead cunt', while if you go to a skinhead gig there's hundreds of you and no-one is going to say fuck all. Fighting all seemed a bit of a laugh, something you'd talk about during the week, show off you scars."

Though sharing similar views, Charlie and Steve rarely spent time together, separated by their age difference and involvement in different groups. "He was a lot older and he didn't want us around," remembers Steve. "When we used to go down to the Last Resort (a skinhead club in central London), Charlie would be inside drinking while we would be outside on the pavement."

Even in Barnet the two brothers lived separate lives, Steve drinking with his YNF friends in one pub while Charlie was down the round in another with his BM colleagues.

Gradually Steve began to broaden his contacts through meeting other skinhead groups from surrounding areas, mostly at a venue called The Circle near the High Barnet football ground. "We began to know other skinheads from Edmonton, Enfield and Arnos Grove." Together they formed the LBB skins: one of the group worked for the council and was able to steal several London Borough of Barnet donkey jackets with LBB printed on the back. "We'd write 'skins' underneath, so we became the LBB skins." As many of his school friends grew out of the skinhead scene, Steve began mixing with people from further afield, with Arsenal hooligans and with other right-wingers at the weekly drink-up or at punk venues such as the 100 Club. The skinhead scene was fading, with most of his hooligan friends adopting the "casual" fashion of designer-label clothes. This smart look often made it easier to evade police detection; it was also symptomatic of the 1980s "loadsamoney" ethos that accompanied Thatcherism, as opposed to the proud-to-be-working-class image of the skinheads, itself a reaction to the more middle class hippies. Steve was one of the last to make the transformation, though he says this owed more to the fact that he had just bought a new pair of commando boots and did not want to waste them.

Steve created his own niche within hooliganism and the far-right, yet always seemed to be in Charlie's shadow. While Steve was in the Young NF, Charlie was a member of the BM Leader Guard; while Steve stayed at home until he was almost thirty, Charlie left when he was sixteen; while Steve ran with Barnet and Arsenal, Charlie counted the leaders of the Chelsea Head-hunters and the England international scene amongst his best friends; while Steve went to skinhead gigs, Charlie was organising the security; and while Steve attended anti-IRA activities with his NF and hooligan cronies, Charlie was joining the Ulster Defence Association. Quieter but more intelligent, Steve continued to play second fiddle to his big brother as C18 emerged.

Once he started *Redwatch*, information flowed in to Steve Sargent from around the country. Some was gleaned from reading the left-wing press, some from national and ethnic publications. In the summer of 1992, two C18 men posing as potential recruits entered the London headquarters of Militant and had a meeting with one of its organisers. Eighteen months later, a small group of activists attended an ANL-organised festival and proceeded to take photos of anti-fascists. Sometimes information was collected illegally. In 1992, the home of the Anti-Racist Alliance leader Marc Wadsworth was burgled; sections of the group's membership list were later reproduced in *Redwatch*. The following year, the contact book for the radical weekly *The Northern Star* was snatched from its office in Leeds and reproduced. Thousands of names, addresses, phone numbers and photographs were to be publicly advertised in an array of C18 publications over the next few years.

It led to the wave of attacks on radical bookstores and offices in London and to the intimidation of anti-fascists, left-wingers and ordinary people like the Norfolk guesthouse owner Alison McLoughlin. Among those who rose to Sargent's call to take the fight to the Left was a small team of nazis straddling the Nottinghamshire-Derbyshire border. They included Simon Chadwick from Bolsover, Graham Tasker from Chesterfield, and Steve and Adrian Belshaw from Mansfield. Over a twelve-month period, beginning shortly after the formation of C18, they carried out a string of attacks across the region, mainly focused on Mansfield. A local anti-racist was enticed from his home by a brick through his window, only to be set upon with iron bars. Solicitor and ANL organiser Danny Phillips was punched in the street; in a separate incident someone tried to strangle his wife with her own scarf. In Nottingham, Chadwick and Tasker were involved in a street attack on some local students who were petitioning against racism; the petition was stolen and many of the names later appeared in *Redwatch*. Chadwick was also involved in an attack on a Labour councillor in London. At the time he was working at a Department of Employment office in Sheffield, where he tried to access personal information on anti-fascists from the VACS national computer. His efforts were thwarted when *Searchlight* supplied details of his activities to the local trade unions, which immediately set about getting him sacked. It seemed a simple enough task: his undeclared conviction for assault was revealed and fellow workers complained that he kept a rounders bat in his desk drawer and occupied his time by reading gun magazines. However, the management initially refused to dismiss him, transferring Chadwick away from VACS to a job that involved dealing with Sheffield's minority communities. A prolonged and bitter dispute was only ended when Chadwick was arrested for the attack on Danny Phillips, for which he, Tasker and both Belshaws were eventually convicted.

C18 attracted some of the Right's most feared streetfighters. From east London came Alan Thompson, who ran with the Yids of Spurs. From west London came Adam "Butty" Butler, an amateur boxer and ex-BM member. From south-east London came Phil Edwards, known as "Phil the Thug", another former BM activist who in the late Eighties led an attack on protesters outside the South African embassy in Trafalgar Square. Edwards was charged with attempted murder in 1992 for allegedly stabbing a man who had burgled his flat. Thirty C18 heavies, led by Charlie Sargent, subsequently walked into the man's local pub, where he drank with his family, all witnesses to the attack, and told them in no uncertain terms what would happen if anyone gave evidence. The case was dropped when the witnesses, including the victim, failed to appear in court.

C18 only rarely stuck to its remit of stewarding events. In April 1992, with a General Election less than a week away, it provided muscle for a BNP rally at York Hall, Bethnal Green. Charlie Sargent led twenty C18 activists, all wearing BNP armbands, in patrolling the short walk from the redirection point to the hall. Three months later, their services were requested to protect a march in Walsall; the BNP had few West Midlands activists and was reliant on London supporters being bussed up for the day. Twenty of the hardcore – including the Sargent brothers, Phil Edwards, Eddie Whicker, Steve Martin and a young man named Will Browning – were driven there in a

Sherpa van by BNP chief steward Derek Beackon. Minders including Charlie Sargent personally chaperoned party leader John Tyndall.

In early July, C18 provided security for a London meeting hosted by David Irving, the historical revisionist and Holocaust denier, which attracted the top echelon of Britain's nazis. The gang, led by Sargent and drawn almost exclusively from the initial crop of C18 followers from east and south-east London, ushered attendees to meeting place at the International Student House in Great Portland Street. They had been given the job by Anthony Hancock, a Brighton-based nazi printer who was organising the event after a previous Irving seminar in Victoria nine months before had ended in humiliation: *Searchlight* had discovered its venue and alerted the police to the illegal presence of American holocaust denier Fred Leuchter, leading to the arrest and deportation of the guest speaker.

Sargent was on hand again, two months later, at another Irving seminar. Hancock was again arranging security and summoned Sargent to Brighton for a meeting with Roberto Fiore and Colin Todd of the International Third Position, a small ultra-Catholic fascist group. They had provided security for the failed meeting the year before and had been given the job of co-ordinating it again this time. Sargent was bombarded with questions about his own background and that of C18 and left the meeting perturbed, later ringing Hancock to say he wished not to be involved with the Third Positionists. However, when two booked venues were both cancelled after being discovered by anti-fascists, an exasperated Hancock turned back to Sargent days before the event, pleading with him to organise security. Sargent turned out an impressive fifty-strong firm, with over twenty from west London, including several Chelsea hooligans, among them Andy Frain, Mark Alloway, Ian Holloway, Stuart Glass, Ken Walsh and the Oxford-based hooligan and nazi Matthew Osbury. Also present was Mark Atkinson, who, with Frain and Holloway, had been active in the Invisible Empire of the Ku Klux Klan.

But in C18, the BNP had weaned a monster it could not

control. Sargent and his increasingly arrogant troops resented any attempt to boss them. A few weeks after the second Irving seminar, they protected the annual BNP rally which, embarrassingly for the Church of England, was held in Church House, Westminster, the seat of the General Synod. With such a controversial venue, the BNP leadership kept the details secret, even from its stewarding team, who were told no more than the redirection point at Euston train station. This infuriated C18, and in particular Gary Hitchcock, who was seen to have a shouting match with BNP officials as the meeting began. He later told Sargent that if the BNP was not prepared to trust them with details of meetings, they should refuse to provide security. It was the first clear sign of a rift.

CHAPTER TWO

A Word in Your Ear

CHARLIE SARGENT HAD street cunning, but he wasn't especially bright. Despite once describing himself as an "intelligent thug", he was never a deep thinker. It made his rise all the more surprising, especially when his gang began to develop a political agenda and produce an array of publications. With Charlie editing *The Order*, and Steve *Redwatch* and *Putsch*, it was obvious that the group's activities were going to be centred on the Sargents. It also soon became clear that they were receiving advice and inspiration from elsewhere. Combat 18 could not have lasted without some kind of "ideology", however flakey. It came from two outsiders who were to be an important influence on the thinking of the gang.

In 1991, Steve Sargent had seen an advert for an American newsletter called *Resistance*, the fortnightly publication of one Harold Covington, a hardline nazi who believed Jews were out to destroy the white race. Sargent sent off £5 to a nazi book club based in Leeds and received a bundle of back issues. He liked what he read. "I got nearly every single right-wing paper out there, but most of them were crap. In them days I would read Covington's stuff five or six times because he was always slagging somebody off really badly. There was nothing like it, it was basically down to earth. If someone was a wanker, he'd call them a wanker. It was always an entertaining read." Drawn to Covington's work by its amusing style, Steve was also to embrace many of his political views.

Harold Covington was a large, fleshy man with a thick black beard and dark-rimmed glasses. He was born into a lower middle class family and spent the early years of his childhood in

Burlington, North Carolina. He was a child of the 1950s, that post-war period of prosperity and technological change that entrenched the United States as the most powerful nation on earth, yet Covington rejected conventional notions of the American Dream. He grew up in a district with few blacks and certainly counted none among his friends. Moving to nearby Chapel Hill as a teenager, his parents enrolled him in a fully-integrated school, a decision he was soon to resent. His racism was born in the classroom and he began to describe himself as "the school fascist". "I have never been able to keep my mouth shut," he later declared to a journalist. "When I see something I don't like I just have to get up and say so, loudly and publicly." His outspokenness did him little good when, as a college student, he volunteered to write a column on student affairs for the local newspaper. Within a few weeks the editor had shown him the door for using his articles to air personal grievances against black students.

In 1972, he joined the United States Army and the neo-nazi National Socialist White People's Party (NSWPP). Within a couple of years he was ordered out of the Army – for racist agitation, he claimed. Covington threw himself into political activity, joining the staff of the NSWPP at its headquarters in Arlington, Virginia, and becoming editor of its newspaper, *White Power*. Within a year, he was on the move again, this time to South Africa, where he worked as a payroll clerk for an engineering firm in Johannesburg. He said it was here that he really began to study National Socialism as an ideology. In 1974, he moved across the border to Bulawayo, Rhodesia, then in the grip of civil war, and launched the Rhodesia White People's Party and the South African Friends of the Movement, agitating along hardline nazi principles. His time in Africa was soon terminated, as his views became too extreme for even the racist government. Covington was to claim that he was expelled from Rhodesia while fighting as a mercenary and "terrorising Jews", but the truth, according to official documents, is less colourful: it appears he was never a mercenary but worked in the office of an engineering and construction company at a junior level, and his eventual deportation came after he wrote abusive and threatening letters to members of the local Jewish community.

Returning to North Carolina, Covington joined the Chicago-based National Socialist Party of America (NSPA), which, during his absence, had replaced the NSWPP as the principle nazi group in the United States. In 1977, he stood for the city council of Raleigh, a decision that propelled him into the media spotlight. Within a year he was standing for the state senate and, in a political coup, as a nazi on a Republican ticket. Despite Republican Party efforts to distance themselves from his candidature, he secured 885 votes out of the 7,000 cast. Two years later, he achieved national attention when, standing for the position of attorney general of North Carolina, he gained 43% of the vote in the Republican primary. His opponents protested that voters knew nothing of his true politics; Covington countered, rather mischievously, that underneath every Republican lurked a nazi. Covington, if nothing else, was a skilful manipulator of the media: he knew that shocking statements made big headlines, a tactic he was to use repeatedly.

Covington was intent on spreading his wings and for that he needed a support base. His first recruits were prised away from the Ku Klux Klan, the infamous, white-robed secret society founded after the American Civil War to maintain white supremacy. He hosted meetings with a number of Klan groups to organise opposition to an anti-Klan rally in Greensboro. Tensions had been rising over the previous three months as the communist-led anti-Klan movement stepped up its campaign against local racists; two weeks before the march, the organisers had issued a public warning accusing the Right of being "cowards, nightriders who try to terrorise innocent people. They must be physically beaten back, eradicated, exterminated, wiped off the face of the earth." Leaning into the lens of a television camera, one leader issued a direct challenge to the Klan. "We invite you and your two-bit punks to come out and face the wrath of the people."

What happened next would make headlines around the world. At 11.21 on the morning of November 3, 1979, a motorcade of right-wingers approached the Greensboro demonstration. They were met with chants of "Death to the Klan." As the marchers almost engulfed the slow-moving motorcade, one demonstrator kicked the door panel of the lead car. The response was deadly: the nazis had come fully armed. First one gunshot cracked across the narrow street, then another, and another. The defenceless protestors had no chance. In the ensuing bloodbath, five anti-Klan demonstrators were shot dead and another nine were injured.

Despite helping to organise the counter-demonstration, Covington was conspicuous by his absence that Saturday morning, preferring to spend the time selling some stock his grandfather had left him. He was, however, on hand to support the twelve men subsequently arrested for the massacre. "What I regret is that twelve good men are in jail," he told the Associated Press as the trial commenced. To a local TV crew he went further. Standing outside the court in full nazi uniform, fitted tightly over his corpulent figure, he declared, "I don't give a happy damn about their human rights or anything else. They got what they deserved." Asked if he felt any remorse towards the families or the victims, he replied, "One shouldn't show remorse for stamping on a rattlesnake." All of the shooters were eventually acquitted by an all-white jury, which accepted their plea of self-defence.

By 1980, Covington was head of the NSPA but, despite repeated publicity stunts, the party declined. He lost credibility when he announced his intention to organise a national "white motorcade" through Greensboro, only to be forced to backtrack by considerable public outrage. He tried to change the venue to nearby Raleigh, promising "the largest white racial demonstration in the past decade", but this too was terminated. Finally the bulky North Carolinian opted for a "Hitlerfest" at a farm south of the city. While publicly claiming that communists were going to attack the demonstration, Covington told an aide that as the motorcade was going to be so pathetically small that he and the NSPA "would look dumb". With his credibility shattered, Covington called a press conference to announce he intended to disappear.

* * * *

DURING HIS SELF-IMPOSED exile, Covington turned up in the Irish Republic. He married an Irish woman, fathered two children, and worked on the volume that would stand as his "handbook for white revolution". *March up Country* argued that the white race faced extinction if racial mixing was not reversed within fifty years, and placed much of the blame on the right-wing itself. "This movement has been simply drifting for years, with no direction or central guidance, no co-ordination, no effort to prevent waste and duplication of effort, and without the foggiest notion of where we are headed. That must end." What was needed, Covington wrote, was quite simply "a White Revolution".

March up Country outlined four stages required for this revolution: initial cadre recruitment; groundwork within the population at large; political and propaganda attacks on the system; and armed struggle. After recruiting like-minded individuals into a revolutionary group, propaganda would be disseminated to the public, firstly in the form of photocopied sheets but later in a tabloid newspaper. The enemy needed to be softened up before engagement. "Psychological warfare serves several vitally important purposes," wrote Covington. "Psywar unnerves the enemy, demoralizes him, confuses him about his role in the scheme of things. Psychological warfare should make the enemy doubt. It should raise our own morale correspondingly. Play on that fear, my brothers! Remember, an unnerved and rattled Jew is a Jew who makes mistakes."

After parallel structures to society had been established, phase four – armed struggle – could begin. This would be the moment of truth. "At long last the masks of legality and fairness will be ripped from the faces of the Jew and his hirelings and there Yehudi will stand, dripping Talmudic hatred, screaming in his fear and rage, urging his slaves to destroy the hatred Aryan goyishe race. By banning us and 'officially' suspending or revoking the Constitution, the enemy will have admitted defeat. And if he could not hold us down with all his money, his computers, his television, and his Holocaust lie, then how can he keep us down with mere guns and barbed wire?"

One man who found this fantasy plausible was John Cato. Born in 1964, Cato joined the British Movement at the age of thirteen whilst at grammar school in Gravesend, Kent. He remained in the BM for three years but was never more than an interested observer. In the early Eighties, he performed in a punk band, acquired the nickname "Weenie" and briefly considered himself an anarchist, dropping out of organised politics. By the mid-Eighties, he was beginning to question the world again. In the meantime, he met his future wife, Lisa, several years his junior, and together they were to have four children. In 1990, Cato came into contact with Paul Jeffries, a Yorkshire-based nazi who had extensive links with extremists across the Atlantic and, like Cato, preferred to operate behind the scenes. Together they formed Life Rune Books, a book club offering publications and tapes previously unavailable in Britain. Cato read, and was immediately captivated by, Covington's writings: his humorous style, mixed with an honesty rarely found on the Right, was a breath of fresh air for a British man so demoralised with the state of the movement in his own country.

Though aimed at an American audience, *March Up Country* became required reading for Cato and, eventually, the Sargent brothers. They saw it as their blueprint for action, once adapted for a British setting. Steve Sargent – who began to correspond with Covington – was impressed by the book. "I thought it was good, though obviously a bit dated." Photocopy it and pass it on, had been Covington's instructions. They did. They particularly liked the bearded nazi's vision of a small, elite core at the vanguard of the revolution. "This small group will get together and determine that something must be done," he had written. "They will then begin to contact, feel out and recruit other like-minded individuals. There will be nothing in the way of formal organisation at this stage, just a group of people who hold similar views."

Covington's wanderings had finally taken him back to the United States, where he further developed his ideas in a fortnightly newsletter, *Resistance*. It was this newssheet he used to announce that he was once again on the move. "I have a plan of my own, which I have entitled Plan X. What is Plan X, you ask? Ah, there's the rub – I can't tell you."

* * * *

HAROLD COVINGTON FLEW to London. It was late October 1991, four months before the formation of C18. He appeared down on his luck, and moved into a small, ground-floor bedsit in an ageing terraced house in east London. Despite his deep-seated racism, he seemed content to be one of the few white people in the street. His main concern was remaining unnoticed. Steve Sargent began to speak to him regularly on the phone. "I wanted to meet him but he wouldn't do it. He was feeling really paranoid."

Covington was careful to protect the true nature of his stay in London. What little could be gleamed from his writings was that he hoped to develop his Resistance Network, its three components being networking, ideological guidance and *samizdat* publishing. Networking was putting nazis in communication with one another, with his *Resistance* newsletter being the bulletin board. He was especially keen to steer people away from the tried – and failed – paths so often trodden by others. New contacts would be encouraged to produce literature. "I envision whole runs of new work like this, not so much in book form as in loose leaf or pamphlet format where many copies can be made from high quality master copy, swelling outward in a ripple effect." Covington liked the word *samizdat*; it encapsulated his outlook. The word – literally "self-publishing" – had been coined to describe the anti-communist, underground propaganda printed on secret basement presses in the former Soviet Union. Always one for theatre, Covington likened those days with the situation faced by the newly-emerging European far-right. He advised people to read George Orwell's *1984* as an accurate insight into the future. Covington even adopted the pen name of Orwell's hero, Winston Smith, and believed that only he had the ideas to lead the movement forward. "Call me an ombudsman, call me a latter day Tom Paine, call me an egotistical jackass, call me whatever you want, but for Heaven's sake listen to what I say and start thinking about things."

The Britons enjoyed the attention shown them by the colourful and controversial Covington. John Cato was delighted. He found the American an entertaining writer with perceptive views on the state of the far-right internationally. Covington urged them to ignore party politics and organise underground, even when their activities were legal. Soon he and Covington, with Paul Jeffries working secretly in the background, launched a plan to reinvigorate nazism in Britain. Significantly, Cato and Jeffries were also the British representatives of the National Alliance, an American nazi group run by William Pierce and viewed by many as the most dangerous organisation that side of the Atlantic.

The decision of the BNP to form a stewards' group, and the subsequent emergence of C18, provided Cato and Jeffries with the opportunity to launch a new national socialist organisation – one that could translate the vision of *March Up Country* into a reality. Cato became indispensable to Charlie Sargent, with the two men meeting at least once a month and talking regularly on the phone. Cato offered advice, suggested reading and provided Sargent with an intelligent sounding board – something lacking among his friends, In Sargent, Cato saw a keen and committed nazi who had the inclination and influence to pull a section of the British Right away from its existing organisations. Covington's arrival had been timely, coinciding with their own desire for a new national socialist group and the increasing militancy and confidence of the movement's rank and file.

"This is the new era, the silent hunter is the most feared enemy, one it can neither name nor can find, UNDERMINE – DEMORALIZE – DESTROY," the first issue of *Redwatch* announced. By the second issue, it contained an American address: Dixie Press, Raleigh, North Carolina – Harold Covington's post office box. Another piece of Covington advice – disguise your identity, he preached. *Redwatch* was only the start. "There will be other organisations," wrote Covington, "ideally ranging from crude pulp 'hate-niggers' agitational material to slick urbane theoretical publications."

Within a few weeks of *Redwatch* appearing, John Cato launched *The Oak*, a densely theoretical journal by comparison. "We should stress," Cato wrote, "that *The Oak*, though a small and fractional part of an increasing armoury of similar publications, is above all else a tool; a tool for the propagation of the message of White survival." Cato was keen for his readers to know exactly where *The Oak* stood. "We are neither supporting publication of any existing or future organisation, nor the sole vehicle of British National Socialism; nor does this publication presumptuously assume itself as the sole voice of all British National Socialists. The sole purpose of whatever *The Oak* does, in any form, is to maintain and champion the cause of the Aryan peoples – wherever they may reside."

A few months later, another publication appeared. Unlike *The Oak*, it was openly aligned to C18. *The Order* was produced by Charlie Sargent, taking its name from a nazi terrorist group in America in the mid-Eighties. Unlike the theoretical *The Oak*, it was a street magazine for activists. Almost simultaneously, a further C18 publication emerged. *Putsch* was produced by Steve Sargent, using the pseudonym Albion Wolf, and came in a deliberately simple format and a jokey, sarcastic style. The newsletter, which was to run to forty monthly issues, was heavily based on Covington's *Resistance*.

Slowly but surely, what began as a loose mob of nationalist thugs was turning into a distinct nazi organisation. Though Covington broke off his trip to Britain by a couple of months after his presence was exposed in the press, he left behind a group fully capable of operating independently. It now had an ideology – however outlandish – and a goal. And Charlie Sargent, guided by his brother and John Cato, was emerging as its leader. For the first time in his life, the former football hooligan and convicted drug dealer felt important.

CHAPTER THREE

The Right Splits

DEREK BEACKON LOOKED flabbergasted as he took to the town hall stage. Rumours that the contest would be close had been sweeping through the ranks of his supporters outside the building, but no-one had expected this. Yet after two recounts, the startling result was confirmed: by a margin of just seven votes, the British National Party had secured its first-ever council election victory, in the deprived Tower Hamlets ward of Millwall. It was September 7, 1993, and Beackon was now the councillor of a London borough on a racist ticket.

The story grabbed media headlines for the next forty-eight hours as politicians of all persuasions queued up to condemn the result. BNP leader John Tyndall was delighted, describing the vote as a "moment in history" and depicting it as merely the beginning. "Success is infectious," he gloated. "It spreads quickly. And it infuses those dedicated to a great cause with the enthusiasm to preserve and redouble their efforts. Just one electoral victory, even if not a big one, will demonstrate to millions of people around Britain that the BNP is capable of winning, that a vote for it may well not be wasted. If it can win in the Millwall ward of Tower Hamlets, it can win other wards in the same borough – wards where in the past its votes, while quite good, would have been even better if the voters thought its candidates had a chance of being elected. And if it can establish a pattern of winning seats in Tower Hamlets, it can begin to do so elsewhere in London – and far beyond." In the weeks that followed, BNP headquarters would receive over 500 enquiries from members of the public. While few actually joined, this represented the greatest single influx of interest in the organisation's history.

Few of those involved in the campaign had believed they had a chance of winning, though they had expected a far higher vote than usual. Tower Hamlets was exactly the kind of depressed inner-city area that most attracts the far-right. It encompasses much of the old East End docks, and many residents had lost their jobs during the preceding three decades as London declined both as a port and as a manufacturing city. Swathes of factories and warehouses, from Limehouse to Blackwall, had closed. In 1981, the London Docklands Development Corporation was formed to regenerate the area, but the influx of investment had yet to trickle down to the hard-pressed residents, creating considerable resentment. This was exacerbated by the large number of immigrants in the area, many recently arrived from Bangladesh and Somalia. The BNP had banged away at this with its Rights for Whites strategy, telling white residents that they were being ignored at the expense of the Asian community. A few days before the election, the local Labour Party, in the hope of scaring its own vote into turning out, had leaked canvass returns to the press showing that the BNP had a chance. The policy backfired, as voters realised that the BNP was in contention.

By targeting a small area, the BNP concentrated its resources and established itself as an alternative voice outside the existing political establishment, albeit one backed up by a propensity to use violence as a tool. It would repeat this strategy over the coming months, assisted by a string of local council by-elections which enabled it to campaign almost constantly. As its vote increased, the BNP began turning away from potentially violent marches and mass meetings. "By this stage of our development we decided that the unpredictable, noisy and volatile public meetings were a thing of the past," said local organiser Steve Smith. "Although they helped us establish our name in Tower Hamlets, they required a great deal of resources and time to organise. More importantly, we had learnt from canvassing feedback as well as from anecdotal evidence that public meetings were becoming, by this time, somewhat counter-productive."

Combat 18, he intimated, was surplus to requirements.

★ ★ ★ ★

TENSION BETWEEN THE BNP and C18 had been rising over the previous year. Despite C18's origin as BNP muscle, it had become a separate entity and, while still aligned with its progenitor, had stopped giving it uncritical support. Similarly, while most in the BNP were content to have Sargent and his goons on standby, there had always been a minority who were not. Their objections had been sidelined initially: there had been a belief that street mobilisations such as Bermondsey and Eltham would benefit the party, while C18's leaders, for their part, were at first fully behind the BNP. "We support John Tyndall and Richard Edmonds 100%...The BNP is growing and anybody who would try and split the movement will be dealt with by us," wrote Charlie Sargent in an early issue of *The Order*.

This honeymoon period could not last as the obvious contradictions appeared between a political party seeking respectability and a street force hell-bent on confrontation. In January 1993, a BBC television crew was allowed in to a BNP meeting in east London as part of a documentary on British neo-nazis. Tyndall and Edmonds were keen to impress, packing the meeting with supporters from across the south-east region while telling the presenter, Sarah Spiller, that it was just another local branch meeting. But when the camera swept around the room, it revealed that some in the audience were less than happy. A small team from the East End Barmy Army, now the core of C18, began barracking the crew. Outside the hall, the sound recordist was struck on the head with a bottle, an incident that embarrassed Tyndall, undermining the respectable image he sought. A week later, Spiller interviewed Tyndall and brought up the attack, pressing him to condemn it. Increasingly irritated with the line of questioning, Tyndall snapped, ordering the crew and Spiller out of his house. Then, unaware that the camera was still rolling, he told Spiller that the film crew had got what they deserved. The resulting programme was a public relations disaster.

C18 was equally annoyed, though for different reasons. It had protested about the presence of the film crew but its objections had been over-ridden by David Bruce, the party's deputy organiser. In criticising the BNP's handling of the incident, C18 was also attacking the party's general approach. Charlie Sargent, writing before the Tower Hamlets victory in issue two of *The Order*, made plain his growing contempt for the BNP: "Two words can be used to describe the Nationalist movement over the past thirty years – total failure. For thirty years we have held marches, stood in elections, sold thousands of papers and magazines and distributed hundred of thousands of leaflets. In return we have failed to win any elections anywhere; failed to build up a mass movement and failed to gain any political power – ANYWHERE. Meanwhile, the Establishment have passed race-acts, banned our rally's, march's [sic] and meetings, hounded our people from their homes and jobs. The struggle in the '90s has evolved to a new level and our present leaders have failed to respond. The Nationalists are still using the failed tactics of the 1970's – rally's [sic] and elections – to win support."

In turn, a Granada TV *World In Action* documentary on C18 in April 1993 compounded growing BNP unease at the thuggery of its stewards. The programme detailed the group's violence, identified its leaders and revealed its close relationship to the Loyalist paramilitaries of the Ulster Defence Association. Many in the BNP were horrified, none more than David Bruce, who had long called for a separation of the two groups. Despite Bruce's long service to British nationalism and his strong support for John Tyndall, he was widely disliked by the party's rank and file; his slightly dark complexion and his occupation as a taxi driver even gave rise to allegations that he was Jewish. "We do believe that Dave Bruce is a half-Jew and has no place in the leadership of a nationalist movement," declared C18, even while it was still fully behind the BNP. The *World In Action* programme was a turning point in the relationship between the two groups.

A perceived lack of security within the BNP became the next nail in the coffin. C18 was suspicious of Tim Hepple, a BNP officer, and was proved right when he appeared on the *World In Action* programme as an informer for *Searchlight* magazine. C18 also targeted another BNP member, Peter Rushden, a leading figure in the Manchester branch. In the summer of 1993, C18 claimed it had deliberately fed him false information that later appeared in *Searchlight* and had intercepted his correspondence with anti-fascists, proving that he was an informer. Whether C18 really believed Rushden was an informer is unclear, but the group certainly did not approve of his family background. An Oxford graduate, Rushden was one of the few university-educated people in the BNP and as a result was soon travelling abroad on its behalf. "Peter Rushden was a sad little individual," derided Charlie Sargent in one publication, "who because of his middle class accent and his middle class education was allowed to rise to a position of trust in the BNP within a matter on months. He was jetted around the world at the BNP's expense and given access to confidential files on members, etc. The first thing that pissed us off was the way he was pushed to the top of the BNP ahead of decent working class lads from the East End, or Glasgow or Leeds." C18 took its complaints about Rushden to the BNP leadership in December 1992 but with little success. Undeterred, it continued to distrust him. Events turned nasty for the BNP man at an annual nationalist jamboree in Diksmuide, Belgium, the following August. Attending the event in the company of a number of leading BNP officials, Rushden ran into a contingent of C18 thugs. After a short exchange, he was attacked, the first of two beatings he would suffer.

Charlie Sargent was irritated by what he perceived was the diluting of the BNP's politics in a bid to become electorally respectable. He began publicly criticising the party and even discussing alternatives. "*The Order* magazine will be sponsoring a national socialist rally in London, in October," he announced in a direct challenge to the BNP. "This will be the first major NS rally held in London for ten years." In fact Sargent, with the encouragement of John Cato, had planned such a meeting six months earlier, but his inability to get a big-name foreign speaker, and the fallout from the *World In Action* programme, had caused his to shelve the plan, albeit temporarily.

It soon became clear that the two groups were heading their

separate ways. David Bruce felt confident enough to address a BNP meeting in London and declare that the party should rid itself of C18. Even Eddie Butler, the man who established the stewards' group, was thinking along the same lines. He had created a monster he couldn't control. Sargent soon learned what was going on through his friends in the party rank and file. "People like Butler and Bruce are total Tory's [sic] and view most working class people as scum to be used," he wrote in *The Order*. "Such people can have no place in a National Socialist movement who must be seen to protect and help the White working class of Britain."

As the BNP pounded the streets and walkways of Millwall in the run-up to the council election, C18 conducted its own activities. Quaddis Ali, a young Asian man, was badly attacked by a gang of white racists a few days before the vote. A demonstration held in solidarity outside the hospital in which he lay soon turned to violence after police attempted to clear the area in a heavy-handed manner. C18 responded by heading down Brick Lane the following night. The police questioned their thirty-strong mob outside one pub but allowed them to remain in the area, where eventually they ran through the streets smashing the windows of Asian-owned shops with baseball bats, bottles and bricks. Steve Sargent was the group's one casualty; he was caught by a group of locals and slashed repeatedly across the head with what appeared to be a machete.

Meanwhile, C18 was advancing its own agenda. "The October meeting will start the ball rolling, followed by meetings in Scotland, Yorkshire, and in the Midlands, over the next year," Charlie Sargent reported in the autumn issue of *The Order*. "At these meetings, a National Socialist manifesto will be drawn up that suits every group...As the Movement evolves so a natural leader will emerge." He made it clear that the BNP did not feature in his future plans. "Should We Split From The BNP?" Charlie quizzed his readers. "My own view is yes! The BNP is riddled with cranks and informers. Recent history shows that a man with a middle class accent and college tie, who is a member only five minutes, will always be pushed and promoted over a working class lad who has put in years of hard work. However, many may wish to stay inside the BNP, and if that is the case, we propose those cells inside the BNP must work with the aim of taking over the BNP from within, in all forms of power, at every Branch level i.e. the funds and membership must be controlled by National Socialists, and promote our manifesto."

That manifesto, such as it was, clearly favoured the boot over the ballot box. Sargent had no time for people poncing about pretending to be politicians. He wanted action. In this, as in his ideology, he drew inspiration not from his own shores but from across the Atlantic.

★ ★ ★ ★

ROBERT J. MATTHEWS was a right-wing legend. In the mid-1980s, he and a small group of racist followers had declared war on the United States Government. In the space of eighteen months his group, known variously as "The Secret Brotherhood" and "The Order", conducted a campaign of killings and robberies that they hoped would ignite a race war. They assassinated Alan Berg, a Jewish radio talk-show host, after he had made a number of disparaging comments about the white supremacist movement. They murdered fellow right-winger Walter West, who they feared would expose their plans to the police. They killed a security guard during one of their robberies. "By ones and by twos, by scores and by legions we will drive the enemy into the sea. Through our blood and God's will, the land promised to our fathers of old will become the land of our children to be," Matthews announced in his written *Declaration of War*.

To finance its operations, The Order carried out a series of armed raids, beginning with the theft of just $369 from a pornographic store in Spokane, Washington, and working their way up to what was then the largest-ever seizure from a U.S. armoured truck when, in July 1984, they stole $3.8 million. Of the $4.3 million in total the group obtained from robberies, only $600,000 was ever recovered. To compliment their heists, The Order also established a major counterfeiting operation which they hoped would eventually undermine the financial stability of the U.S. economy.

The Order came to an abrupt end when the mundane arrest of Tom Martinez for possession of counterfeit money led the authorities to the heart of the operation. Though on the fringes of the group, Martinez was a trusted friend of Matthews and, despite warnings from those around the leader, had been allowed to know too much. Fearing prison, he struck a deal with the authorities, telling them all about the group, its leaders and plans. The FBI, which had had few previous leads on the group, began making arrests.

Matthews made a last stand, single-handedly occupying a building on Whidbey Island in Washington state and holding off the police. A twelve-hour stand-off ensued. Rather than surrender to face possible life imprisonment, Matthews died under a hail of bullets and a fire that ripped through the building. The demise of The Order had come just in time: the group had intended to disrupt the 1984 Los Angeles Olympics and had even devised a plan to poison the water supply of three major cities.

Matthews instantly became a right-wing martyr. His defiant stand and his uncompromising belief in direct action enticed thousands of other extremists disillusioned with the political process. He was presented as an ordinary American aggrieved with society. His death also did much to publicise the novel that had been his inspiration: *The Turner Diaries*, a fictional account of one man's fight against the American system.

Set in the late 1990s, *The Turner Diaries* depicts a right-wing underground army taking up the battle with the American Government, which it claims is under Jewish control. A race war develops after the Government outlaws the right to bear arms and attempts to enforce racial integration. Leading the revolt is a white underground movement called the Organization, with a secret leadership known as The Order. Members conduct a terrorist campaign, from the blowing up of FBI buildings to a rocket attack on Congress. Supply lines are cut as the economic infrastructure of America is slowly destroyed. Finally the white population wins, but only after Israel is destroyed by nuclear weapons. Described by some as a modern-day *Mein Kampf, The Turner Diaries* became a core text for thousands of nazis throughout the world. It introduced the term ZOG – the Zionist Occupation Government – to describe its conspiracy theory of a Jewish-run society, a myth adopted by nazi movements in several countries. While the Jewish conspiracy has long been a central plank of far-right thinking, *The Turner Diaries* provided it with a demonic catchphrase, and the acronym ZOG became ubiquitous.

The Turner Diaries had been written in 1978 by Andrew Macdonald, a pen name for William Pierce, arguably America's most important white supremacist. Pierce began his political involvement with the John Birch Society, before moving over to the American Nazi Party under the leadership of Lincoln Rockwell. Shortly after a fellow Nazi Party member assassinated Rockwell, Pierce left to join the National Youth Alliance, its mottos "Free Men Are Not Equal" and "Equal Men Are Not Free". In 1974, he founded the National Alliance, through which he built up arguably the most important and well-funded nazi organisation in America. Twenty years on, the National Alliance has chapters in most states, a comprehensive book service and a radio station that beams Pierce's message across the continent.

Robert J. Matthews had idolised Pierce, believing he was a possible leader of the future, and gave the National Alliance leader $100,000 from his robberies. The respect was mutual, though Pierce did think that Matthews acted too impulsively. "Bob gave us a very important symbol," Pierce later claimed. "He did what was morally right. He may have been a bit premature ... and he may have made many tactical errors. But he reminded us that we are not engaged in a debate between gentlemen. Instead, we are engaged in the most desperate war we have ever fought. A war for the survival of our race. Bob elevated our struggle. He took us from name-calling to blood letting. In the long run that will be helpful." (*The Turner Diaries* is still influencing right-wing terrorists. In April 1995, Timothy McVeigh planted a bomb which devastated a federal building in Oklahoma City, the single most destructive act of domestic terrorism in US history. It followed, almost to the letter, a scene from *The Turner Diaries*, McVeigh's favourite book. In Britain, the book was a favourite of David Copeland, the London nail bomber).

While The Order catapulted Matthews and his followers into legendary status among America's nazis, some were determined to learn from their mistakes. One was Louis Beam, a fiery orator and rabble-rouser with a life-long dedication to national socialism. Beam captured international headlines when he tried to strangle Deng Xiaoping during the Chinese leader's visit to Houston in 1980. A year later, he was again in the news, offering assistance to a group of West Coast fisherman who were under increasing competition from Vietnamese immigrant crews. Beam and his supporters rallied to their cause, burning Vietnamese-owned ships and threatening their crews. There was no disputing his political zeal. At five foot seven inches tall, Beam was a small, thin man with dark, piercing eyes. Wherever he went he attracted support, for if nothing else he was a formidable public speaker. In a cleverly deceptive manner, he seemed to often lose control when speaking to an audience, his mouth frothing with an unhealthy mixture of rage and passion, his arms gesticulating wildly.

The federal authorities attempted to link a number of prominent right-wing extremists to The Order's conspiracy of bombings and assassinations, including Beam who, after a period on the run, returned to face trial. He defended himself in court and was acquitted. "They call me a seditionist," he said a short time after. "If you look at the definition of seditionist, it's one who opposes the established authority. And I am a seditionist." Soon after his trial, Beam wrote probably his most important document, *Leaderless Resistance*, a strategy for guerrilla warfare. Instead of the standard type of centralised nazi group with a hierarchical leadership, Beam advocated a cell system consisting of up to four individuals, acting secretly and independently from others to prevent police infiltration. If one cell were exposed or destroyed, this would have no effect on other cells.

The story of The Order and the writings of pseudo-intellectuals like Louis Beam had a significant effect on the development of C18. "It was less than ten years prior to us being formed," one C18 supporter says. "It was within our generation, our lifetime. It happened in 1984, a lot of our lads were in their mid-to-late teens, and while most wouldn't have remembered it, they could relate to it because it was in today's society. No one could really relate to the German era. Robert Matthews was a hero of mine. He just went out and it did it." But it was more than that. Many inside C18 believed the strategy was right, in theory at least. "It was the right way, the cell structure and everything. He didn't succeed, but it was the only way to do it. Maybe it failed because America wasn't ready, or Tom Martinez was a grass, I don't know, but it certainly was the right way to do it, at least compared to any other right-wing group."

There was another factor influencing the young C18 crew. The violence, the mystique and the glamour of armed resistance was more compelling than the boring drudgery of electioneering offered by the BNP. "Of course there was romanticism in it," admits the former C18 supporter. "They said, 'Fuck it, we'll declare war on America.' Some people can't comprehend what they actually meant, declare war on America. There was nothing that would supersede that. It was just fucking mental. Then they actually went out and tried to do it. The plans they had, before it all came on top, were phenomenal. There was the well-documented one about the Los Angeles Olympics. If they had got away with some of these things, it would have destabilised America unbelievably. One man through his beliefs was prepared to take on the most powerful country in the world."

Another young man, in another country, would take this message to heart. Will Browning had become an indispensable part of C18. He was a fearless fighter and a fanatical activist. But Browning – or "Wilf the Beast", as he was sometimes known – wanted much more than street brawls. He devoured the stories of Robert Matthews and The Order. That was the way to go. The thoughts and deeds of Matthews, Pierce and Beam fitted his own view of what a nazi should aspire to: ideology and action, hand in hand. He also had an irresistible urge to prove people wrong. Browning was obsessed with how others viewed him, and when the Union of Jewish Students produced a pamphlet outlined a number of terrorist groups operating in Britain – and disparaged the threat posed by C18 – he was incensed. Browning became determined to prove the Jewish students wrong.

CHAPTER FOUR

The Beast

WILL BROWNING'S THIRST for violence may owe much to his unsettled upbringing. He was born in north London on April 19, 1970, but his parents separated when he was only four, and his mother took him back to her birthplace on the island of Jersey. Though she had a close family network around her, and soon remarried, her young son became increasingly detached, and his relationship with his new stepfather was poor. He was constantly in fights with other boys. At the age of nine, Browning was allowed to take up boxing as a means to channel his aggression. It failed. He continued to be involved in fights and petty vandalism and within a year was arrested for violence.

Though he was later to recall his childhood as being "ordinary" and "no different from anyone else's", it clearly was different. After further trouble in and out of school, the eleven-year old Browning was sent to a secure school, where he was to spend the next three and a half years. He was locked in outside school hours for the first six months, then was able to earn weekend visits home for good behaviour. It was a place hardly conducive to educational success: twelve young people, all but two boys, and all too disruptive to be incorporated into mainstream schools, being taught in one classroom and sleeping in dorms. Browning learned the guitar and adopted a skinhead appearance for the tough image it transmitted. His spell at the secure school did little to rehabilitate him, as he continued to get into trouble during his visits home. Finally, when Browning was just fifteen, an exasperated judge used a provision in Jersey law whereby foreign nationals who commit crimes can be excluded to order him off the island for three years.

Browning was to claim that his time at the secure school had no negative affect on his personality or ability to relate to other people, but being shut away from family and friends at such an early age must have done little to improve his social skills or respect for others, especially in positions of authority. One unlikely consequence of his unconventional childhood was a puritanical streak that would later mark him out from others in Combat 18. When, years later, his friends liked nothing better than to watch strippers and visit the red light areas of foreign cities, Browning would be appalled. And when Steve Sargent would send him hard-core porn mags through the post to wind him up, Browning would lock his girlfriend in the house while he burned the publications outside. "Sex is all right once in a while," he once confided, "but it's not like the feeling you get when you wedge someone's head by a kerb and kick it."

The exiled teenager returned to London to live with his father, who ran a building company in which he would serve an apprenticeship. He dreamed of joining the elite Parachute Regiment of the British Army and had begun the admission process when he courted trouble again. Browning had become involved with nazis, initially through the skinhead music scene in the capital, and was made guitarist with a band called Brutal Attack in 1989. One night, he and an Italian skinhead attacked a gay man in Kings Cross and left him bleeding in the gutter before going on to assault a group of black people in a nearby burger bar. Browning was arrested and later sentenced to three years for grievous bodily harm and one year for affray. A spell in Feltham Young Offender's Institution, followed by a transfer to Warren Hill adult prison, hardened his already damaged outlook on life. He laughed when, years later, he heard of attempts to improve the regime at Feltham. "I was in there when it was much worse," he boasted, which says more about his own warped outlook on life than any assessment of penal policy.

Browning's hopes of a career in the Paras were now in tatters, and he saw injustice all around him: from the gay man who "only got a bloody nose", to his Jewish lawyer who had advised him to plead guilty to GBH in the hope of a lighter sentence, to the judge who had punished him so severely. He inwardly vowed revenge on a society he already despised.

On his release, Browning became a strict vegetarian and also gave up alcohol in his bid for total fitness, spending up to three hours a day with his weights and punch bag and developing a powerful, muscular physique. He also immersed himself in the far-right, principally with the British National Party, which was becoming increasingly active in the east London neighbourhood where he lived. He was never a party member but attended meetings and demonstrations and became friendly with the East End Barmy Army. Though one of the youngest in the group, Browning quickly earn a reputation for being "game", and with it the nickname Wilf the Beast. He lied about his past convictions and political beliefs to join the Royal Marine Reserves, based in south-east London, with the sole motive of learning how to use a gun, though the combination of a knee injury and his arrest for C18 activities some months later would force him to leave. By early 1994, Browning had moved into a modern two-bedroom house in Bermondsey, having taken advantage of a 100% mortgage he saw advertised in the *Evening Standard*, and converted the second bedroom into a gym, where he worked out feverishly. He was also working as a carpenter and making good money.

Browning shared his house with a long-term girlfriend he had met through the nazi music scene. Theirs was an unconventional relationship, with his girlfriend playing second fiddle to the movement. Even when Browning made an effort to be romantic, it invariably backfired. On one of his trips abroad he bought her a tin of biscuits as a present. On another, left to his own devices in an airport duty free shop, he presented her with a bottle of Polo Sport for men. More recently, he claimed that he did not have time to buy the Christmas dinner; this went down so badly that, in order to have a roof over his head for the festive period, he was forced to search south-east London at gone 10pm on Christmas Eve for anything resembling a fowl.

There was, however, never any violence in their relationship; Browning had a rigid, though unconventional, sense of honour.

Indeed, his girlfriend gave as good as she got. She doted on her two German shepherd dogs, which she described as "her babies", and on one occasion was forced to choose between them and her boyfriend. One of the dogs had jumped up at Browning and bitten him across the face. Furious, he decided that it had to die and chased it around the house. He eventually caught up with the animal as it cowered in its kennel. His partner sat between the dog and the entrance to prevent Browning from spearing it with a long knife he had attached to a broom handle.

Dysfunctional in many ways, Browning was no respecter of tradition or authority. His impulsive and aggressive behaviour would see him confront and threaten more of his political allies than his opponents, including some of the most respected nazis internationally. It was also not unknown for him to extend his threats to police officers. During a trial for producing racist material in 1997, Browning was teased by one of his arresting officers.

"It looks like you're going down, Wilfy boy," the officer mocked. "You're not so brave now."

Browning was furious. After offering out the policeman for a fight around the corner, he told him that his friend owned a boxing gym in south London. "You and me in the ring," he said. "We can both put up £5,000 and it's winner takes all."

The officer laughed but Browning was determined not to let the matter drop. He returned to court the next day with a business card for the gym. On hearing that the officer was not in for the day, Browning gave the card to a colleague to pass on. On the back he had added his own phone number. "Tell him the offer stands," he fumed.

★   ★   ★   ★

DESPITE THE BNP'S electoral success in Millwall, Charlie Sargent remained unimpressed. "While we certainly don't wish to take anything away from Derek Beackon, or even the BNP 'leadership', apart from the media and Establishment embarrassment, what has been achieved?" he wrote. "A few red faces, a couple of sleepless nights, perhaps even a few Whites may have come out in sympathy and vote for the BNP again. Big deal. To some of us the lack of option now open to the BNP has been obvious from the outset. Yes, the BNP makes no other pretences than that it is, as a political party, attempting to enter government through nothing other than up a democratic path. Great. Good ol' British. Tally-ho. Well now they have done that and with some measure of tiny 'success'. Fundamentally it is a failure. Complete and utter failure." Sargent even ridiculed the party's surprise at the opposition to Beackon's victory. "Since when has 'democracy' guaranteed any rights to Whites? *Worse, why does the BNP expect it to?*"

His conclusion was clear. "If White Britons want to secure the existence of our people and a future for White children we are going to have to begin answering the answering the questions that the BNP has ignored. It is simple: If the System continues to exist, to continually batter down White families, if necessary kill them …then there is only ONE answer. It is either the System and its paid agents….or it's us. Whose side are you on?"

Any hopes of reconciliation between the BNP and C18 were shattered just three days after Beackon's election. The BNP, despite police opposition, decided to proceed with its weekly paper sale in Brick Lane. Buoyed up by the election victory, some sixty supporters turned up on the day, but this comparatively large turnout was dwarfed by several hundred anti-fascists protestors, especially when police prevented many of the nazis from entering Brick Lane itself. Barriers erected to protect the BNP from the anti-fascists proved to be their undoing when the action began.

A prolonged stand-off ended when a small group of young men came walking down the street singing the National Anthem and "Rule Britannia". Assuming they were right-wingers, the police allowed the baseball cap-wearing group behind the barriers and towards the increasingly nervous BNP contingent. By the time everyone realised they were anti-fascists, it was too late; the police were trapped behind the barricades while the BNP contingent felt the full weight of bottles and punches. The Anti-

Nazi League, massed on the other side of the road, cheered as the BNP ran in every direction.

Simon Chadwick, a BNP member who had previously been an active and violent supporter of C18, headed straight for The Sun pub, knowing that a large group of C18 brawlers were drinking inside.

"Quick," he shouted, out of breath, "the Reds are attacking the paper sale."

"The BNP can go and fuck themselves," came the reply, to laughter. "They said that they didn't need us, well that's fine by us. Fuck off and tell them that."

In late November, C18 released a glossy issue of *Redwatch*: over fifty pages of pure hate. The *Black Mag*, as it became known, bore the fingerprints of the increasingly influential Will Browning. All restraints were off as Browning set out his outrageous priorities: "To ship all non-whites back to Africa, Asia, Arabia, alive or in body bags... To execute all queers... To execute all white race mixers... To weed out all Jews in the Government, the media, the arts, the professions. To execute all Jews who have actively helped to damage the white race and to put into camps the rest until we find a final solution for the eternal Jew."

Jews faced the bulk of abuse. Like all nazi groups, including supposedly respectable organisations such as the British National Party, C18 saw Jewish people as the root of all evil. Nazis are still preoccupied with their alleged domination of society, even in countries with tiny Jewish populations such as Poland and Austria. The Jews are seen as a homogenous unit, working together to undermine Western societies. Nazis contend that communism and capitalism are Jewish creations, and that the arrival of black and Asian people into Britain is a ploy by Jews to dilute and weaken the Aryan race.

"They run the world," one C18 supporter told this author. "They've got this committee of three hundred. It's an international conspiracy."

I asked him who exactly was part of this committee.

"It's the bankers and the people who run the newspapers."

He insisted that Rupert Murdoch, owner of *The Sun*, the *News of the World* and *The Times*, was Jewish. When I pointed out that he was in fact a born-again Christian, he seemed surprised. "Yeah, but he's a Zionist, isn't he? He's pro-Israel, so it's the same really."

Asked again to name names, he admitted that he couldn't. "But that's how successful it is. It's there, but no-one knows whose part of it."

It is a classic conspiracy theory. Rather than exploding the myth as nonsense, his inability to say who was on this mysterious committee was proof of the deviousness of those behind the conspiracy.

As Browning ascended the small C18 hierarchy, so the Jew-baiting increased. In the summer of 1993, a group of C18 supporters led by Mark Atkinson, Ian Holloway and Matthew Osbury used an England football match in Poland as an opportunity to visit the German concentration camp at Sachsenhausen. They posed for photos at the entrance to the camp, vandalised the museum, gave Hitler salutes, stole and later broke a pendant commemorating the dead, and lay on the slabs used by nazi scientists to conduct experiments. This trip was recorded in *Combat 18* magazine under the headline, "The Holocaust is a load of bollocks! C18 experts examine the myth." Will Browning authored the accompanying article:

> Why is it after fifty years people still go on about the so-called Holocaust? We know it's a load of bollocks and so must anyone else with half a brain. Yet still we're bombarded with films and documentaries about these poor little Jews, not a day goes past without some hooknose kike weeping on our TV screens, 'A vea, A vea I lost my daughter, I lost my mother and father, A vea I was gassed six times and my wife she's a table lamp'. Is there no end to this dribble, of course not because all ZOG's TV channels are controlled by the Jews. It doesn't matter that there weren't even six million Jews in the whole of German-occupied Europe or that most of these so-called gassed

Jews fucked off to New York, Israel and Whitechapel before there was any smell of danger. We at C18 decided to send a team of experts to examine these so-called death camps.

A trolley used to transport the bodies of dead Jewish people to the ovens was described as being "purchased as Billingsgate Fish Market in 1958"; poles on which Jewish people were tortured and whipped were described as being "used by the SS for drying their washing on"; and Mark Atkinson was pictured posing in the camp ovens above the caption, "On further investigation we found that you couldn't cook a cheeseburger in them, let alone six million stinking Yids." The conclusion, the magazine announced, was that the "Holocaust is absolutely bollocks, there was no way six million Yids were gassed and even if they were, who gives a fuck because next time we're gonna incinerate every last stinking one of 'em! No Fuss! No Mess! Just pure cyanide."

Two years later, the same person who had told me about the committee of 300 was more candid about the use of anti-Semitism. "All the anti-Jewish stuff was done because we knew it would offend people. In recent years the TV is full of programmes and films about the Holocaust, the newspapers are always carrying stories about Germany having to pay compensation for what happened over sixty years ago. If there is one issue that really winds people up it is the Holocaust. This in itself gave us a real laugh. No-one really believed that the Holocaust didn't happen, though many questioned the six million figure, but we knew how people would get worked up about it. Laughing at Jews and denying that the Holocaust happened was the ultimate way to offend people. It had become such a taboo subject."

Though *Combat 18* was an infantile and offensive comic, with grotesque caricatures of Jewish and black people intermingled with the now common hitlists and death threats, it did explain C18's rejection of the BNP's electoral strategy by highlighting the failure of far-right parties abroad: "But what about Le Pen in France, isn't he doing well? Or Vlaams Blok in Belgium? I hear you ask. Doing well? Are they fuck. Le Pen has reached his zenith at around 15-17% of the vote. He has been like this for years; he will never break through this let alone be Prime Minister. The same in Belgium, they've got five MP's and are stuck at this level, they will stay at this level until their support fizzles out. They are going nowhere. As said before, just another pressure valve. No – this is not for us. We must change tactics."

It explained what these tactics would be. "We must build at grass roots level a movement which is not interested in playing political games but is prepared to take control of our peoples' destiny when the shit hits the fan and the Jewish multi-racial powder keg blows up in their face. These so called parties and movements are nothing more than pressure valves that the state uses to release any steam which might otherwise blow up against them. Do you think for one minute that they would allow a movement to legally exist which would stand a chance of wrestling power from the Jews? NO WAY!"

The publication of *Combat 18* was the final straw for the BNP leadership. John Tyndall called for C18 to be proscribed in a special bulletin distributed to members in December 1993:

> It has come to our notice that representatives of that organisation have been exploiting their contacts with BNP members and supporters in a deliberate drive to undermine the latter's loyalty to the BNP. The methods used to this purpose have included not only cheap and nasty 'tittle-tattle' against BNP personnel but downright attempted physical violence. In addition to this, Combat 18 seems to have assumed the right to set itself up as the disciplinary enforcement apparatus of the BNP, picking upon party members who for one reason or another have incurred its dislike, and condemning them for acts of 'treachery' against the nationalist cause, then administering 'punishment' to them by way of random beatings-up.
>
> Many of those who have read this material and listen to the talk of Combat 18 spokesmen say that their language bears a close resemblance to the 'class-war' rhetoric of the extreme left, attempting constantly to divide nationalist

from nationalist by exploiting differences of social and educational background. These disruptive tactics have no place in the nationalist movement. Things have now reached a pitch at which the BNP is no longer prepared to tolerate this divisive behaviour, and it is hereby issuing a notice of complete repudiation of Combat 18 and declaring that group to be a hostile organisation. All BNP members who have hitherto maintained links with both sides should be informed that henceforth and with effect from now they must decide where their loyalties lie. If they wish to remain in the BNP they must sever all connections with Combat 18. If they wish to remain with Combat they must consider themselves no longer members of the BNP.

Less than two years after its formation, C18 had been ostracised by its founders. Charlie Sargent feigned outrage. "Those involved in the struggle now have a straight choice," he wrote, "between the failed policies of Tory nationalism or the ideology of Adolf Hitler. The two groups cannot work together, one must be crushed." Sargent had been planning a split of his own for some time. "It is now time that the voice of the extremist and militant was listened to, for years the only words uttered by the British racist movement have been that of moderation and compromise for the sake of a few votes. It is time we faced the truth that elections are a waste of time. ONLY A WHITE WORKING CLASS REVOLT AGAINST THE STATE WILL EVER WIN US ANY FORM OF POWER...Robert Matthews, our great Aryan prototype, made a declaration of war, not one of appeasement and cowardice. It is now your decision, do you follow Tyndall or NATIONAL SOCIALISM?" His brother Steve responded in his own style, using the pages of *Putsch* and *Thor Would* to ridicule the BNP leader, calling him Tinpot or Tindole. The combination of vitriol and ridicule got the message across.

The Beast was more direct. His first victim was Tony Lecomber, a BNP London organiser who had little time for C18. Lecomber had tried to establish a stewarding group in

1989, shortly after being released from a three-year sentence for attempting bombing, and firmly believed any such group should be under strict BNP control. He was in prison again when C18 was launched, serving a three-year sentence for attacking a Jewish teacher caught peeling off a BNP sticker, and became an outspoken critic of the gang when he was released in late 1993. He was keen to reassert his authority over the London membership and, as a close ally of Eddie Butler, was a supporter of the community politics that saw the party win Millwall.

On a personal level, Lecomber had little time for Will Browning, remembering an incident in 1990 in east London when he had received a nasty beating at the hands of anti-fascists Browning had wandered off to get a burger. On hearing Browning was now C18's supposed hardman, Lecomber simply laughed. "The man's a coward," he remarked to a close friend. What Lecomber failed to realise was that Browning was now quite different from that day in 1990: four years older, considerably broader and as fit as an athlete. This Lecomber discovered to his cost in January 1994 when, on his way to a leadership meeting at BNP headquarters, he bumped into a Browning. Despite putting up brave resistance, Lecomber was badly beaten, falling down a manhole in the process.

A similar fate befell Eddie Butler, the architect of the stewards' group and the Millwall by-election victory, whose private condemnation of C18 had earned him the nickname "Snake Lips". Soon after beating up Lecomber, Browning was collecting a C18 magazine from the printers when he learned that Butler was due there the same day. He waited for him and sliced him across the face with a knife; according to C18 literature, it was an attempt to cut out Butler's tongue.

The attacks had two effects: they raised the Beast's standing considerably with his peers, and they ended any chance of a rapprochement with the BNP. A couple of meetings did take place between Richard Edmonds and the C18 leadership to try to heal the split, or at least call a truce, but they came to nothing. The divisions were not only too deep, but personal. C18 believed it was now in the ascendancy and set about establishing its own alternative political wing, the National Socialist Alliance.

All of this came at a cost. John Cato, who had played such an important role in advising Charlie Sargent during the birth of C18, became increasingly disenchanted with the group and with Sargent in particular. He was annoyed by C18's open contempt for anyone with a brain and was disgusted at the violence meted out to fellow nazis and the infantile nature of *Combat 18*. Likewise, he was also loosening his links with Harold Covington because of the American's increasingly vitriolic and negative attacks on the National Alliance in the States. While Cato and Sargent continued to talk on the phone, their chats became increasingly infrequent and inconsequential. Not that that seemed to bother Sargent much. He was enjoying his role as leader of a national socialist gang.

CHAPTER FIVE

Favours for Loyalists

WATERLOO STATION WAS heaving with commuters as Eddie Whicker and Matthew Collins made their way across the concourse. Though their meeting was not for another thirty minutes, neither of them dared to be late. Whicker was a rugged streetfighter, the Loyalist tattoos colouring his thick forearms covered by his familiar green combat jacket, his sturdy frame exaggerated by the jacket and his swagger. But he was apprehensive. It had been a couple of weeks since he and Collins had responded to an advert seeking volunteers for a London branch of the Ulster Defence Association. They had been given the name of a pub at Waterloo where, tonight, they were to ask the barman for "Billy".

As the clock approached 7pm, they became aware that they were being watched. Special Branch, they presumed. Why else would a fat Italian dressed in a shell suit be so interested in them? Still, they weren't about to stop now. They headed to the pub and ordered drinks.

Pondering whether they would they be whisked off to another meeting place or shown into a back room to be met by hooded terrorists, they were greatly disappointed when the fat Italian reappeared, in the company of two others, and asked if they had come for Billy. They were led to a little booth in the corner of the pub and finally introduced to a dark-haired, bearded man who was clearly in charge. The man looked into their eyes for a moment or two, before delving into a sports bag and bringing out a number of press cuttings. One was the December 1988 issue of *Searchlight*, its front cover depicting Whicker sporting a white leather tie on a black shirt, a shiny grey jacket, black trousers and white shoes, and his customary shades.

"You're Eddie Whicker, aren't you?" asked Billy. The tension broken, they fell about laughing.

Whicker was a close ally of C18. Billy was Frank Portinari, the new London commander of the UDA. Together they intended to forge a link that would provide the Loyalists with vital mainland support and give C18 a lift into an altogether higher league of terrorism.

British nazis had long supported the Loyalists of Ulster. At first, they favoured the paramilitary Ulster Volunteer Force (UVF), with its historic tradition and role in resisting the civil rights movement in Northern Ireland in the Sixties. In the Seventies, the then-NF leader John Tyndall proudly marched through London with the former leader of the B Specials, a Loyalist militia. From the mid-Eighties, the NF became increasingly enamoured of political developments within the UDA, a less-centralised but arguably more militant paramilitary group. Under a new and younger leadership, the NF had shifted politically, developing a more anti-capitalist and environmentalist stance. In 1980, NF man Steve Brady wrote to Andy Tyrie, a leading member of the UDA, suggesting "the establishment of friendly and useful liaison" with a number of nazi organisations across Europe, many involved in terrorist campaigns. While a letter is no measure of mutual support, the fact that Brady was later flown to Belfast to discuss his proposals does illustrate that the UDA was at least willing to consider his ideas. Mark Cotterill, a member of the Front's national executive, was also a strong supporter of the UDA: in 1991 he laid a UDA wreath during Protestant celebrations for Twelfth of July, the anniversary of William of Orange's Protestant victory over Catholicism at the Battle of the Boyne.

Others had gone further than laying flowers. In 1974, three men were convicted at Winchester Crown Court for their involvement in a conspiracy to run guns to the UDA. One was a member of the NF, another was a former Conservative councillor in Leeds and the third was a member of the right-wing Monday Club. In 1980, Joseph Bennett, an UVF supergrass, had contact with the nazi Flemish Militant Order (VMO). In testimony against eighteen other UVF members, Bennett admitted that he and Jackie 'Nigger' Irvine met VMO leader Albert Eriksson, who offered £50,000-worth of weapons, with free explosives thrown in, if they would bomb Jewish targets in Britain. Bennett claimed they had turned on their heels and walked out, Irvine telling the nazis to "fuck off." Eriksson had a different version of events: after being told that the two Loyalist representatives had no authority to conclude a deal with such a proviso, he and some of his supporters travelled to Belfast and underwent explosives training. The UVF was unwilling to launch an anti-Semitic war in Britain, and, with the arrival of a large arms shipment from the United States, felt able to decline the VMO offer.

By the late Eighties, what links that did exist between British nazis and Loyalists were usually confined to individuals acting independently of their organisations. They also tended to be one-sided, with British right-wingers generally helping the UDA. They collected money, publicly argued their cause and very occasionally transported guns across the Irish Sea. As was shown in the Belgian gun case, when the right-wing attempted to extract favours in return they were usually given a cold shoulder.

The relationship between C18 and the UDA was different from the beginning. Charlie Sargent, Gary Hitchcock, Rob Hilton and Alan Thompson, the men who had met in Steve Martin's north London flat to cement C18 a week after the BNP stewards' meeting, all had some links to the UDA or other Loyalist groups. Then there was Eddie Whicker. The former NF activist became involved in C18 at the beginning and participated in many of its early activities. When Ian Paisley addressed a Loyalist rally in Bristol in 1990, a ten-strong contingent from London UDA travelled up in a minibus. Accompanying Eddie Whicker and Frank Portinari were Rob Hilton, Charlie Sargent and Matthew Collins.

To understand this umbilical link between London UDA and the founders of C18, it is important to chart the development of the Loyalist cause during the early Nineties.

* * * *

BETWEEN 1990 AND 1994, the UVF and the Ulster Freedom Fighters (UFF), the military wing of the UDA, were responsible for more killings than their Republican enemies, the Provisional IRA. They had entered a new phase in their terror campaign. Random attacks on Catholics increased. The number of murders rose. In 1990, the Loyalist paramilitaries claimed responsibility for nineteen deaths, a four-fold increase on the previous year. By 1991, this had risen to forty-one, with only a slight drop to thirty-four in 1992. Few were known Republicans or had any connection to paramilitary activity.

Orchestrating this violence was a new generation of remorseless young gunmen. For the UVF, they included the notorious Billy Wright, known as "King Rat", from South Armagh. He was only nine when the Troubles erupted and knew nothing else but conflict. When he was sixteen, his future wife's brother was killed by the IRA. His own cousin died at the hands of an IRA bomber. Billy Wright went to war and by the age of thirty had served eight terms in prison. When news began filtering through of secret talks between Sinn Fein and intermediaries of the British Government, the Loyalist paramilitaries became increasingly concerned with London's intentions. If Republican violence could bring the British to the negotiating table, the Loyalists hoped that their violence would keep them apart. "The object is to hurt the Provos and teach the Catholic community what they have inflicted on their fellow Ulstermen. You can create a stalemate in suffering," Wright told the *Sunday Times* in 1991. "The Protestant community has the ability to destabilise Ireland. Dublin would have a field day hanging Protestants, but they know that's what they would have to do to rule us."

The changes within the UDA were even more pronounced. By 1990, the old leadership had been discredited and replaced. Their intelligence officer, Brian Nelson, had been exposed as a British informer and *agent provocateur* and the racketeering activities of James Pratt Craig, their one-time military commander, were exposed on British television. John McMichael was shot dead in what seemed an internal UDA feud and other leaders such as Tommy "Tucker" Little were imprisoned. The old regime was replaced, leaving no one from the pre-1974 leadership in senior positions.

One of the most feared of the new breed was Johnny Adair, commander of West Belfast UFF. Adair began his political life in the early Eighties as a skinhead and lead singer of the racist band Offensive Weapon; in 1985 they performed at the Rock Against Communism festival in Suffolk and paraded through Belfast on a National Front march. Many of Adair's most loyal supporters in the Second Battalion UFF shared his nazi background. Adair changed the pattern of sectarian violence. Living so close to the Catholic community of West Belfast, he brought random and indiscriminate killings to a previously insulated area, earning the nickname "Mad Dog". His battalion was believed to be responsible for over twenty Catholic murders. He would eventually be arrested and convicted for "directing terrorism", the only man to have been convicted of this charge to date.

The post-1990 UDA was also politically different. Determined to revitalise an ailing organisation, this new generation, most in their late twenties and early thirties, became more secretive and hostile towards Britain and the security forces. There was no single, identifiable leader. All interviews with the press were now conducted by the UDA inner council. Even the removal of the large oval table in the chairman's office, around which the inner council had previously met, was symbolic of a more collective leadership.

Underlying these changes were deep suspicions about Britain's true intentions towards Northern Ireland. While the old generation of UDA leaders seemed content that the British would never sell them out, the younger activists were unconvinced. They saw the secret talks with the Provos as a sign that the British were attempting to untangle themselves from the Union. When Sir Peter Brooke announced in 1989 that the British Government had no "economic interest" in the province, the young Turks in the UDA vowed to fight to the death. They believed that the

British would never have contemplated talks with the IRA, or withdrawal, if the previous UDA leadership had been more firm in their dealings with the British. "The UDA was always the line of defence between us and an enforced United Ireland," a senior Loyalist told journalists in the early Nineties. "Some of the old leadership was corrupt, sitting back, not rocking the boat. In this way the Government was able to introduce the Anglo-Irish Agreement without any fear. We can't trust the British Government and we can't trust anyone else. Without us being here, it would be so much easier for our country, and our way of life, to be taken from us."

This hardening of the UDA position led to a deadly approach that went beyond sectarian murders in Northern Ireland. Drawing up what became known as the Doomsday scenario, the UDA developed a two-pronged strategy in the event of any further British concessions to the IRA. Having seen the relative success of the IRA bombing campaign against economic targets in Britain, principally in the City of London, it decided to adopt a similar tactic in the Irish Republic. In 1992, the UFF was responsible for attacks in Dublin, Donegal and Dundalk. While its bombs were rudimentary, its intention was clear. As another senior Loyalist declared, "One day we will get it right … it is coming." The second element of their new strategy was political assassination, including targets on the British mainland. For that, they needed an efficient and active British base of support.

The UDA began to reorganise on the mainland. It had always been well represented in the Protestant strongholds of Scotland, but England was a mixed bag of five brigades, London being the principal unit containing the inner council. Some mainland members had direct links with Northern Ireland and friends and family there, but others became involved simply through supporting the cause. Despite his father being an Irish Republican, Matthew Collins was drawn towards the UDA. "The main reason for joining the UDA on mainland England was simple, it was anti-IRA," he says. "Eddie Whicker and myself only got involved in the UDA because we hated the IRA. We were not Protestants, we didn't care about Protestants; we were Loyalists."

Many of the English brigades underwent change. The London UDA commander, better known for his late-night socialising than his militarism, was replaced by the younger, more bullish Portinari. On first sight he was an odd recruit. Born Francis John Portinari, he was an Anglican, though he married a church-going Catholic, Lisa. They had two children, both of whom went to Catholic schools, one to a convent. London-born but of Italian ancestry, Portinari had no family ties to Northern Ireland; his closest link was the marriage of his stepsister to an Ulsterman, though this relationship had long ended.

Growing up in Islington, he developed a passion for football, and it was this that eventually led him to the UDA. As an avid Spurs supporter in the 1970s, he became involved in football hooliganism and, like many hooligans of this period, joined the NF, adopting its anti-IRA position. From there it was a short journey to Loyalism. He joined the UDA in 1985, rising through the ranks of its London Brigade. With a small group of friends and political acquaintances from east London, Portinari began training on some land in East Anglia. This was mostly weekend adventure stuff – survival techniques, play fighting and unarmed combat. However, there was also some weapons practice.

In 1990, the London UDA was still badly organised. It had carried out a few street attacks on its Republican opponents during the Eighties but these were largely uncoordinated and insignificant, and it had little information on its opponents. Amid speculation that the British Government was planning to ban the UDA in Northern Ireland, instructions were dispatched to recruit and re-organise. Portinari took over the reins of the London Brigade and set about rebuilding it. In his search for support, he held a detailed and prolonged discussion with the NF leader Ian Anderson and his assistant Peter Cox. Cox was keen to form a partnership, but Anderson was cool. The talks came to nothing and Portinari left the meeting with a poor opinion of the NF.

By the time Portinari met Whicker in a Waterloo pub, the bearded school janitor was already firmly in control of the

London Brigade. Under orders from Belfast headquarters, he was determined to place the UDA on a more active footing in the capital. He and Whicker bonded quickly. Whicker had provided security for virtually every British nazi leader since the early Eighties and was a man of action. Wooed by Portinari, he moved into the UDA orbit, becoming distant and secretive. He ferried senior UDA officials around London while they were on brief trips over from Belfast, and he and Portinari became regular visitors to the Loyalist drinking dens of Belfast. Whicker's stocky build, no-nonsense manner and colourful past made him a popular recruit.

The purge of the old order had left the brigades with younger, less anti-Catholic attitudes and a greater emphasis on intelligence gathering. Whicker in particular never missed an opportunity to pull out his camera and shoot a few snaps, either at Republican events such as the annual Troops Out march in London, or of anti-fascists with known links to the Republican movement. Newspapers of all political persuasions and none were bought solely to increase the archives on their opponents. The underlying aim was to turn their moribund sympathisers into active service units. One key supporter obtained a job in the Royal Mail sorting office in Kentish Town, north London. He was able to intercept a considerable amount of mail destined for the Troops Out Movement, arch-enemies of the UDA. Most of it was insignificant, but some letters were important, including one from Joan Ruddock, a former head of CND and a Labour MP.

Despite his extremism, Whicker was warm and approachable. "Eddie Whicker is a perfect gentleman," says Matthew Collins, who was his closest friend in the NF. "He is one of the most genuine and honest people I have ever met. He does not partake in racial violence, in fact he is the de-facto landlord to two Nigerian families in his block and treats them very well. Outside of politics, there is no Eddie Whicker. He is very much a homebody, and a hard worker. He is also a fashion victim. He was always trying to persuade Ian Anderson [NF leader in the early 1990s] to accept an old suit or two that he had picked up on the bin rounds. His home is immaculate; he told me that he nearly burst into tears when the Anti-Terrorist Squad ripped up his new carpet to look at the floorboards."

During 1991, Whicker had switched allegiances from the NF to the BNP, providing muscle for its activities and attending the weekly Sunday drink in east London. It was here that he and Portinari met Charlie Sargent, Hitchcock and the others. Whicker became involved in many of C18's early activities but was never entirely comfortable. After participating in the attack on left-wing paper sellers on Brick Lane, he threw up down a side alley. He later told Collins that this attack went too far.

With the Labour Party seemingly certain of victory in the 1992 General Election – with a manifesto commitment to the notion of a united Ireland – the British political situation began to dominate UDA strategy. "The Loyalist magazines were full of articles about Britain and the treacherous behaviour of the British Government," says one UDA sympathiser who was active in C18. To many involved, it finally seemed as if the UDA was about to launch its doomsday scenario, combining a prolonged assault on economic targets in the Irish Republic with political assassinations in mainland Britain. Two targets widely floated amongst the UDA and C18 leadership were the London MPs Ken Livingstone and Diane Abbott. According to one UDA source, an attack on Livingstone was only aborted because one long-time Loyalist and C18 supporter who knew about the plot talked too much and compromised its secrecy. In 1992, a West Midlands-based woman received a phone call from the police informing her that she and her family were named on a UDA hitlist that they had recently obtained. Her husband was involved in Sinn Fein. C18 members were to be responsible for executing these hits.

Portinari didn't confine his activities to the capital. Because the London Brigade played such an important role in the UDA's entire English operation, he was also advising and directing other units. The West Midlands Brigade was based in Coventry and, during the 1992-3 period, was actively encouraging C18 to attack Republican opponents in the region. "The West Midlands UDA would hand over the lists of targets," admits one former

C18 man in the region. "They provided us with the information which they claimed had originated from the London UDA brigade but it was us who were supposed to do the hits."

They were also to provide the hardware. Guns later found in the possession of Portinari were obtained through Will Browning, who in turn had got them from an older C18 supporter with close ties with the criminal fraternity of south-east London. Six of the guns were supplied in the Lord Stanley pub in Bermondsey, the other in the Shakespeare in Bethnal Green. The Lord Stanley is close to the house of one leading C18 member while the Shakespeare was a regular drinking hole for C18 followers on Sunday evenings. It is believed that as many as twenty guns found their way to the UDA via Browning.

London UDA was acting on instructions from Belfast, which by the beginning of 1993 was considering an even more violent strategy. Despite Labour's defeat in the 1992 General Election, word was sweeping through the streets of Northern Ireland that the IRA was preparing a ceasefire. Loyalists became increasingly concerned, despite repeated assurances from the Conservative Government that the province would remain part of the United Kingdom. According to David McKittrick, the Northern Ireland correspondent for the *Independent*, the Loyalists, who had already overtaken the IRA in sectarian murders, intended to step up their activities. "There are fears that they are planning political assassinations and the use of no-warning bombings," he wrote. "Loyalists have already openly warned that they will intensify their violence 'to a ferocity never imagined'. Security sources say that this is no empty threat and intelligence reports indicate plans for violence on a scale not seen since the Seventies."

To support this campaign, the Loyalists had two further requests for C18 and its underworld connections. The UFF had a seemingly endless supply of killers but lacked the sophisticated weaponry enjoyed by its IRA rivals: sub-machine guns were adequate for pub killings, but striking into the Irish Republic or London required bomb-making equipment. The three attacks it did carry out in the Irish Republic were less than impressive, highlighting its primitive bomb-making capabilities. Several other devices had failed to explode because of ineffective detonators.

A request for detonators was so sensitive that the Brigade Commander of East Belfast UFF made it in person to Charlie Sargent during a secret trip to England sometime towards the end of 1993. In a pub in Holborn, he also asked the C18 boss to supply ecstasy tablets. While the new leadership had frowned upon the racketeering activities of the old guard, they did so more because they believed it led to the individuals becoming corrupted and complacent rather than for any moral reasons. Indeed, Johnny Adair, the West Belfast Mad Dog, was known to use the drug scene to fund his activities, as was another leading figure in the UDA who earned the street name "Captain E" for his dominance of the ecstasy trade in Belfast. Despite his own background in drug trafficking and criminality, it seems that Sargent was unable to assist. He was, however, hugely flattered to be approached.

While there is no evidence that C18's inception was ordered from Belfast, the nazi group certainly provided a function for the UDA and could not have emerged without its knowledge. Frank Portinari was travelling over to Belfast at least four times a year, often accompanied by Eddie Whicker and, with several other leading UDA activists present within C18, the UDA must have given it some tacit support. In 1991, the London UDA unit provided security for South African racist Clive Derby-Lewis as he attended a meeting with right-wing Conservatives and neo-nazis in central London. Derby-Lewis was head of the Western Goals Institute, a coalition of far-right groups that brought together supporters of the apartheid regime. Among its world-wide affiliates were European neo-nazis, Central American death squad leaders and British Conservative MPs. The UDA security included Frank Portinari, Eddie Whicker and Matthew Collins.

Under Portinari's leadership, London UDA also became embroiled in the simmering feud between the NF and the BNP. In 1992, while C18 was still aligned to the BNP, Portinari stepped in to prevent a Loyalist marching band performing at the NF's annual Remembrance Sunday demonstration. Portinari and the other UDA/C18 activists had been enraged to hear about the band, partly because NF officer Terry Blackham had gone behind their backs to organise it and because they had no intention of allowing anything that would boost the ailing NF. After urgent consultation with Belfast, the UDA pulled the plug on the engagement. Blackham was told in no uncertain terms that if the event had gone ahead he would have been marching with two broken legs.

Portinari and Whicker welcomed the hardline attitude coming out of Belfast and were eager to replicate it on the mainland. From the middle of 1991, Whicker told close friends that the UDA was stepping up its activities. One suggestion that had circulated within the organisation was to confront an Irish meeting at Islington Town Hall on April 20, 1991, the anniversary of Adolf Hitler's birth. While the NF wanted to organise a picket outside the event, the London UDA brigade discussed the possibility of putting bombs on the supporters' coaches. Whether through a lack of technical equipment or orders from Belfast, this attack never materialised, but the following year – after C18 had been established – London UDA was ready for battle. Fresh from its successful attacks against left-wing targets in London, C18 turned its attention to mainland Republicans. One target was the annual Troops Out march in central London on January 30, 1993. For several years the Troops Out Movement, which supports British withdrawal from Northern Ireland, had organised a demo to coincide with the anniversary of the Bloody Sunday massacre, when thirteen Catholics were gunned down by British soldiers in Derry. The nazis had long opposed these marches, though rarely had they managed to mobilise more than fifty counter-protesters. This time would be different. "This is the big one, we'll do the march and then we'll torch Kilburn," Eddie Whicker told friends.

Come the day, over 600 nazis, football hooligans and Loyalists massed to attack the march, a small army of hardened rowdies. In soccer parlance, these were boys out for a ruck. "They said that it was time to make a stand," says a former West Midlands C18 activist. "The UDA were attending all the right-wing meetings in the months leading up to the march, urging people to go. Some of us would have gone anyway, but a lot more went because of the UDA's active involvement."

They came from everywhere. Some Chelsea met up at Waterloo, while others met at Earls Court. Most of the east and north London C18 rendezvoused at a pub by Euston, while another group met at the Wellington pub on the Strand. Still more went straight to Hyde Park: many hoped to get among the protestors at the assembly point and "kick off" from there. "It was organised," said one Chelsea hooligan present, "but everyone tended to go around in their own small groups, especially when it started to get on top for us. Charlie [Sargent] had put it around that the Reds were coming up to do the security but most of the football boys were there because they were anti-IRA. Chelsea had a large Loyalist following, it's a patriotic firm."

For the UDA, the day turned into a nightmare. The planned attack failed and many of its activists were arrested. In total the police pulled in 376 people. More than eighty were convicted football hooligans. Though only five were later charged – for public order offences and possession of offensive weapons – the mass round-up dissipated the attack. C18, however, was greatly encouraged by the turnout, not least with the 300 football hooligans from twenty-two different gangs. Brought together by word of mouth, there were hooligans from Chelsea, West Ham, Spurs, Arsenal, Oxford, Newcastle, Wolves, Portsmouth and many other clubs.

A few weeks later, the Provisional IRA planted bombs at a gas works in Warrington, shortly followed by another device in a crowded north London shopping area, injuring eighteen people. The IRA was reaching the height of its mainland campaign. In March 1993, two more bombs exploded on a busy Saturday lunchtime in Warrington, killing two children, Jonathon Ball, aged three, and Tim Parry, aged twelve. Over fifty others were injured. The revulsion and shock at the attack stunned even the IRA and its leaders made a statement claiming that it would abandon bomb attacks in public areas from then on, concentrating instead on military and political targets.

Four days after Warrington, the England football team played Holland in a World Cup qualifier at Wembley. Perhaps the anti-Irish feeling of the hooligans would have been galvanised anyway, but the death of the two children provided C18 with a perfect opportunity to repair the dented morale from January. "We were playing Ireland quite a lot during these times and Kilburn was known to be quite strong for IRA support," recalls a Chelsea hooligan. "We had spent the early evening in a pub in Piccadilly waiting for the Dutch, and though they brought a firm of sixty or seventy, we had such a firm that they didn't come anywhere near us. During the game we were drinking up in Park Royal, one of our boys had a pub up there. After that about three hundred of us came down and just ran through Kilburn High Street. Quite a few pubs got smashed, a lot of people got whacked. We just went down to Kilburn to cause mayhem." Street cameras caught the scenes as up to 300 hooligans and C18 supporters ran amok, attacking pubs and breaking shop windows. Two police cars were overturned and an Indian restaurant was attacked. No one was arrested.

C18 would mobilise another anti-IRA force for the Troops Out march the following January, but the arrests at the previous protest deterred many, including the UDA, from attending. While a pub was attacked in Kilburn and six C18 and football hooligans were later sent to prison, only eighty were involved.

* * * *

SOME LOYALISTS FELT a degree of sympathy with C18 that went beyond tactical support. One was Shaun Leighton, a convicted terrorist who had joined Ulster Resistance, a small paramilitary group, before switching his allegiance to the UVF. In 1989, he and a UVF colleague were arrested in a hijacked car containing two loaded Browning pistols and a sledgehammer, on their way to a house of a senior IRA figure in North Antrim. Leighton was in regular correspondence with leading members of C18, particularly Steve Sargent, and his letters praising them and National Socialism appeared in their publications and in Harold

Covington's *Resistance* newsletter. In exchange, Sargent dispatched material for Leighton to distribute around prison. The UVF man eagerly told Sargent that everyone was very impressed with the material.

Perhaps the most infamous Loyalist terrorist to have open links with C18 was Steve Irwin, the UFF killer sentenced to life imprisonment for his part in the attack on the Rising Sun pub in Greysteel which left seven people dead. On entering the pub on Hallowe'en night, Irwin shouted, "Trick or Treat," before opening fire with a sub-machine gun. In 1994, he sent over a number of photos of himself taken in the Maze Prison posing in front of Combat 18 posters.

However, not everyone in the Loyalist movement was happy about the links between the UDA and the British nazis. They could never have been so close under the pre-1989 UDA regime, with the likes of Tommy Little being bitterly opposed to nazi connections. Even in the early Nineties, Eddie Whicker was severely reprimanded when he came out with a crudely racist outburst while ferrying a leading Belfast UDA officer around London. Whicker and his wing of the mainland UDA were aware of this unease and were keen to reassure, as in an article that appeared in the Loyalist magazine *Warrior*:

> Many Loyalists do not feel comfortable with the ideas and beliefs of these groups in regards to immigration, crime, homosexuality, work, housing and so on. However it must be remembered that regardless of beliefs, when it comes to Ulster the British right-wing detest Republicanism as much as we do and have shown a lot of loyalty to our cause and people. It must be stressed that over the years this support for Ulster has led to many young men in Scotland, England and Wales being sent to prison – from weapons offences to attacks on pro-PIRA groups on the mainland. On a regular basis members of C18 organise counter-demonstrations against pro-PIRA groups such as 'Troops Out Movement', 'Red Action' and so on. At a Sinn Fein meeting in Glasgow late last year, a number of C18 members were involved in

an attack on the meeting, resulting in a number of injuries to Sinn Fein supporters.

Whilst no one is being asked to support groups such as the NSA [the National Socialist Alliance] and C18, beyond their support and struggles for Ulster, we would be damned for not showing our appreciation for their support. Especially when so many have and still are in prison, due to their support for Ulster. Many of these young men, members of C18 and various right-wing groups, risk their liberty and lives for Ulster regardless of what you think of their political beliefs, their sacrifices on our behalf make them worthy of our gratitude, indeed they can easily be classed better Loyalists than some of our so-called political representatives here in Ulster!

However, three events during the first half of 1993 damaged the UDA-C18 alliance: the mass round-up at the Bloody Sunday counter-demonstration, which brought the UDA and its supporters unwelcome attention; a *World In Action* programme that April highlighting Eddie Whicker's leading role in C18 that again handed the paramilitary organisation unhelpful publicity; and the arrest and later imprisonment of Frank Portinari.

★ ★ ★ ★

ON THE MORNING of Saturday, May 29, 1993, Eddie Whicker drove up the M1 motorway. He had been told to head for Perry Barr Stadium in Birmingham, where a man in a maroon-coloured Escort would be waiting. Whicker was to hand over a Puma sports bag and then return home. The instructions were simple enough but, approaching Birmingham, Whicker mistook road signs to Great Barr for Perry Barr. When he finally came across a greyhound track shortly after 4pm, almost two hours before his arranged meet, he presumed he had the right venue. He sat around for a while, but feeling increasingly nervous and conspicuous, he left, returning shortly before six. Whicker brushed aside a security guard, claiming that he was waiting for a friend.

His friend never showed. After twenty minutes of nervous fidgeting, Whicker got into his car and drove back to London.

The following day, Whicker headed to Brick Lane to meet Frank Portinari and explain the botched exchange the day before. Portinari was annoyed, and worried that such amateurish behaviour would reflect on him. After a brief conversation, the two men went to retrieve the bag from Whicker's hire car. Portinari decided to take the bag up to Birmingham himself the following day.

He arrived at the Little Crown pub slightly ahead of time, accompanied by his wife Lisa, whom he had placated by the promise of a shopping trip after his work was done. They wandered into the pub and ordered some drinks and, while at the bar, Portinari recognised a man sitting in the adjoining room. He asked the barman to carry the drinks through, approached the man and, after a brief discussion, he and James McCrudden left the pub. No sooner had McCrudden taken the light blue Puma sports bag and placed it in the boot of his own car than they were surrounded by armed police. Inside the bag were six handguns that had been destined for the Loyalist paramilitaries in Belfast.

Whicker was arrested and taken to Birmingham for questioning. While he was later to be released without charge – with police unable to prove that he knew guns were in the bag – it was the culmination of a bad few weeks for the dustman. Six weeks earlier, he had been named on *World In Action* as a leading C18 organiser. "He's the daddy," said an actor, reading the words of reformed nazi Matthew Collins, Whicker's close ally. "He's the one everybody looks up to. Running C18, he's getting at what he sees as his natural enemy, which is the IRA. Eddie Whicker's very secretive. He's the UDA man. He was the courier between the two. He's a regular visitor to Belfast, where he's well liked and respected. When you're invited to join C18 that's it, then you're no longer doing things that are British National Party or National Front but things that have the blessing of who's running it, of the UDA."

With Portinari remanded in prison, London UDA again reorganised, on the orders of Belfast. The approaching ceasefire, coupled with the arrests of some of the more violent Loyalist paramilitaries including Johnny Adair, reduced the group's sectarian campaign. Changes were also occurring within C18 as it forged ahead with a new political outlook that reduced its desire for big street confrontations. Eddie Whicker, whether under orders or through choice, began to withdraw from C18 and concentrate on Loyalism, though he would attend and provided security for a number of C18 events over the next couple of years. Other Loyalists such as Steve Martin, Alan Thompson and Rob Hilton also began to fade from C18 activity, as a younger generation came to the fore. Links continued but the relationship had changed: C18 supporters regularly turned out at Loyalist and Apprentice Boys marches in Britain, but largely in the hope of confronting Reds; a UDA speaker addressed a C18-sponsored meeting in the West Midlands in 1995, but seemingly in a personal capacity due to his own extreme political views. Some C18 members were even becoming indifferent to the battle over the water. As C18 developed its "Our Race is Our Nation" policy [see Chapter 9] in preference to the simple nationalism of the BNP, it saw the Irish conflict as increasingly futile and counter-productive. Interestingly, when C18 established the National Socialist Alliance as a political front, Charlie Sargent drew comparisons with the IRA/Sinn Fein relationship rather than the UDA/UFF.

* * * *

FRANK PORTINARI WAS jailed for five years at Birmingham Crown Court for running guns to paramilitaries. One month later, another London-based racist appeared before a Scottish court. Terry Blackham, a twenty-four-year-old NF officer from Beckenham, south London, pleaded guilty to possessing two Czech-made sub-machine guns, an automatic pistol, a grenade launcher and 1,000 rounds of ammunition. On Friday, November 16, 1993, Blackham had hired a car in Kent and driven to Scotland, stopping briefly in Birmingham to collect £200 off friends, before continuing his journey to Cairnryon, where he bought a return ticket to the Northern Ireland port of Larne. It was a designated port under the Prevention of Terrorism Act and security was tight. During what was claimed to be a routine search of Blackham's car, an officer became suspicious of a loose door panel. The police uncovered the lethal weapons hidden in the front doors.

At first Blackham pleaded ignorance of the cache, claiming that he had been set up, but he later changed his plea to guilty of possessing weapons. The first person to visit him in jail was Eddie Whicker, which was slightly surprising, as there had been no love lost between the two men after Whicker left the NF for C18. Clearly UDA work overrode personal disputes. The two men Blackham had been to see in Birmingham were both former NF activists and Aston Villa football hooligans who had recently switched their allegiances to C18. One of them, Neil Keilty, received a one-year prison sentence for his part in the mob attack on Kilburn in 1994.

In March 1995, fifty C18 supporters came out to provide protection to the annual Derry Apprentice Boys march, a mainstay of the Loyalist calendar, in central London. Led by Charlie Sargent, the mob included activists from London, the East Midlands, Bristol and Scotland. It was an impressive turnout but was not needed, as the march was ignored by the Left and by Republican groups. C18 did, however, attempt to gain entry to the Labour Party's special conference on abolishing Clause 4, which was taking place at the Methodist Central Hall in Westminster, but were forced back by the police. The following year, only thirty C18 activists showed for the Apprentice Boys march; this time they were physically attacked by anti-fascists as they gathered in Holborn. By 1997, their numbers had dwindled to fifteen. It signified a downgrading of Loyalism within C18 circles and vice versa. By then, C18 had found other outlets for its violent tendencies.

CHAPTER SIX

Men Behaving Badly

THE MOBILISATION OF Britain's most notorious football gangs gave Combat 18 a massive boost. Given the background of many of C18's initial activists, it was only natural that they would seek to recruit the soccer firms. Steve Sargent, a former hooligan with Barnet and England, was particularly excited about this turn of events. "At the pro-IRA march," he wrote in his magazine *Thor Would*, "fans from throughout London's teams and further afield joined together as one. From London there was Arsenal, Spurs, Chelsea, Millwall, Charlton and Orient. From the Midlands there was Birmingham, Wolves and Forest. From up North there was Leeds, Bradford and a good few Geordies. From the South, Portsmouth and Southampton and from the East, Peterborough and Norwich. The list is endless but it shows it's possible for rival fans to join together and fight the common enemy. Getting all the football fans, or firms, mobs, whatever and getting them all behind a Nationalist cause as one, that's when we start to get progress."

The courting of hooligans coincided with the break from the BNP. From the beginning of 1993, C18 began looking outside the ranks of the established Right for young white males inclined to violence. In issue one of *Combat 18*, hooliganism was given its own section combining reports of gang fights with complaints about heavy-handed policing. "99% of football thugs are white and 99% of those are nationalistic and patriotic," claimed the magazine. "The authorities are attempting to destroy our race and what they cannot afford is groups of patriots dotted around the country. The can't afford to have white youths displaying the warrior instincts which made Britain and our race great

...They know that if hooligans got together they could take liberties with the police, with any mob of niggers, and with any red marches."

The mentality of the average hooligan and the average C18 supporter was similar. The connection went beyond the "buzz" of a good ruck: it was about gaining respect, a sense of power and a desire to shock. "It's just natural to rebel," believes Ken, a long time follower of the Chelsea Headhunters. "This is the way to do it. It seems to be the nationalist thing, people don't look much further into it. They're proud of being British. If you have nothing and are from a working class estate, you say, what's wrong with this – I am white, I am working class, I haven't got a job and it's your way of rebelling back. Rather than just taking it, you hit back at society. The right-wing is the most shocking thing because it's constantly put to us through the television, the press, everything, that the worst thing to ever happen is the Nazis. So the biggest way to rebel is to be seen to endorse it."

Typically for C18, there was no systematic enlistment drive, no membership forms to fill in. "All this stuff about Combat 18 recruiting on the terraces, it just didn't happen," says Ken. "It tends to be that you know someone who knows someone else who would come out with you. The greater the likelihood of there being trouble, the more people would want to come out with you and during that period we were involved in a lot of fights. I think a lot of people who became involved weren't particularly right-wing, not in the C18 sense anyway."

The Headhunters, however, were undoubtedly right-wing, heirs to a racist tradition at Chelsea that went back to the late Sixties and the early skinhead scene. As the Kings Road became a focal point for the skins, the close proximity of the Stamford Bridge ground was always likely to attract them, and several nazi skinhead bands openly associated themselves with Chelsea. It became a vicious circle. The more skins were attracted to Chelsea, the greater the level of fascist violence; the greater the violence, the greater the pull for racists and yobs to follow the club. During the late Seventies, both the NF and the loutish British Movement targeted Chelsea fans recruitment through leafleting and paper sales. At the time, the NF produced *Bulldog*, a youth publication focusing strongly on music and football and intended to "win the hearts and minds of young white males". *Bulldog* was sold at football grounds around the country. Its back page was dedicated to a "Football Focus", where the racist antics of fans were proudly recounted and violence was glorified. An accompanying "League of Louts" allowed thugs an opportunity to compete with each other to claim the coveted title of the most racist support in the country. Chelsea was invariably in the top three, often battling it out with northern rivals Leeds United. "Chelsea is a right-wing club," says Ken, a veteran of Headhunter campaigns. "It always has been. I can remember the Seventies, the ground was just full of skinheads. As a right-winger I feel comfortable down there."

During the mid-Eighties – as the skins were replaced by the more trendy casuals – Chelsea's fascist connection gained new blood from a fusion with Loyalism. Links were established with Loyalists groups in Scotland and Northern Ireland. A number of friendly pre-season fixtures against staunchly-Protestant Glasgow Rangers over consecutive seasons cemented this connection, which was soon followed by the first of what became almost annual trips to Belfast to meet the Loyalists. The so-called "Blues Brothers" friendship was formed between followers of Chelsea, Rangers and Coleraine (who all play in blue strips). Simultaneously, a number of nazi activists came through the ranks of the Chelsea hooligans.

It was a time when the Headhunters earned the reputation as the most feared gang in the country. The gang, itself composed of a number of smaller groups, became infamous for causing trouble at home and abroad. During one match against arch-rivals Leeds in 1983, 199 people were arrested in fighting before, during and after the game. The same year saw another 200 arrested in two matches against Sunderland. In one particularly nasty attack, a Newcastle supporter was waylaid by thirty Headhunters at a motorway service station and left unconscious with wounds that required 140 stitches.

The Metropolitan Police targeted the gang in Operation Own

Goal. Two undercover operations, involving months of observation and surveillance work by plain-clothes officers, led to the
arrest of the alleged ringleaders and the seizure of various
weapons and NF literature. Some of those arrested were jailed
but serious doubts were subsequently raised about the reliability
of notes taken by the officers in the case and some of the verdicts
were overturned on appeal. A series of similar trials involving the
fans of other clubs also collapsed in what was a major embarrassment for the Met.

Several years later, in August 1994, the Combat 18 campaign
at Chelsea came to life.

★ ★ ★ ★

AUGUST 20, 1994, was designated "Kick Racism out of Football
Day", when supporters, players and officials were to show their
public opposition to bigotry on the terraces. Around the country,
leaflets and newsletters were distributed, players made public
statements and clubs reiterated their determination to deal firmly
with racist abuse.

At Chelsea, the anti-racists had company. In a pub on the
Kings Road, twenty C18 nazis finished their drinks in a mood of
anticipation. They left their empty glasses and headed outside,
taking a long, convoluted route through back streets to avoid
police detection. Nearer the ground – where 30,000 were heading
to watch the match – Steve Sargent and three others were
coming out of Fulham Broadway Tube station to join them.
Their destination was the Finborough Arms, the regular drinking
hole of the Chelsea Independent Supporters Association (CISA).
The nazis identified CISA with anti-racist activities at the club.
They were determined to teach them a lesson.

Steve Sargent would fail to join rest of the gang. Walking past
a house with an ANL placard in a window, he couldn't resist
banging on the door. The flat belonged to a young woman who
had gone to an anti-racist music festival a few weeks before and
liked the placard. One of the nazis demanded that she get "the
man" of the house; on hearing she was alone, they directed their

venom at her, demanding she take down the poster and threatening her when she refused. The woman rang the police. Sargent and his sidekicks were arrested moments later and would be held on remand for seven days.

Oblivious to this, the main C18 group continued its march through west London. It was led by Mark Atkinson, a violent thug with a long history on the nazi scene. The son of a Northamptonshire mushroom farmer, Atkinson became involved with the NF in the 1980s and was later a leading member of the British chapter of the Invisible Empire of the Ku Klux Klan. One KKK activity, carried out with several other members who were later to become involved in C18, was the desecration of Jewish gravestones in Staines, a few miles from his home in Egham, Surrey. His involvement ended in 1991 when KKK leader Alan Beshella was exposed as a sex offender. With the inception of C18, the then-dustman soon joined their ranks, taking on the responsibility of organising security for the Blood and Honour music scene. Atkinson was not really interested in football but was close friends with several of the leading Chelsea hooligans, many of whom lived nearby. He recognised the sport's importance as a recruiting ground and so attended matches, especially with England abroad. In 1988, a photograph of Atkinson giving a nazi salute appeared in a national newspaper during the European Championships in Germany.

Atkinson's group finally reached the Finborough Arms and went in. Twenty minutes before the end of the match, they took up position around the pool table. The pub was quiet but soon filled up after the final whistle. The CISA group arrived and sat together in a corner, discussing the game. None of the C18 firm knew them by sight; they relied for identification on a leading Headhunter who had been a childhood friend of one of the CISA leaders. He, along with a few older Headhunters, watched events unfold from the pub doorway.

Many of the pub regulars soon realised something was wrong. One even approached the landlord to say he thought the group around the pool table was out for trouble. In the toilets, a CISA supporter unwittingly approached one of the nazis.

"There are some nasty looking people in the pub today," he cautioned.

"Are there?" replied the C18 man, feigning surprise.

There was nothing the landlord could do. The pub was by now too full and the group too big to eject. The signal for the attack came when Atkinson jumped up on the pool table and began shouting, "Sieg heil." It triggered a barrage of bottles, glasses, stools and tables aimed at the CISA group. Atkinson remained on the table throwing pool balls, while Will Browning waded into the group with a bottle and a knife.

There was nothing the CISA group could do. They were seated, caught by surprise and above all, not fighters. They were ordinary football supporters enjoying a peaceful drink after a game. They included women and children. None escaped. One eight-year-old boy cowered in a corner, covered with the fragments of smashed glass.

"It was like a tidal wave," recollects Phillip Martin, the pub's landlord. "It was something I had never seen in my life before and I hope never to see again. There were women screaming, kids screaming, glasses, bottles, pool cues, pool balls, tables and chairs flying all over the place. All you could hear above the din was, 'Sieg Heil!'"

After less than a minute, the nazis stopped and headed for the door, still chanting. The Headhunters parted to allow them out. In the street, the nazis split up. Browning was the only one in need of immediate attention – he had been covered in the blood of his victims. The friend of another attacker lived nearby and so Browning was able to wash and change his clothes.

The attackers left carnage. Four people needed hospital treatment, the most serious for a depressed fracture of the skull caused by a pool ball to the temple. Another person suffered a gashed neck caused by flying glass; a fraction of an inch further across and his jugular vein would have been severed. A third needed twelve stitches in the back of the head, again from a thrown glass. The fourth person who required hospital treatment was Ross Fraser, the editor of the CISA fanzine. He had a bottle smashed in his face, resulting in seven stitches and a number of abrasions on his left cornea. "This has left me with blurred vision in my left eye, which has if anything deteriorated in the time since. The whole thing was a nightmare," he says.

★ ★ ★ ★

ROSS FRASER IS not easily frightened. Broad shoulders match his six-foot three-inch body, and his scarred face bears testimony to a few previous battles. "What I can't understand," he said, reflecting on the incident, "is why they are coming after me. I'm not political, I've never done anything against them."

The Chelsea Independent Supporters became a target because they were considered a challenge to the Right at Chelsea. They had made a series of statements during the preceding season in their publication, *Chelsea Independent*, deploring racism. Beyond that, there was little or no politics; they all had their own personal views on life but these never intruded into the magazine. What made C18 see red was an advert in the fanzine for Anti-Fascist Action stickers. CISA had no allegiance to AFA, having merely reacted positively to a request to support the anti-racist cause, but C18 took a different view. They vowed to make CISA "reap what you sow".

C18 was making football a priority area, as demonstrated by the involvement of Will Browning, who actually disliked the game intensely. "Why would anyone want to watch twenty-two grown men run around a pitch in a state of half undress?" he would ponder to anyone who would listen. Despite this, he made the targeting of Ross Fraser a personal crusade. The horrific attack in the Finborough Arms was only the beginning. As he recovered from shock and his injuries, Fraser received a letter addressed to his magazine containing two C18 stickers. This was followed a week later by another letter, sent directly to his home. Inside were several BNP leaflets; on one was scrawled, "Hello Ross, hope you are well," and "See you around then Ross, but not in the Finborough Arms though, eh!" The message was signed, "CHELSEA BNP WHITE POWER."

C18 was convinced that Fraser was a prominent left-winger.

"This made him a legitimate target," smirks Headhunter Ken, like an infant who knows he's done something wrong. "He bore the brunt of it." The fact that he was a Chelsea fan made his victimisation all the easier. "I don't think we would have got away with it so easily on somebody else's patch," says Ken. "If we had gone to Arsenal and tried it there, we would have ended up fighting with the Arsenal firm. Not just with the blacks but because we didn't have the contacts or the mutually-known friends that we had at Chelsea."

C18 was able to call on leading Headhunters for support. Many originated from the west London housing estates of Hounslow and Queens Park but had moved out to London commuter towns and the "Silicon Valley". Reading was one such place: amid the relative prosperity of Berkshire's county town is a toughness that is often ignored. Just off the main shopping centre lies a dark, dingy pub that is the haunt of the "Nightmare". Flitting between tables, the short but powerfully-built man in his thirties has a word or two for everyone. He is amiable but not one to cross. Every town has someone similar, a man whose reputation precedes him. For Reading, this man is the Nightmare, otherwise known as Andy Frain.

Considered by police to be one of the most violent hooligans in the country, Frain has thirty-five criminal convictions, mostly for violence and drunken behaviour but also for drugs, burglary and fraud. In 1984, he was convicted of attacking an Asian with a baseball bat. He has been associated with the Headhunters since the early Eighties, and later in the decade joined his friend Mark Atkinson in the Invisible Empire of the Ku Klux Klan, travelling to the U.S. on one occasion for training, only to be deported for violence. To him, involvement in the Klan was all a bit of a laugh; that was until its British leader was exposed as a child molester. Then it was time to move on. He joined C18 at its inception, though he is at pains to say that they are merely acquaintances and claims he is no longer involved.

Everyone in his circle has a story about Frain. Whether they are all true is largely immaterial; that's how legends are made.

Towards the end of one spell at Her Majesty's pleasure, he was called in to the governor's office.

"I think we'll be seeing you in here again before long," said the governor.

"Yeah," replied Frain. "I really don't give a fuck."

The stories take on added authenticity when one meets him face to face. Though below average height, he has a frightening physical aura, with his thick neck, big shoulders and huge fists. In 1995, he was one of only two hooligans in Britain to be banned from travelling abroad to watch Chelsea and England. It was reputations such as Frain's that gave C18 much of its credibility among the hooligan fraternity.

* * * *

THE SECOND HALF of 1994 saw C18 at its height of street activity. C18-linked mobs became active around the country, taking the fight to their political opponents. Leeds, Oldham, Scotland and the West Midlands all saw incidents, while in London the death by stabbing of Richard Everett, a fifteen-year-old from Camden, at the hands of a gang of Asian youths, provided another excuse to whip up racial tension. C18 supporters distributed posters and roamed the Camden area late at night, looking for targets.

A week after the Finborough Arms attack, the Belgian seaside town of Diksmuide played host to the annual Flemish nationalist celebration, which had expanded into an international right-wing jamboree. A sizeable C18 contingent made the journey to what was little more than an excuse for a twenty-four-hour drinking binge. Problems arose when one of them spotted a Belgian nazi wearing a shamrock tee-shirt. While the British far-right has traditionally supported the Loyalist cause, on the Continent the Flemish and Dutch especially have tended to side with Irish Republicans, viewing them as a nationalist movement struggling for independence from imperialism. For C18, the sight of such open Irish support was a red rag to a bull.

Will Browning began the fight, virtually ripping the tee-shirt off the man's back, and before long it escalated into a mini-riot.

The Germans sided with C18 against a larger mob of Dutch and
Flemish extremists. Six of the English, including Browning,
Charlie Sargent and Rob Hilton, and fifty Germans were
subsequently arrested and deported, and several people needed
hospital treatment, including the sons of two Flemish MPs.
Sargent was deported for possession of racist tee-shirts.

This period also witnessed a changing balance of power
within C18. West London became increasingly important, a
trend confirmed by the turn to football at Chelsea. "Many of
the east London lot simply began to drop out," says Ken.
"Some of them began to get paranoid that their luck was going
to run out, while others simply decided that things were
beginning to get too heavy for them. They had run and fought
on the streets for a few years, but the growing police interest
was making it increasingly unattractive." The west London
links extended to the local BNP branch. This was under the
control of Warren Glass, the younger brother of Stuart Glass,
who had been a defendant in the second Own Goal hooligan
trial and was himself a strong C18 supporter. While Warren
Glass was a member of the BNP, he also believed that a C18-
type group was necessary as a parallel organisation.

A council by-election in the autumn of 1995 clearly illustrated
the overlap between C18, the Headhunters and West London
BNP. Warren Glass stood as the BNP candidate. Having
thwarted an anti-fascist attack on their paper sale the week
before, the nazis decided to mobilise for the count itself. The
evening got off to a fractious start when a fight broke out within
their own mob. Andy Frain had just returned to Reading after a
period on the run in Liverpool: he had bottled an Irishman in a
pub who, it emerged, was connected to the main crime family in
Kilburn. The word was out that they wanted revenge. Frain
initially sought the support of nazi and hooligan friends,
suggesting they mob up and confront the Irish in north-west
London. Despite their anti-Irish bravado, they thought better of
it, and Frain was forced to lie low until the situation calmed
down. He may have wished he hadn't, because during his time in
Liverpool he became involved in a pub fight which saw him

stabbed in the buttocks. Frain returned south an angry man, and it was with a view to releasing his aggression that someone convinced him to come out that night.

As his gang mobbed up near the town hall, Frain approached a young skinhead wearing a green flying jacket over a blue football top.

"Is that a Chelsea top?" Frain enquired.

"Of course it is, you muppet," answered the skinhead cheerfully.

The bystanders winced: they knew exactly how Frain would react. Weeks of anxiety were released as the Nightmare punched the young man square in the face, sending him crashing to the floor. Frain pulled out a blade and moved in to finish the job. Further injury was only prevented by Frain's friends holding him back.

The nazis knew that the ANL had prepared a picket outside the town hall. Banter between protesters and police was sharply curtailed as news of the imminent arrival of the BNP-led mob spread. Officers huddled together, engrossed in their radios, collecting and relaying instructions, while the demonstrators organised themselves for the usual verbal assault on the nazis. Up the street, the first faces were spotted, but rather than the usual dozen or so faces, the trickle turned into a stream – about eighty in total. Most had shaven or closely-cropped hair and wore designer clothes: an equal number of C18 and Headhunters.

The eerie moment of silence that followed the sighting of this mob was shattered as the gang broke into a run. The police attempted to restrain them but it was never going to work. A shower of bottles and bricks rained down on the officers and the protesters. The Tactical Support Group, London's specialist riot police, were called into action but took thirty minutes to arrive. By then the local police had lost control and the damage was done. Many of the ANL supporters, some in tears, fled into the council building to escape the missiles. Less fortunate was the victorious Labour candidate, Les Bawn; he arrived at the height of the violence and, without realising what was occurring, strode towards the entrance. With a shout of, "Get him," the mob made one last surge and Bawn was struck on the back of the head with a brick.

Inside the hall, a couple of national BNP representatives, oblivious to events outside, pondered the absence of their candidate and his local unit. Colin Smith, the party's election officer, turned to Steve O'Connell, the Newham organiser, and asked if he should go and fetch them from the pub.

"No, I don't think that would be a good idea," replied O'Connell. He had been in the pub earlier that evening. "I don't think you will like what you see."

Down the road, election candidate Warren Glass was brushing himself down, removing any traces of his involvement in the evening's fracas. Then, to loud applause from his supporters and a raucous rendition of "God Save the Queen", he strolled into the hall to take part in the democratic process. Turning to the press, he blithely disassociated himself from the violence. "The BNP," he asserted, "were not responsible."

* * * *

AFTER TWENTY-TWO years, Chelsea FC were back in Europe. In September 1994, the club had been drawn to play a team from Prague, Czechoslovakia, in the first round of the European Cup Winners Cup, though the game was switched to Jablonec, sixty kilometres away, as a security precaution. About twenty C18 made the journey to Prague and about forty hooligans, including a few from other clubs who went along for the ride. While the hooligans were eager to take on any local opposition, C18 had the sole priority of getting Ross Fraser.

Fraser knew something was up. A few days before the game, the landlord of the Finborough Arms had found graffiti saying, "Left wing scum, you're going to die in Prague," on the toilet walls. However, C18 had no intelligence on Fraser's whereabouts other than rumours that he would be drinking out of town. The Headhunter who had been to school with Fraser said he was travelling on a CISA-organised coach. Will Browning stomped around the coach park at the ground, more in hope than anticipation. The match began with Fraser still nowhere to be seen.

Chelsea came through the tie unscathed, though as the cameras panned the travelling crowd, one man was not participating in the celebrations. Browning, who hated football, was bombarding the players with stones. His boredom was growing and he wanted action. Outside the ground, the Beast led the search for Fraser once more. Eventually the parked CISA coach was spotted. Mark Atkinson was first aboard, demanding to know where Fraser was. The fanzine editor, unaware of the danger, stepped forward to introduce himself. Atkinson lunged, punching him in the face and causing Fraser to fall back into a seat. Browning, who had boarded the bus with Atkinson, screamed, "Come on you Chelsea Reds!" and rushed forward, plunging a screwdriver towards Fraser's face, missing it by centimetres. Seconds later, the doors closed and the coach sped away.

Fraser has no doubt he could have died in this attack. An *Evening Standard* journalist sitting next to him concurred. "If they had connected then he could have been killed," he told fellow reporters back in London. For his part, Browning would gloat about the attack in the next issue of *Combat 18*: "Frazer [sic] got a slap and just managed to dodge a chisel which was almost plunged into his throat ... Frazer might have survived that assassination attempt but his luck is gonna run out sooner than he thinks, and Chelsea will be cleansed of this piece of shit and all the other so-called anti-fascists."

To justify its actions to the Headhunters, C18 circulated a series of unfounded stories about the CISA. A number of leaflets appeared around the pubs of Chelsea declaring that support for the CISA meant support for the IRA. They even claimed that buying a copy of the *Chelsea Independent* was "contributing to the next bombing atrocity in the capital". This allegation, though absurd, appealed to many Chelsea hooligans, who prided themselves on their strong support for the Loyalist cause. At least one leading Headhunter was taken in by the propaganda. "While Fraser is a Chelsea fan and I have no problem with him

personally, the *Chelsea Independent* supported the IRA and so
was fair game," he says. C18 also claimed the CISA coach was
flying a hammer-and-sickle flag on the trip to Prague.

The nazi campaign had turned directly against Fraser. A few
weeks after Jablonec, he received yet another C18 letter at home.
"There is a motto that goes: Lay down with dogs, get up with
fleas," it said. Fraser was given an ultimatum: "Stay away from
Chelsea because C18 are going to kill you."

"It became a personal vendetta against Fraser," says Ken.
"Rightly or wrongly, he had been put up to be what he was. I
don't think he over-endeared himself to people with his actions
after it, milking it in the press. He then turned up on these sports
programmes on Saturday mornings. He seemed to make a right
celebrity of himself. It appeared to us to be rubbing it in. He was
bleating about why he had been attacked and yet on the other
hand he seemed to be clawing in the money over it. He just
seemed to be a hypocritical bastard. Calling people no-neck
monsters in the *Evening Standard* didn't help him. That went
down really well, didn't it." Never mind that Fraser was not the
author of the *Evening Standard* article and that his – unpaid –
appearance on Sky TV was in his capacity as a fanzine editor,
talking about football.

For his part, Fraser returned from Prague determined to get
action taken. He wrote in desperation to David Mellor, then the
Conservative MP for Putney and a keen Chelsea supporter and
radio pundit. "This letter is a plea for help," he wrote. "Without
over-reacting, I do feel extraordinarily intimidated by this whole
episode and feel that in a civilised society an innocent citizen
should not be exposed to this sinister level of threat and terror.
Surely the State has a duty to protect anyone who finds
themselves in this situation." His plea fell on deaf ears. He felt
even more let down by the woefully inadequate response from
the police. It took six weeks for them to take witness statements
after the Finborough Arms attack. Even then, and despite CISA
identifying a number of possible suspects, not a single C18
supporter was ever questioned.

Eventually even the football club was forced to take note,

coinciding as the attacks did with the return of racist chanting by a small section of their crowd. Club chairman Ken Bates, though no friend of the CISA, condemned the racists in a match programme. In the same issue, the programme editor noted that "the dark clouds are once again coming over Chelsea." He had an unequivocal message for the followers of Combat 18: "Hitler lost. He died. He blew it. There's no room for losers at this club any more."

The next round of the European competition saw Chelsea drawn against an Austrian side in Vienna. After receiving yet more threats, Fraser watched the game from the safety of the press box and left the city immediately afterwards. Chelsea emerged victorious and, with the next round not for several months, Fraser hoped his troubles would be over.

* * * *

AS POWER SHIFTED towards the west London crew, *The Stormer* appeared. It was produced by Mark Atkinson and was the organ of West London C18. *The Stormer* was typically part comic and part politics. It carried reports on events of interest – usually the glorified recounting of fights and music gigs – and contained the usual hitlists, including a selection of Jewish synagogues which supporters were urged to desecrate. While Steve Sargent's *Putsch* was more of a witty commentary on events and Charlie's *The Order* was more serious political reportage, *The Stormer* followed the example set so crudely in Will Browning's *Combat 18* magazine, one of base humour and vile abuse. LibDem leader Paddy Ashdown, issue five reported, "doesn't deserve to live". His address was given to readers. Celebrities and public figures such as Anna Ford, Jacob Rothschild, Vanessa Redgrave and Bernard Levin were also targeted.

Another target was Lynette Bruno. Her crime was to be the mother of the popular black boxer Frank Bruno. *The Stormer* editors, too cowardly to go for the heavyweight champion directly, instead published his mum's address: it led to a prolonged spell of threats. First came a letter telling her to "go home and die", followed by a series of terrifying phone calls. "Bang," one caller shouted, "it's that easy to blow your head off." Mrs Bruno, a sixty-seven-year-old lay preacher, endured many sleepless nights and more than a year later was still too scared to go out of her house alone. Eventually she was forced to move home.

The Stormer also gave its readers a running commentary on the persecution of Ross Fraser: with so many of the west London C18 crew connected to the Headhunters, football featured prominently in the magazine. Fraser became a central topic of debate. A blow-by-blow account was given of various trips around Europe, interwoven with more threats and jokes against Fraser.

> Q. Why can't 'Ross Fraser' see the light?
> A. Cause he's always wearing other people's glasses.

Chelsea were next drawn against the Belgian side Bruges. For the hooligans and C18, this was a big one: the "Mother of all Battles", as it was described in *The Stormer*. The relative proximity of Bruges, the growing infamy of Belgium's own hooligan gangs and the belief that Chelsea were unlikely to progress much further in the competition meant that many Headhunters saw this as their last chance to stamp their authority as the undisputed kings of soccer thuggery. They would go out of the competition in a blaze of glory, regardless of the consequences.

"Getting England banned again from Europe would be definitely seen as one in the cap: 'they got England banned from Europe and Chelsea did it,'" admits Ken. "It's like the World Cup; everyone would like to see England win, but given the choice of that or having two weeks of violence, it just doesn't compare. Two weeks of riots and taking liberties in somewhere like Italy or Germany and you'd really be respected and feared. Everyone wants to win, but there's more to life than that, there's national pride. I think you stamp more national pride on people by the actions of hooligans than England winning the World Cup."

That sort of bizarre logic underpins much of the hooligan and right-wing mentality. While some might say such a thing just to shock, others genuinely believe it. "Every other generation has had a war, but we have been deprived of that," asserts Ken. "It is our generation who are the hooligans and this is the strongest generation of any race. We are the best army, aren't we?"

Andy Frain puts it slightly differently. "There's always been people like us, the cannon fodder. Two hundred years ago they would be putting medals on our red tunics and sending us out in the front line." His view has an uncomfortable ring of truth. During the Napoleonic Wars, men in British prisons were given a way out by joining the army. If they survived frontline duty, they could return free men. "Without a good share of violent psychopaths," claims one former football intelligence officer, "Britain could hardly have expected to rule a third of the world. We've always had these sort of people."

The C18 contingent arrived by car at the port of Ostend and slipped past the police while several hundred others were being detained and later deported. Before leaving the port they painted a warning to Fraser on the harbour wall in letters several feet high. Again they had no idea of their target's movements and searched pubs across Bruges city centre to no avail. Fraser stayed out of town until moments before the game. Despite a chance meeting outside the ground with his treacherous former school pal, he eluded C18.

In any case, the nazis were preoccupied. The Belgian police had decided to round up hundreds of people without match tickets and hold them in a disused aircraft hangar. Water cannons were used to dampen the spirits of the detainees. At one point, Stuart Glass thought he had escaped. Wearing his obligatory sunglasses, designer clothes and gold jewellery, he broke out of the compound and made a dash to a river, diving in despite his wrists still being bound by plastic cuffs. The police were waiting for him on the other side.

Ross Fraser, in contrast, had got away once more.

*　*　*　*

THE C18-HEADHUNTER alliance was always a volatile mix and, as the season progressed, some within the Chelsea mob began to resent the nazis' presence. With C18 being blamed for every outbreak of violence, some Headhunters believed that they were not getting the "credit" they deserved. A death threat placed on the car windscreen of a leading black Headhunter annoyed others, not least the man himself. It is odd but true that at Chelsea, and among football firms in general, some of the most racist thugs will tolerate or befriend black hooligans if they are on "their" side. While the man in question did not make an issue of his colour, even to the point of resenting how others attempted to use it, neither did those who in any other situation were thoroughly racist. They were bonded by a love of Chelsea and the respect they had for one another in the firm.

Conscious of the tension, *The Stormer* attempted conciliation. Mark Atkinson penned a prominent item on the editorial page of issue four: "We also hear that some Chelsea lads are not happy with C18. The Chelsea lot think C18 are taking over – all we can say is we are not. We cannot stop the media labelling us as Chelsea Headhunters, most of the Chelsea lads know who we are. We were asked to sort out the red scum, which you were supposed to have done a long time ago, so we did. We were honoured to have the privilege. I hope this gets across." This statement, and a drop in C18 activities, soothed much of the resentment. There were too many links between the two groups for any real division.

Chelsea's final foray into Europe was against the Spanish side Zaragosa in the competition's quarter-finals. While a group of C18 made the journey, there was no Browning or Atkinson, the two men at the forefront of the "Get Fraser" campaign. Rather, the gang, led by Stuart Glass, consisted of older Headhunters, many of whom had been active since the late-Seventies. They were known amongst themselves as the "West London Deviants", or sometimes the "Northstandi Family" because they want in the North Stand at home games. The Deviants had travelled the world together for football, politics, holidays and, most importantly, sex. Among them were several veterans of the notorious South American trip in 1984, when they made headlines for abusing England footballer John Barnes on the plane home. A few years later, Ken Walsh climbed up a floodlight during an England under-21 game in Istanbul and dropped his trousers, much to the annoyance of several government dignitaries in the crowd. Getting deported was quite an honour for them: on one trip to Cuba, they refused to leave the airport until their passports were stamped "deported" after they had been arrested for fighting with the Argentinean Boco Juniors football team.

The group thrived on adventure, even scouring through the Foreign Office list of destinations best avoided by Britons. On one such trip, to Colombia, they insisted on going to the cocaine-growing region. They stopped for liquid refreshment in a hut along the way, only for their quiet drink to be interrupted by an armed gang of bandits who burst in demanding money and possessions. Stuart Glass looked up and knew they were in trouble but before they had to relinquish their belongings, Paul Jones, another veteran Chelsea hooligan and nazi, got up and introduced the leader of the bandits to "Don Corleone Northstandi". With that, he bent down and kissed Glass's hand. The bandits, clearly impressed with so distinguished a visitor, put their guns down on a table and joined the Deviants in a game of dominoes.

Not everyone in the group abided by Glass's own immaculate dress sense. On a trip to Mexico, Ken Walsh arrived at the airport dressed in jeans, tee-shirt, Dr Marten boots and donkey jacket. His baggage for a two-week trip consisted of a spare Chelsea Headhunter tee-shirt, a spare pair of pants and a four-pack of bitter. The label Deviants was also well-earned. On a trip to Thailand, two of the group were in a blowjob bar playing cards while women plied their trade. They were joined by a third member of the group, who warned that many of the women in the bar were actually "ladyboys". One of the two pulled at the hair of the "girl" who was at that moment crouching between his legs, only to find the young man's wig coming off. Asked later if he did the boy over, the Deviant replied, "Yes, but I waited 'til after I came."

Ken still giggles when he remembers the trip to Zaragosa. They hired a minibus and set off overland to Spain, though not before Glass had pinned a sign on a window. "It was a normal minibus but with a simple piece of A4 paper stuck in the window with 'hate bus' written on it with marker pen. It was so stupid it was funny. People got in with crates of beer and one person, who will remain anonymous, brought a blow-up doll. That was getting serviced along the way."

The excursion epitomised their mentality: a desire to shock, abuse and insult, to act freely without restriction or comeback. "The thing about the Spain trip, it was only partly to do with football," says Ken. "It was just a group of blokes like in *Men Behaving Badly* – but they had nothing on us lot. A weekend of going over there, getting really, really drunk, causing loads of trouble and shagging loads of dodgy birds. It was outside the parameters of normal life. It was mental. The football was just an excuse for going. The main reason why we wanted the team to win was so we could do it all again next month. It's a social thing, especially going away from home. You go somewhere like Spain and you know it's going to be brilliant. You go over in a pair of shorts and just be really obnoxious. That sounds really childish, but that's half the attraction I suppose."

Ken admits that such behaviour also fulfils an urge for power. "It's good because when you are [in England] the rest of your life is dull and boring, especially if you are in the right-wing, you are even more alienated from society. It's just our way of getting our own back. We go across to Europe, everyone hates us but at the same time everyone is wary of us. It's a power position. It's about getting respect."

Respect is a recurring theme. Coming from a life where they feel downtrodden, belittled and ignored, they yearn for it. They perceive their actions as bringing them respect – either through fighting or through fear. Respect leads to power. Whether you are a football hooligan on a Saturday afternoon or a C18 warrior on a Saturday night, people take notice. For a day, you are on top.

Fraser and the CISA took a three-day break to Spain but

encountered no trouble. "The omission of certain people from the trip led it to being a more relaxed atmosphere," says Ken, in reference to Browning and Atkinson. "There were other things going on and Spain was quite a long way. The novelty of doing Fraser was not as fresh then and there were other problems raising their heads in the movement, internal things." In the event, Chelsea lost and went out of the tournament. And in C18, interest in football was already waning as Will Browning became increasingly influential and other priorities reared their heads.

A footnote to the story: two years after his last run in with C18, Fraser and a group of friends made a trip to Milan to watch a mid-season friendly between Chelsea and Internazionale at the remarkable San Siro stadium. As Fraser enjoyed a quiet drink before the game, he saw a group of men in designer clothes heading in his direction. He quickly realised that they were right-wing Headhunters and managed to flee without serious injury. For his own safety and that of those who had made the journey with him, Fraser was forced to miss the game, which was fortunate as his attackers spent the match searching the stadium for him. One C18 supporter laughed about the incident afterwards. "It's just become like a bit of fun now, it's nothing political. If we can't find someone else to fight, we'll just look for Fraser. It's sport."

CHAPTER SEVEN

White Noise

WILL BROWNING WAS being nosey. The small, tatty office of Music Media Manufacturing was a temple of information that he was eager to plunder. He needed to learn everything he could about the compact disc production process

"So where's it done then?" he casually asked the assistant.

"Mr James, you said?" enquired MMM owner, Mike Spenser, glancing at the name on the order form.

"Yeah, that's right," replied the Beast nonchalantly, as he pulled £1,100 from his back pocket.

Browning never got the answer to his question: while the CD broker was keen to encourage the interest of his customers, there was a limit to how much he would divulge. CD manufacturing was a cut-throat business and, with small profit margins for the broker, he was keen to prevent bands making direct contact with the pressing plant and cutting him out of the loop.

Browning couldn't hang about. He faced a busy schedule as he carried his newly-pressed CDs back to his car for the drive to Harlow, where he would drop off 200 with Charlie Sargent. He also had to collect the printed CD sleeves, put the newly-pressed discs inside and post them out to his distributors on the Continent. C18 was now in the music business. It had launched the first nazi CD label in Britain. Browning hoped it would make his gang self-sufficient and provide the financial means to fund its ultimate goal: racial war.

Music has long been a lucrative and component of the British far-right. Ever since nazis became dominant within the skinhead scene in the late Seventies, they had viewed the skins as a pool of recruits and revenue. The icon of this worldwide scene was Ian

Stuart Donaldson. He had first formed a band while at grammar school in Lancashire, changing its name to Skrewdriver a couple of years later while he was the Young National Front organiser for Blackpool and Fylde. Skrewdriver were heavily influenced by punk and their first album, *All Skrewed Up*, was regarded by some critics as one of the best of the genre: simple guitar chords, rasping vocals and lyrics spitting with alienation. As a singer and songwriter, Donaldson appeared to have a lucrative career ahead of him, but was already set on a racist course. He was linked to the NF until 1987, when he became increasingly annoyed at their financial exploitation of the skinhead scene and launched Blood and Honour as an independent umbrella organisation for right-wing bands and their supporters.

To young men who followed the far-right, Donaldson was a star. His records were played until they wore out. As his songs became more and more extreme, they drew increasing numbers into what became a skinhead cult, particularly in continental Europe and the United States, where large numbers of nazi skins began to appear on the streets for the first time. Skrewdriver travelled extensively across Germany and Scandinavia and helped build up links between extremists from different countries. By 1988, Donaldson was telling the *Sunday People*, "Eventually there will be a race war and we have to be strong enough in numbers to win it. I'll die to keep this country pure and if it means bloodshed at the end of the day, then let it be." His idea of bloodshed was beating up an elderly Nigerian man in Kings Cross, central London, near the flat he shared with Charlie Sargent (their friendship soured when he was imprisoned for assault and Sargent sold a picture of him with the Madness singer Suggs to *The Sun* for £500). On his release from jail, Donaldson vowed never to return, and his music was tame in comparison to that of later C18-aligned bands. Several beatings at the hands of anti-fascists convinced him to leave London, but to the nazi movement he remained a hero.

When C18 emerged in 1992, Blood and Honour was controlled by Neil Parish, a Milton Keynes-based BNP activist, and Paul Burnley, a British Movement supporter from south London.

While Parish had been the stereotypical working class skinhead since his school days, acquiring over forty convictions, Burnley came from an altogether more comfortable background. Born Paul Bellamy, he was the youngest son of the Scottish artist John Bellamy. He went on to produce the *Blood and Honour* magazine while Parish ran the merchandise operation, which at its peak brought in orders worth £1,000 a week. Such success inevitably attracted interest. Charlie Sargent had been involved in the skinhead scene for years and was keen to grab a slice of the spoils. But with Parish aligned to the BNP, and regularly giving them donations, Sargent knew control would not be handed over voluntarily.

C18 hovered like vultures around the skinhead scene. At the same time, Parish hit bad luck. He was arrested for possession of CS gas following a joint C18/Blood and Honour attack on a gay bar in Kings Cross, and faced almost certain jail. Compounding his problems was an *Evening Standard* article depicting London as a haven for terror groups: mentioned alongside Islamic and Kurdish terrorist networks was Parish's Blood and Honour. His politics fell by the wayside as he increasingly dipped into Blood and Honour funds to feed his drug and alcohol addictions. All he had built up was disintegrating. To make matters worse, his wife, who was expecting their second child, gave him an ultimatum to sort himself out or lose her and the children.

Depressed and increasingly paranoid, Parish accepted an offer of help. He met Charlie Sargent through Steve Martin, who Parish had befriended during the weekly BNP paper sale in east London. Ignoring Ian Stuart Donaldson's advice to steer clear of Sargent, Parish struck a deal: C18 would protect him from antifascists during his weekly trips to London to collect mail, and in return he would furnish them with details about the music scene and its merchandising operation. He knew C18 had designs on Blood and Honour but believed he had little alternative. Before long he had agreed to Sargent's suggestion that C18 temporarily take over the running of the music business while he served his prison sentence, with the promise that it would be returned on his release. Sargent promised to pay Parish's wife £50 a week during his incarceration as an act of good faith. Within days, Sargent and Martin had hired a van and collected over £9,000-worth of stock.

Of course, it was a scam to gain control of Blood and Honour. Parish had scarcely begun his prison when Sargent began discrediting him. He first contacted Donaldson and claimed that Parish had milked the movement dry, failing to mention the considerable amount of stock he had secured. He then set about writing articles in *The Order* attacking Parish as a low-life thief and informer. It was classic Sargent: sly, treacherous and selfish.

C18 turned its attention to the concert and magazine wings of Blood and Honour, controlled by the British Movement and Paul Burnley respectively. It was again assisted by incidents outside its direct control. In September 1992, a London concert billed as the biggest skinhead gathering since 1989 was organised by the BM. Waterloo Station was given as the re-direction point. Over 1,000 anti-fascists, led by a couple of hundred AFA activists from around the country, took over the station, forcing the assembled nazis to flee under police protection. Although Waterloo had been a smokescreen, with the bulk of the nazis meeting at the South Mimms service station on the M25, the anti-fascist victory overshadowed the concert, which was attended by over 400 nazis. Some C18 supporters from west London did turn up to lend a hand but the majority stayed away, content to monitor the ensuing chaos from a north London pub.

The Waterloo fiasco had been a blow for the organisers and C18 was quick to take advantage. Three months later, its thugs attended the annual "White Christmas" concert in Mansfield *en masse*: forty made the journey by coach from London in what was their first organised trip out of the capital. Many in the audience were seeing C18 for the first time. It was a dramatic clash of subcultures. On one side were the Londoners, cocksure and glib, all flash labels and arrogance. On the other were the largely-provincial skins, tattooed and shaven-headed, cumbersome dinosaurs facing a new breed of interlopers. The skins for once were wary: they had heard much about the C18 mob and knew many of them were veterans of scores of terrace

battles. Ian Stuart Donaldson, fearing trouble, introduced Charlie
Sargent to the audience. His intervention established C18 as *the*
firm on the scene.

Seven months later, another high profile BM-organised concert
went askew, as police in the East Midlands banned a weekend
Aryan Fest, confiscating stage equipment and thousands of cans
of beer on the eve of the event. Widespread anger greeted the
organisers from the hundreds who had made the trip, many
from abroad. With the BM seemingly incapable of organising a
successful concert, its followers turned to C18 for leadership.

On the foggy morning of September 23, 1993, Ian Donaldson
was with friends driving north along the A38 in Derbyshire
when their car left the road and overturned. Donaldson and
another passenger were killed. In one stroke, the umbilical cord
holding the movement together was cut. C18 and Paul Burnley
each tried to claim Donaldson's legacy, with the shameless
Charlie Sargent even saying that he had been the singer's guiding
political influence.

Burnley proved no match for C18 and in particular Will
Browning, who loathed him. Browning had played guitar in
Burnley's band, No Remorse, until an incident in 1991 when the
Beast performed drunk on stage during a concert in Germany.
Only when Browning later watched a video of the gig did he
realise that Burnley had been standing behind him making
obscene gestures. From that day the two men never shared a
friendly word, and Browning was only too eager to lead Sargent's
campaign against Burnley. He only once came across Burnley
again and immediately struck him in the face, causing a large
swelling. Soon after, No Remorse called it a day. Also quitting
the scene was Alex Allui, a Chelmsford-based nazi who was lead
singer with Battlezone and a close friend of Burnley. He received
a visit from Browning and was pinned him to the wall with a
machete at his throat. He took the hint. Blood and Honour was
now firmly in the control of Combat 18.

★   ★   ★   ★

ISD RECORDS TOOK its name from the late Skrewdriver singer who, in the manner of rock stars, became bigger in death than in life. His hero status was ironic given that he had become increasingly disillusioned with the skinhead scene in the couple of years before he died. ISD was a new departure for the British nazi scene, its first attempt at launching its own CD label. It gave the movement control over the entire production process, from the recording of material to its production and eventual distribution.

Previously, Neil Parish had been forced to deal exclusively with Rock-o-Rama Records, a company run by the German-based Herbert Egoldt, who produced nazi music for financial rather than ideological reasons. During the late Eighties, Egoldt established the world's largest nazi music empire, stretching from Europe to the United States. Through a deal with Donaldson, Rock-o-Rama exclusively produced Skrewdriver material and subsequently the work of every other British nazi band, with the exception of No Remorse. It was a bad deal for the British bands. Not only did they receive few proceeds from their work, but strict German race laws meant Egoldt banned overtly nazi imagery, lyrics and images. Blood and Honour also suffered financially, with Parish being forced to buy British racist music through intermediaries at £8 an album. The £2.50 profit he gained through mail orders was miniscule compared to the £8 profit available to ISD through the production of its own CDs. When the police finally closed Egoldt's operation they confiscated over 30,000 nazi albums and tapes.

One man was not happy at the arrival of ISD Records. Gary Hitchcock was not impressed with Will Browning's initiative and was even less pleased that he had not been consulted before it was launched. When Browning had first raised the idea of a right-wing record label in Britain a couple of years before, Hitchcock had managed to talk him out of it. What Browning didn't know was that any new incursion into this scene would damage Hitchcock's own business interests. Hitchcock was very secretive about his work; few within C18 knew of his connections to the Oi! music scene, fewer still that he had become the sole importer of Rock-o-Rama records during the last months of Parish's reign. The formation of ISD took away a large slice of Hitchcock's business. "I know he was very fucking bitter when the first CDs came out," says Steve Sargent. "He was really bitter, saying, 'These cunts have done this behind my back.' You see he's always done CDs himself. He's a very money-motivated geezer." Too scared to confront Browning directly, Hitchcock pleaded with Charlie Sargent to intervene, with no success. Eventually Hitchcock dropped out of C18.

Browning was oblivious to Hitchcock's anger; like the majority of people in the movement, he knew nothing of his secret business dealings. He was more concerned with making ISD Records a success and before long had persuaded several British bands to sign up. Taking advice from people who had produced their own material, and speaking directly to CD companies, Browning found the business far easier than he had imagined. Most of the discs he produced went through commercial CD brokers, music middlemen who get the material pressed by manufacturers around the world. All that was required was a DAT (digital audio tape) master copy, which Browning either paid the band to record in a studio or, with live material, simply recorded himself. Browning was to use at least three CD brokers and other activists who carried out work for him used a further two. All of the brokers subsequently claimed ignorance of the political content of the music. "I had no idea what the lyrics contained," claimed Mike Spenser, of MMM, which produced some of the group's most extreme material. "We never listened to them and he [Browning] seemed a nice bloke. He took a great interest in the business, always asking questions about how things were done." Spenser was convinced Browning was some sort of Mod but never actually enquired about the music.

Browning was able to get his music produced without even having to supply his real name or address to any of the brokers. The manufacturers were equally blasé. Browning's most inflammatory CD was produced by Nimbus (UK), a British subsidiary of the giant American multi-national that produced the world's first CD. In the spring of 1996, they mastered and pressed several thousand copies of *Barbecue in Rostock*, every song an apparent breach of the Public Order Act. Later it emerged that the company had made no checks on the legality of the material it produced. Like most of the industry, Nimbus simply accepted the integrity of the customer.

Browning organised the production of the CDs but was content to leave the mail order business to Sargent and others. This reduced the potential profit available directly to ISD but avoided strict tax or legal liabilities, to say nothing of the mundane administrative work involved. Browning would collect the newly-pressed CDs from the brokers, split them up into the required bundles and post them off around Europe at a discount to chosen distributors. In Britain, Charlie Sargent took a couple of hundred of each CD to sell through *The Order* and *Blood and Honour* magazines, while smaller quantities went to other UK-based mail order outlets. Most distributors were charged between £5 and £7 a CD, but Charlie received his quota for nothing, using the money raised to subsidise the less profitable propaganda wing that he and his brother controlled. Abroad, Browning was quite choosy about ISD distributors, limiting his network to one operator per country or region. In Scandinavia, the CDs were sold through NS88 Records, while in Belgium the distributor was Yannick Pollet's Excalibur Records. In Italy, Browning's contact was Ciao, the lead singer of the Italian band Peggiore Amico, while in North America a deal was struck with Wolfpack Services. The final few hundred from every batch of 1,000 would be sold by Browning or one of his cohorts at gigs at home and abroad.

Most bands that signed up to ISD would get ten percent of the proceeds as royalties, made up of either 100 CDs or £1,000 in cash, though sympathetic bands occasionally waived even this. ISD covered all the recording and studio costs. While £1,000 was not much, few complained, at least initially. Some musicians who had been ripped off by other companies in the past were happy just to receive something; others simply did it for the cause. To most of the bands, the music was a weekend hobby, something that elevated their status in the movement.

"While the financial returns were small, there were benefits," one band member says. "It was an easy way to get music produced and then sold on, and you basically have a captive audience. You can easily become pop stars within a small scene. Other people who are a lot more talented could play the pub circuit for years in front of only five or six people and a dog without the hope of ever getting a CD produced. You also had a ready-made market for your material. In many ways it wasn't a bad life either. Some bands got to travel around Europe, while Celtic Warrior and Squadron even managed to get gigs in North America and Australia."

Concerts abroad were a perk of playing in the band, an all-expenses-paid opportunity to travel with your mates. The flights or other transport were covered, as was accommodation, and beer was often free. Some bands made a long weekend of a trip, seeing it as an opportunity for a two-day drinking binge. There was the added benefit of being the centre of attraction, not least for foreign skingirls, something that was of great motivation for many band members. One or two gigs a month in Britain and the occasional trip abroad probably explained why most band members were content while times were good.

Blood and Honour was reorganised, with Simon Dutton, another BM defector, running the southern division and Derby-based Chris Hipkin, a long-time skin who ran the *British Oi!* magazine for many years, running the north. Security at gigs was organised by Mark Atkinson and Del O'Connor, a neanderthal Wigan nazi who had been involved in Skrewdriver Security and had been a close friend of Donaldson. The two divisions were supposed to alternate events every few weeks, though it rarely worked as efficiently as this. Generally gigs were held monthly. Many were relatively small, attracting sometimes fewer than 100 people, with larger events every few months. Surprisingly, they rarely made much money. Despite entrance fees of as much as £10, overheads were high, especially when travel for foreign bands had to be paid, and it was not unknown for the smaller gigs to make a loss. Still, the financial incentives attracted people other than the two divisional organisers. Charlie Sargent, ever on the look out for new ways to make money, quickly got in on the act and during 1995 and 1996 staged a number of well-attended events in north-east London and Essex. The performing bands were rarely paid for their efforts, though they would generally get travelling expenses. They were, however, allowed to sell their own merchandise and this could yield decent money. Leading bands like Celtic Warrior and English Rose produced not only their own CDs but also a range of other merchandise, from tee-shirts to badges. Foreign bands would have their travel paid and, during this period, bands from the USA, Germany, Sweden, Finland, Italy and France played in Britain.

The audiences at gigs were a combination of traditional skinheads and the football casuals of C18. The former was a decreasing group, as the skin image had long gone out of fashion, even amongst nazis. The casuals tended to view gigs as social rather than musical functions. Not everyone was happy with this mix. Years later, Steve Sargent would blame the move into Blood and Honour as a major reason why C18 collapsed, claiming that the group suffered because of the absence of young people in the music scene.

Though few concerts were ever stopped by the police or anti-fascists – in marked contrast to the British Movement days – there was the odd noticeable exception. Blood and Honour's first major event under C18 control was held in east London at the beginning of 1994. Billed as a memorial for the late Ian Stuart Donaldson, the concert was due to attract hundreds of nazis from across Europe. It was a complete flop. First the police, and then anti-fascists, prevented Blood and Honour from staging the event. On hearing that the concert had been cancelled, a group of East Midlands nazis vented their frustration in a cowardly attack on Mushroom Books, a progressive bookshop in Nottingham. Over thirty skinheads were involved, knocking the manager over with a blow to the back of the head and assaulting a disabled member of staff. Leaving the shop in chaos, they were arrested as they left the area by public transport.

However, the vast majority of concerts went ahead without trouble, though all had to be clandestinely organised with no

external publicity. Most of the larger events occurred outside
London: one on the Isle of Sheppey, in Kent, in 1994 attracted
over 500 people. Another large bash was a Donaldson memorial
concert in Caerphilly, South Wales, two years after the death of
the Skrewdriver leader; it attracted over 400 people. The concert
was booked for a community hall, with the PA and other stage
equipment being arranged by Celtic Warrior's lead singer Billy
Bartlett. His band was first on stage, followed by Warlord,
Razor's Edge and the Swedish band Swastika. Last to appear
was a reformed No Remorse, starring Will Browning on guitar,
Daniel "Jacko" Jack on vocals, Gary Smith on bass, and the
diminutive French nazi Jean-Charles Tanzi on drums. Such
larger gigs were highly profitable. Even allowing for the few who
got in without paying – principally the band members and local
organisers – there was a lot of money to be made. At a
conservative estimate, the 300 paying customers at Caerphilly
made the organisers £3,000; on top of that were the proceeds
from the sale of beer, provided privately. Around the room were
a number of merchandise stalls, some selling ISD CDs and
general Blood and Honour material, others the merchandise of
individual bands.

Twenty miles away from the Caerphilly concert was an even
bigger event, a world title boxing match between Cardiff-based
Steve Robinson and Sheffield's Prince Naseem Hamed. Four of
the C18-aligned football hooligans were not interested in skinhead
music and so went to a pub to watch the fight on TV. They
immediately found themselves at odds with the strongly partisan
Welsh locals. Banter between the two groups deteriorated as the
Londoners stood up and joined in the National Anthem at the
start of the boxing match while giving nazi salutes. The locals
responded with derision, which infuriated the hooligans. They
headed back to the community hall and spoke to Mark Atkinson,
who was dutifully performing his role as head of security. Atkinson
took to the stage to announce that there was "a pub full of Reds
down the road". It was all the incentive the crowd needed. Two
hundred nazis piled out of the hall.

The pub door was kicked open and Ian Holloway, a leading

Chelsea Headhunter, stood with his arms crossed over his chest, clutching a bottle in each hand.

"Come on you Welsh cunts. Who wants it first?" he shouted.

He lashed out with each bottle, smacking Welshmen to his immediate left and right. Another west Londoner was next in, also armed with bottles. It was the signal for others outside the pub. First the ground floor windows were smashed, then, with the aid of scaffolding poles, the upper windows went. Those who had armed themselves with bottles from the community centre began hurling them through the broken windows. When their supply ran out, some attempted to make weapons out of the wooden window frames. A couple of cars were overturned and set alight in the street.

"It was a frenzy," recalls one resident who was in the pub at the time of the attack. He, like the majority sitting in the lounge, had only gone to watch the boxing. "I have never seen anything like it before, and I doubt I will again."

The Caerphilly police, who seemed to know nothing of the concert, turned up well after the damage had been done. They then took some while to arrive in numbers, by which time the pub had been wrecked. "The first police didn't turn up for at least five minutes," recalls one skinhead who attended the concert, "but that's a long time when it's a continuous assault on the pub." Most of the culprits had already headed back to the hall. The few officers who arrived first went to the hall, having been told to gauge the mood and numbers. While there was general antagonism towards their presence, no-one impeded their entry.

Twenty vans were scrambled from Gwent and neighbouring forces, with many kitted out in full riot gear. The mood inside the hall turned sour. Most of the audience were eager to get away from the area unharmed but some discussed the possibility of taking on the police. Charlie Sargent, was one. Grabbing the microphone, the small, squat C18 leader smashed a beer bottle on the side of the stage and urged his followers into battle. "Let's kill the pigs," he screamed, to general bemusement. He repeated his call to arms but before he could incite further bloodshed, another activist quietly took him off stage. The majority of the audience filed out of the hall to their parked transport, under the watchful eye of the law. Baton-wielding officers turfed out the few who refused to leave.

Steve Sargent became separated from his mates and missed his transport back to London. Confronted by some angry locals, he initially denied being part of the attacking group, but this cut little ice with his accusers. Irritated, Sargent headbutted one man, unaware that police had gathered behind him. "I felt myself going backwards, and I was thrown in the back of a meat wagon, as were the two birds I was with," he later reminisced. "The two skinheads who were with them ran, typically." Steve thought that he was heading for the cells in Cardiff and so was surprised when the van stopped in what appeared to be a small village. He was told to get out. "I looked at the two birds and thought, nah, if I get out here they're gonna shoot me or something, saying I was trying to escape. I really didn't want to get out so I made the birds go first, being the Aryan warrior that I am. Then [an officer] said, 'Are you getting out or what?' So I got out and I'm looking at him and he's looking at me and then he said, 'Be good,' and drove off."

★　★　★　★

THE CAERPHILLY GIG signalled Browning's return to playing onstage after a four-year absence. His reformation of No Remorse was a further dig at Paul Burnley, who Browning believed had used the band's name to make himself into a pop star, not to promote the cause. Few concurred with this interpretation. To the majority on the scene, even many who aligned themselves with C18, Browning's band was privately known as No Remorse Mark II. Unsurprisingly, the Beast's version of the band was extremist: the songs, mostly written by Browning, were inflammatory and highly racist. Their first album was called *Smash the Reds*, followed soon after by *No Remorse Live*, both produced by ISD Records. Several songs were covers of music originally performed by Burnley but, of course, there was no acknowledgement.

In 1996, No Remorse produced *Barbecue in Rostock*. It was,

and is, arguably the most repulsive CD ever produced, even by a right-wing band. Every one of the songs dripped with hatred. The title itself was a sick reference to the pogrom against a refugee hostel in Rostock, Germany, in August 1992, when nazis ran riot and burnt the hostel to the ground:

> Didn't want their town filled with scum
> So they got together and made petrol bombs.
> Then one cold, starry night
> They set them filthy Turks alight.
> There's a barbecue in Rostock, you better come.
> How do you like your Turks? Do you like them well done?

Other songs were, if possible, even worse. The chorus to *The Niggers Came Over* ran:

> Shoot the Niggers! The Pakis too!
> Hang the Reds and we'll gas the Jews.
> If you're black you're going back
> With a bit of luck in a body bag.

Every track was littered with references to "wogs", "niggers" and "Pakis" and with repeated exhortations to murder.

Such outrageous lyrics made Browning's No Remorse a big attraction at gigs, especially in Germany, where nazi imagery was banned. During 1996, the band may have played as many as nine concerts abroad, making it the most popular British band on the scene. One concert was held in Rostock, attended by many of the same skinheads who had participated in the firebombings from which the album was named. So popular was the title track that No Remorse had to perform it five times. The band enjoyed playing in Germany. The audiences were considerably larger than those held in Britain and, more importantly for Browning, the scene was considerably more militant. With police interference much greater than in Britain, it wasn't unusual for German skinheads to travel for most of the day to reach a concert, a trip often involving several re-direction points in an attempt to shake off the authorities. By comparison, many within the British scene were lazy and uncommitted, the slightest inconvenience deterring them from leaving their homes or, more commonly, the pub.

One of the closest links established by Browning during this period was with Thorsten Heise, a man many considered as being the Beast's equivalent in Germany. He had a similarly unenviable record, having been in and out of trouble since his exclusion from school for racist graffiti. At the age of eighteen, he was held by police following an attack on a Turkish immigrant after an event to commemorate the anniversary of Hitler's birth. The following year he was in the company of another German extremist when a policeman was shot. He was also caught attempting to run over a Lebanese man, though the intended victim managed to jump out of the way; not one to be put off, Heise later caught up with the man and attacked him with teargas. All the while, Heise was rising up the ranks of the German nazi scene, becoming regional organiser for the ultra-violent Freiheitliche Deutsche Arbeiterpartei. Increasing responsibility failed to curb his violence. In 1995, while protesting against the deportation of an Austrian nazi, he confronted anti-fascists with a scythe and Molotov cocktails. Twenty people were injured in the ensuing melee. Heise was also active in the growing German skinhead scene, organising several concerts, some attracting over 1,000 people.

One such event cemented Heise's relationship with Browning, whose No Remorse were heading the bill. The German authorities got wind of the concert and immediately banned the nazis from using the hall in Adelsleden. Refusing to be beaten, Heise arranged for everyone to return to his house, a detached building with a large open yard to the rear. There the concert went ahead, though without a PA system, which had been confiscated earlier in the day by the police. A stand-off developed as officers surrounded the building and ordered Heise to stop the event, initially to no avail; despite being virtually unable to hear the music, the nazis danced to No Remorse's racist lyrics while Heise's masked supporters displayed makeshift weapons from the windows of the

Charlie Sargent caught on camera outside a BNP meeting in east London in 1990. In front of him is Gary Hitchcock. The pair were instrumental in forming Combat 18 two years later. © *David Hoffman*

Sargent in C18 tee-shirt on a demo in Denmark in 1995.

Sargent in an Essex pub the week before Chris Castle was murdered.

Will 'the Beast' Browning reacts violently to the attentions of a
World in Action camera crew in a London street in March 1995.

Browning (centre) on a BNP
march in Thamesmead,
south-east London in 1991.

Browning attending court with his
right-hand man Darren Wells (right).
© *David Hoffman*

Charlie Sargent acts as minder to British National Party leader John Tyndall (in suit) on a march in Walsall in July 1992.

Eddie Butler (left) leads a C18 security team to a BNP election meeting in Bethnal Green in April 1992. The gang was set up to steward BNP events.

London UDA leaders Frank Portinari (left) and Eddie Whicker brandishing weapons in Loyalist regalia. Insets: Portinari (left) on an National Front anti-IRA protest and Whicker at a speech by Holocaust-denier David Irving.

C18 supporters, including Stuart Glass (third from left in sunglasses), greet photographers with nazi salutes outside the Old Bailey in 1995.

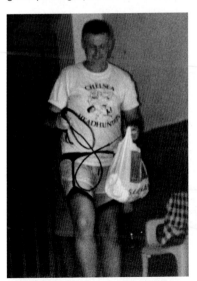 

Left: Ken Walsh of the West London Deviants in Chelsea Headhunters tee-shirt, stockings and suspenders and brandishing a whip.
Right: Andy Frain, aka 'the Nightmare', on an anti-IRA protest in 1998.

NO REMORSE

BARBECUE IN ROSTOCK

Leighton Jones (left) was jailed for producing the racially inflammatory *Barbecue in Rostock* CD (above). The album's lyrics celebrated the burning of immigrants and exhorted listeners to 'kill niggers'.

Left to right: Gary Smith, Jean-Charles Tanzi, Will Browning and Daniel Jack of the band No Remorse, which recorded the album.

Nazi skinheads battle with anti-fascists at Waterloo in 1992.
The trouble opened the door for C18 to take over Blood and Honour.

A typical scene at a skinhead gig: Andy Nolan (Razor's Edge) and John
Henderson (Blackshirts) on stage at a C18 concert in Coventry in 2000.

A selection of CDs produced by Combat 18 in the 1990s. £200,000
profit was raised through the production of twenty-five albums.

Will Browning earned a reputation for violence on the Hess demonstration in Roskilde, Denmark, in August 1995.
He and Charlie Sargent (above) face anti-facist protestors.

Browning hurls a bottle at the Danish demonstrators while carrying a large pole. His crazed attack was captured by a film crew.

The Beast punches a protestor in the face, watched by a line of riot police. His thuggish display inspired nazis in Scandinavia.

building. Deciding that storming the building could result in considerable casualties, the police waited, arresting anyone who strayed outside the compound. Heise donned his trademark long leather coat and opened a cupboard full of weapons, including knives, bats and an air rifle that was used to take pot shots at the police. Browning put on a German Army helmet and stormed from window to window, waving an axe. At one stage the No Remorse drummer, Jean-Charles Tanzi, decided to take a leak outside the building, only to get arrested, to the general amusement of the others. He was forced in lie face down in the snow, his hands cuffed behind his back. Finally, the police massed for what appeared to be a raid and the remaining nazis made their way onto the roof for a defiant last stand. They found Steve Sargent, who had taken refuge there, supplied with a box of biscuits and some coffee. After holding out a short time longer, the nazis eventually emerged into the custody of the waiting police.

Sometimes the London band Chingford Attack accompanied No Remorse on their travels. Their lead singer, Mick Dunne, was a close friend of Browning and the two bands shared Jean-Charles as drummer. It was common for one or two friends to ride with them, and the events proved more of a social occasion than anything else, with band members enjoying the free beer that was often provided and the adoration of local skingirls. In the autumn of 1996, both bands were due to play in Chemnitz, East Germany. Browning planned a number of meetings with representatives of NS88 and some East German record labels and insisted that everyone behave themselves. Not trusting his bassist, Gary Smith, he assigned two Germans to chaperone him until the band was due on stage. Nevertheless, during the evening Browning broke off from one discussion only to see a drunken Smith slumped in the corner of the venue with a girl on each leg. Jean-Charles was also the worse for drink, having taken advantage of the free bottles of schnapps on offer. Within minutes of starting their set, Browning had to unplug the bassist's guitar, as he was so drunk there was nothing remotely tuneful coming out of his instrument. A short time later Browning looked round in horror to see the bassist and the drummer exchanging blows. He was hopping mad – but sure nothing worse could happen – when Jon Hodgins, better known as "Dr Death", drunkenly stumbled through the crowd and threw a glass of beer over Jacko. The set was abandoned and Browning stormed out of the hall.

His problems were not yet over. The concert organiser had provided a chalet for the visiting C18 contingent. Browning, already in a bad mood, arrived there to find Dunne and Tanzi parading round in stolen Nazi regalia. The others were interrogating a German who some believed was a police informer. Convinced of his guilt, Darren Wells rammed a champagne bottle into the German's face. 'Great shot,' remarked Gary Smith, to break the silence. Some time later, police arrived and dragged the English from their beds. 'Stasi harassment,' shouted Browning.

Bass player Smith was considered the prankster of the group but the joke was on him during a No Remorse gig in Milan in 1996. Unable to book all the band members on the same flight home, Browning decided that the bassist would have to take a flight the next day but, knowing that he was unlikely to agree to the trip under these conditions, decided to not tell him. At the airport for their return flight, Browning, Jean-Charles and Daniel Jack suddenly ran through the check-in, leaving their bemused colleague arguing with airline staff. Furious, Smith rang the gig organiser Ciao, lead singer of the Italian fascist band Peggiore Amico, and ordered him to collect him. Ciao drove for nine hours to the airport, but the Englishman was nowhere to be seen; he had wandered from one bar to another in a drunken stupor.

On another occasion, Smith was left with a bag of CDs, including copies of *Barbecue in Rostock*, and some money to catch a separate flight home. He decided to return the joke by going back to the city centre to spend the airfare on drink, then raise more beer money through the sale of the CDs to local skinheads. Several days and hangovers later, he finally ran out of money, and approached the British consulate claiming he had been robbed. The officials were unsympathetic to his plight, as it appeared that this was not the first time he had pulled this stunt. A few very reluctant and annoyed Milano skins were forced to pay out for another air ticket.

★ ★ ★ ★

WILL BROWNING KNEW exactly what he was doing when he wrote and released the *Barbecue in Rostock* album. He was not only trying to whip up racial strife amongst his followers, but was sending a defiant message out to a society he despised and to the other nazi bands. In an accompanying newsletter, Browning wrote, "What is the point talking about smashing ZOG if you're too scared to even break the Government's race laws?" He went on to boast that this album was "guaranteed to incite racial hatred" and concluded the article by asserting, "I mean, if the Jew is your enemy, then you shouldn't be scared to say that either. FUCK THE RACE LAWS!" Browning knew he was risking prison by producing such material. While he covered his own tracks by getting other people to organise the production of the CD and open a Post Office box, he was not too bothered about possible consequences. He had long been urging others to take up the battle that they advocated in their publications and was annoyed at what he perceived to be the cowardice of many in the movement. Even in the early days of C18, Browning had wanted to go beyond simple street confrontations, but found no takers.

The Beast became increasingly strident towards the end of 1994. His vehicle was *Combat 18*. Issue one contained general propaganda, lists of opponents and threats. Missing out issue two – to confuse his enemies – Browning's literary masterpiece was issue three, an eighty-eight-page magazine that said much about his state of mind. It was littered with images of death and violence and contained simple instructions for home-made bombs gleaned from manuals he had obtained while in the Royal Marine Reserves. "Now you have the technology, so bomb the bastards!" he urged his readers. All nine bomb types listed were later built successfully by police technicians at a lab in Kent. Under lists of the names and addresses of what he thought were left-wing activists, Browning wrote, "Kill'em all." The original draft had included the names and addresses of 300 MPs, something Charlie Sargent removed in a fit of panic.

C18 publications regularly contained thinly-veiled threats, but *Combat 18* plumbed new depths. While *Redwatch*, for example, urged its readership to harass and intimidate their opponents, *Combat 18* explicitly called for their murder. Worse still, Browning believed what he was writing. Time and again he had shown that he had little regard for human life. The magazine also illustrated the immaturity of Browning and his followers. Grotesque and silly caricatures made up much of its content. One could imagine Browning giggling like a child as he put in one picture of the black athlete Linford Christie eating a banana. It was puerile stuff that reflected the limits of their politics.

Browning's desire for terrorism infected the small group closest to him. Among them was Darren Wells. He came from a relatively comfortable, middle class family in Putney, south-west London, later moving with his family to Hatfield in Hertfordshire, where he attended a grammar school. He went into London when finances permitted to watch Chelsea play and arrived in the C18 orbit in January 1993 while attending the Bloody Sunday counter-demonstration with Chelsea hooligans. His had been a political journey well-trodden by others on the Right: from football hooligan to Loyalist, from Loyalist to patriot, from patriot to nazi. Like most other English hooligans, he professed to hate the IRA and people he believed put down his country. In C18 he found men proud of who they were. As if to proclaim his views, Wells had swastikas tattooed on his chest and leg. He got to know Browning well during a trip to Scandinavia in October 1995 and the two became inseparable. In early 1996, Wells, like Browning several months before, gave up his job in the insurance business to commit himself full time to the cause.

★　★　★　★

BROWNING HAD ESTABLISHED ISD Records primarily to fund C18 operations and this it certainly did. The potential profit from each batch of a 1,000 CDs was large. When ISD organised the production of *Whatever it Takes* by Razor's Edge, they paid the London CD broker MMM about £1,350. With recording costs and sleeves, the total moved up to somewhere between £3-4,000. Had Browning chosen to establish his own mail order company, the potential profit on a 1,000-CD run would have been £6,000, but farming out the CDs to other distributors reduced his profit to between £2-3,000. However, Browning's real money was to be made in re-pressing. Without the costs of recording, royalties, and the master tape, the only expense incurred was for the pressing and additional sleeves. For every re-press of 1,000 CDs, ISD Records stood to gain £5,000, even taking into account the discount given for bulk sales. More money still was to be made through direct sales at gigs, while live recordings immediately cut out studio costs and often royalties.

It is estimated that ISD Records produced twenty CDs with a total pressing of about 35,000 units between 1994 and 1997. Even allowing for thousands of CDs confiscated in police raids, ISD earned, at a conservative estimate, £100,000 profit, and possibly double that amount. The Scandinavian NS88 re-pressed several of the more popular CDs, while *Barbecue in Rostock* had two pressings in Britain, one or two more in Scandinavia and another three or four in Germany, making it the most popular ISD album by far. As Browning became more experienced in managing a record label, he sought to cut his overheads still further. He was conscious that performing in a commercial recording studio could create difficulties for right-wing bands, quite apart from the costs involved, and so began purchasing his own recording equipment.

The volume of profit made ISD unique on the British far-right. Even in the skinhead heyday of the Seventies, it was always the commercial middlemen who creamed the profit. Will Browning, almost single-handedly, made the entire British right-wing aware of the possible financial rewards to be made from the music business. While some bands became resentful of ISD and sought to produce their own material in later years, Browning had, for the first time, made the movement financially self-sufficient.

More importantly, he now had at his disposal funds to further the war.

CHAPTER EIGHT

Our Race is Our Nation

"IT'S TIME TO fight," declared Charlie Sargent from the stage. "We've had enough of talking, of false hopes and betrayals by our so-called nationalist leadership. Within a short time we must begin the war."

His audience, in a packed room at a Birmingham hotel, clapped in appreciation. A chorus of "Sieg Heils" was accompanied by nazi salutes. On-looking staff at the Stephenson Hotel, tucked away behind New Street Station, had never heard anything like it. Nor, for that matter, had many of those at the meeting. Sargent spoke of hitlists having been drawn up and said the day of reckoning was fast approaching. At the top of the pile of people to be murdered was their arch-rival, *Searchlight* journalist Gerry Gable. The mere mention of his name brought howls of abuse. There could have been few prouder moments for Sargent as he returned to his seat, surveying the 150 applauding nazis gathered before him.

It was the inaugural meeting of the newly-formed National Socialist Alliance (NSA), an idea first discussed in the summer of 1993. Sargent had hoped to launch the group at a high-profile event in central London, but American ideologue Harold Covington, his choice to address the first meeting, had continually let him down. Still, as other speakers took to the floor, there was an unmistakable feeling of excitement. "Stuart", an Ulsterman involved with the UDA, spoke about the Loyalist cause; the host of the meeting, Nigel Bromage, talked of the need for right-wing unity; and Max Wegegg, a former Luftwaffe airman living in Coventry, spoke of the struggle before them. But no one matched the aggression of Sargent. He had derided the BNP and NF as right-wing Tories, and ridiculed the BM for its inactivity. "The NSA", he boasted, "is the first true national socialist group in Britain for many years." Moreover, it was about to embark on what others only ever talked about – war.

The National Socialist Alliance was a network of semi-autonomous groups united by core beliefs: a rag-tag cabal of extremists, conspiracy theorists and lunatics. It brought together a number of people committed, at least on paper, to the violent destruction of "the system". Aside from C18, it was made up of the Blood and Honour music scene and sections of the largely inactive British Movement. There were also a number of previously unaligned smaller groups and individuals, including some of the most hardline nazis in Britain: David Myatt's National Socialist Movement, Adrian Blundells's White Aryan Resistance and the Bradford-based Women's Patriotic League. At its peak, the NSA would claim the support of fourteen different publications, including *Putsch, Thor-Would, The Order* and *The Stormer* from C18 and *Sigrun* and *Europe Awake* from renegade BM groups. From the Blood and Honour network came *British Oi, Blood and Honour Scotland, Rampage,* and *Blood and Honour* itself. Adding to this list was David Myatt's *National Socialist* and Jeff Dunn's *Wodin, Backlash* and *Blitzkrieg.*

The NSA's ideology aped Hitler's National Socialism and was an extension of the political theory that had led C18 to split from the BNP. There was none of the fudging or confusion over goals that had characterised of much of C18's early propaganda. The NSA rejected not only the BNP's election strategy, but also its parochial nationalism. "Nationalism is merely a political solution to a political problem – it aims to cure some of the ills of the present System, rather than replace the whole rotten system," one supporter wrote in *The Order.* "The fundamental mistake made by many nationalists is in believing that National Socialism was some ephemeral, German phenomena and that it died in the ruins of Berlin in 1945. The reality is that our present problems – racial, social, spiritual and economic – stem from the so-called Allied victory in WW2. With this victory, the materialistic, multi-cultural order triumphed. The diagnosis offered by

Nationalism is only half a cure: an ineffective one. Were a
nationalist movement to triumph, what it achieved would only
be temporary – as the triumph of Franco in Spain: today, it is
just another multi-racial, 'democratic' State dedicated to material
consumerism." In opposing what he described as "the reactionary
'right wing' BNP with their 'Fly the flag', 'God Save the
Queen' philosophy", the author claimed that only true National
Socialism could be an answer. "National Socialism is, in fact, a
revolutionary movement which seeks the complete overthrow of
the present order and its replacement with a new order: its aim
for a complete re-birth, a renaissance. National Socialism is, in
fact, a revolutionary movement which seeks to create an entirely
new type of society, based on noble idealism – and, ultimately,
seeks to create new ways of living." The NSA adopted the
slogan "Our Race is Our Nation".

★   ★   ★   ★

WHILE SOME OF those who attached themselves to the new umbrella
group were simply paper organisations, others were quite
effective. The biggest success for the NSA was its West Midlands
region, run by the Phoenix Society. Unlike others, the West
Midlands NSA was not only truly independent of C18 but also
very active. It was established by Nigel Bromage – using the
name Jason Ball – and Rob Wild, two close friends who had been
together since the early Eighties in both the National Front and
the British Movement. While Bromage was made West Midlands
BM regional organiser, the long-haired Wild served on the NF
national executive. Bromage shied away from publicity; Wild
was more reckless. In 1991, he and five other NF members were
arrested after a late-night brawl in an Indian restaurant in south
London, having gone for a meal after an executive meeting. In
the same year he was seen heading a trade union march against
the Gulf War through Coventry city centre: with his long hair
and scruffy appearance, he appeared a typical peacenik, until he
threw down his banner and pulled out NF posters from under
his jacket. Three years later, reinforcing his image as a practical

joker, he replaced a Mandela Road sign with one reading "PC Blakelock", after the policeman killed in the Broadwater Farm riots in 1985. News of his handiwork appeared in the NF paper.

The emergence of C18 coincided with Bromage's growing disillusionment with the BM, especially over the question of Ireland, where, unlike other right-wing groups, they sympathised with the nationalists. In July 1992, Bromage and Wild attended the BNP march in Walsall which was protected by C18, but left without making any decision about joining. The new NSA provided them with a solution: Bromage could support national socialist unity but remain within the BM. However, this position soon became untenable as the BM refused links with the NSA, viewing it as a rival. Having seen much of its London base shift allegiance to C18 in 1992, the BM leadership was in no mood to open up the rest of its organisation to Sargent. Bromage grew frustrated at the intransigence of the leadership and began to voice his views in the pages of *Europe Awake*, a magazine he had established.

Bromage was excited about the launch of the NSA. "If unity into one movement can't be achieved then we must unite into a network, exchanging information, publications and helping each other out when we can," he wrote in the autumn of 1994. He announced that the Phoenix Society, an alliance of right-wingers in the West Midlands, was joining the NSA. "Phoenix hopes wholeheartedly that the British Movement will unite with other National Socialists and decide to affiliate to the NSA. Phoenix seeks NS comradeship with all National Socialists, we are too few to fight amongst ourselves." In one last attempt to pull the Right together, Bromage invited the BM to address the first NSA rally in February 1995. The invitation was ignored.

Others were deserting the BM, men like Kevin Watmough, a leading light in its West Yorkshire branch. He believed that that the NSA offered the only realistic chance for an openly national socialist organisation in Britain. He was closely connected to Yorkshire BNP, several of whose members were attracted to C18 because of its violence, and saw a potential alliance, despite having some political differences with C18. He too deserted the

BM and took others from West Yorkshire with him. "For far too long now," he wrote in his leaving statement, "National Socialists in this country have been divided into several groupings, most of which have had little or no impact. It was against this that the NSA was formed as an umbrella organisation for the various NS groups who had decided that the days of squabbling and fighting amongst ourselves was over."

The NSA developed strongly in the West Midlands, hosting several well-attended meetings in the months following its inaugural meeting in Birmingham. Around 100 attended a gathering at the Britannia Hotel, Wolverhampton, to hear Charlie Sargent again speak about the looming confrontation with "the system". There were some new faces, including a group from the Black Country. Speaking alongside Sargent was Hugh Llewellyn Hughes, a long-serving British nazi whose presence confirmed the growing status of the NSA. Approaching sixty, Hughes was a veteran of the Right. The former Welsh Guardsman had been convicted at the Old Bailey in 1966 for a series of arsons against synagogues and other Jewish targets in London, having led one of a number of commando units drawn from the ranks of Colin Jordan's National Socialist Movement and John Tyndall's Greater Britain Movement. The arson campaign went on for over a year, during which a young theological student was killed in one attack and another man was crippled after leaping from a blazing window. Hughes received a five-year sentence. After several years behind the scenes, he re-emerged with an interview for the prominent US Nazi publication *New Order*, in which he boasted about stealing army equipment for the nazis.

Charlie Sargent spoke at another NSA meeting in Derby in the autumn of 1995. Other speakers included Jeff Dunn, Blood and Honour organiser Chris Hipkin and Tony Williams. While Dunn, the publisher of *Wodin*, devoted his entire speech to Nordic mythology and Odinism, Sargent launched an all-too-familiar attack on ethnic minorities, telling the audience that he wanted to read headlines about burning "niggers out of their homes". The presence of Williams confirmed the rise of the NSA. Aged in his forties, he was an important player, with links extending from the post-war nazi godfather Colin Jordan to William Pierce's National Alliance. An NF organiser in East Anglia during the late Seventies, Williams later moved over to the International Third Position but dropped out after a dispute over a business loan he gave to Nick Griffin (now the BNP chairman). Williams came from money – his father had run a large independent drinks import business and a very up-market deli in Constable country. According to Steve Sargent, his allowance from a trust fund alone was £2,000 a month. While the significance of Williams's presence at the NSA meeting would have been lost on most of the audience, other older and equally-important figures in the movement would have been impressed. One was David Myatt, a highly secretive figure who, while not attending public NSA activities, was to play an increasingly influential role behind the scenes, particularly on the political development of the Sargent brothers. He was also one of the few NSA supporters who really understood nazi ideology.

★ ★ ★ ★

DAVID MYATT WAS not a typical C18 supporter. In his late forties, he was well-educated, polite and shy. He sported a long ginger beard and would regularly be seen in a tweed flat cap, a green Barbour jacket and beige corduroys. On other occasions he would appear in a yellow cycling outfit, still wearing his tweed cap. He would also, according to Steve Sargent, carry a dagger emblazoned with the German SS insignia. He spoke quietly and would use flattery to convince those he spoke to. He was as different as you could possibly get from the street thugs in London, to the point of being an oddity.

Born just after World War Two, Myatt moved at an early age to what is now Tanzania, his father working for the British Empire. When he was eleven, they moved to the Far East but never settled, with his father yearning for a return to Africa, the continent where he was to die. Myatt returned to England in his mid-teens – after an upbringing in overseas public schools – to complete his education. His childhood prompted a wanderlust and over the next thirty years he spent a considerable time abroad, largely retracing the path of his early years. "It gave me a perspective which perhaps I wouldn't have had otherwise," he later recounted. It also instilled a loneliness that is apparent in the man and his writings.

His political opinions formed as he turned sixteen. Reading books about Nazi Germany, Myatt became engrossed in what he saw as the "loyalty, honour and duty" of the Germans of that period, particularly of the SS. These three themes became the central planks of his own writings. Myatt admired the "heroic warrior nature of National Socialism" and set about discovering the ideas behind Adolf Hitler. His search eventually brought him into contact with Colin Jordan, the father of British post-war fascism. At that time Jordan was the British leader of the World Union of National Socialists, an organisation established by American nazi Lincoln Rockwell. Jordan was soon to launch the British Movement, which Myatt was to join.

Myatt threw himself into political activity. Even as a student, he was proud to announce himself as a national socialist at a time when other fascists were trying to disguise their politics. After dropping out of Hull University, where he was studying physics, Myatt moved to Leeds and helped form the National Democratic Freedom Movement (NDFM). It lasted less than a year but during its short life its members were involved in a series of physical attacks on black people, trade unionists and socialists, and Myatt was sent to prison. He became disillusioned with the right-wing, though his frustration was more with a leadership he believed was woefully inadequate.

Turning his back on politics, Myatt joined a monastery. He found the eighteen months a period of reflection, an opportunity to gather his thoughts, but eventually decided that the Church wasn't for him. "I had a great struggle between my political beliefs and my religious dogma. In the end I decided that the religious dogma of the Catholic Church was not compatible with what I felt," he said. He did, however, use this time to write *Logic of History*, his so-far unpublished political philosophy in four volumes.

After further travelling, including a visit to the grave of his father in East Africa, Myatt returned to the political fray a harder and more determined man. By now he was close to finalising his own theory of national socialism. In January 1984, the American right-wing publishing house Liberty Bell produced Myatt's *Vindex: The Destiny of the West*, a condensed version of *Logic of History*, in which he concluded that Western civilisation was the most advanced and sophisticated in history. Adapting the work of Toynbee, Spengler and Nietzsche, Myatt saw the history of the world dividing into seven civilisations – Sumeric, Egyptaic, Hellenic, Indic, Sinic, Japanese, and Western – each defined by a distinct "ethos" or cultural identity that bonded it together and marked it out from what had gone before. Whilst the West derived much of its ethos from the Hellenic or Greek civilisation, including language, law and art, it was distinct in its own right, due primarily to science and its application in technology. According to Myatt:

> This search for the truth which created modern science derives from another trait peculiar to the West: the desire for exploration. Western civilisation is characterised by the desire for exploration. Other civilisations have conquered, for power or wealth, but no other civilisation, except our own, has explored the world (and latterly the planets and space itself) purely out of curiosity. This burning desire to know what is over the sea, and under it, this energy is, above everything else, the ethos of the West. But perhaps the greatest and surely the most noble expression of this truly Faustian will-to-knowledge is space travel, particularly the manned flights to the moon. Space travel exemplifies the West as nothing else – not art, not even science itself can, because space travel successfully combines the three elements that are so ineluctably Western: Science, technology, and the desire to know.

For Myatt it followed that if Western civilisation was the most advanced society ever, then its people, the northern and western

Europeans, including those who moved to the United States – in short, the Aryans – were the most advanced race on earth and so needed protecting from racial dilution. For the West to achieve its ultimate destiny, which Myatt described as a New Order and the creation of a new type of man, the Aryan race had to remain pure.

Myatt viewed National Socialist Germany as the embodiment of this Western ethos. "Everything about National Socialism confirms this," he wrote, "its vitality, the spartan joy of its followers, its attitude to all forms of degeneracy." In Adolf Hitler, Myatt saw a Caesar-type figure of the like not previously seen in Western civilisation. He contended that the anti-Nazi propaganda of the post-war period, particularly that surrounding the Holocaust – which he argued never occurred – was simply an attempt to demonise this Faustian spirit by its detractors, among whom he counted the Jews and the Communists:

> This propaganda – particularly that relating to the ob-
> noxious myth of the six million – has hypnotized several
> generations and all but paralysed their will to resist the
> invested values of Marxism and its brotherhood of
> degeneracy. This propaganda has made everything anti-
> Western acceptable: Negro music (with its most odious
> offshot 'rock') is preferred to the Western traditions of folk
> and 'classical'; the literature of Dante, Goethe, and the
> Icelandic Edda is replaced by the neuroeroticism of Kafka,
> and the modern disposable novel whose plot revolves
> around money and sex and whose characters increasingly
> resemble either Shakespeare's Shylock or Eliot's Hollow
> Men. This propaganda has allowed the West to become
> dominated by the psychology of the Magian – the psycho-
> logy of Freud, Fromm, Klineberg and Maslow. This
> psychology, with the help of the six million and other
> 'invented' horrors, has defined National Socialism and
> similar expressions of the Faustian ethos, as 'perverted'.
> People who uphold National Socialist views are, therefore,
> sick and require 'treatment'.

Myatt saw religious, philosophical and spiritual dimensions to Nazism that he believed had been overlooked by others. He regarded Nazism as a harmonising influence which linked man and his environment in a "natural way" through irrational mystic bonds of racial kinship and the "folk community". In many ways this view was merely an updated version of the pre-war theory of "Blood and Soil", which argued that identity was created by one's racial heritage and link with nature and the Fatherland. However, Myatt's emphasis on the religious, even messianic, aspects of National Socialism was evident in his spiritual terminology. The struggle, he believes, is a holy racial war. "For the Destiny of the Aryan to be fulfilled," he wrote, "there has to be a holy war against all those who oppose National Socialism."

There was another side to Myatt, hidden from virtually everyone in the NSA. He was the High Priest of the Order of Nine Angles (ONA), a Satanic church which he established. Espousing "traditional Satanism" and rituals involving sexual acts and claims of human sacrifice, Myatt and the ONA are considered dangerous extremists even by other Satanists. It was unsurprising that Myatt was less than keen for his C18 friends to discover his extra-curricular activities.

Myatt's Satanism did not derive from some rigid form of devil worshipping but from the ancient Greek word for adversary, in this case meaning opposition to the present order. "Expressed simply," ONA literature read, "the aim of the ONA is to create a new species." To Myatt, Satanism represented the Black Order, the only force that could unlock the stranglehold the White Order had on modern society, particularly through Christianity, which he believed had enslaved Western society. Only with its replacement by paganism could the West possibly reach its potential. "What the West has achieved," he wrote, "its science, technology, and its conquest – has been not achieved because of Christianity but in spite of it. However tame Christianity may have become in most of the West, it is essential to realise that as an attitude of life Christianity is the antithesis of all that is healthy, noble and instinctive. Christianity exhorts the virtues of the slave – meekness, forgiveness and guilt – and even its ultimate symbol, the crucified Christ, is a symbol of rejection of life. In contrast the Western spirit, exemplified by the Vikings, rejoices in life and its vitality. Christianity, in its approach to life and the world, is essentially Judaic."

For Myatt, Satanism and fascism are inextricably linked. "National Socialism is the only real theory in existence, since it is based solely on the highest ideals of Honour, Loyalty and Duty, championed over and above selfish individual pursuits. It calls for a revolution of the Soul; a Triumph of the Will; a return of racial pride and defiance. In a very important sense, National Socialism IS contemporary Paganism."

Myatt kept most of these views deeply hidden from C18. Few would have wanted to associate themselves with some of the less savoury aspects of his rituals, which included bizarre sex, drugs and role-playing scenes. The Mass of Heresy, contained within the ONA's *Black Book of Satan*, is performed before an altar adorned with a swastika banner, a framed photograph of Hitler and a copy of *Mein Kampf*. With black candles and incense of Mars burning, the congregation, dressed in black robes, chant:

> We believe Adolf Hitler was sent by our gods
> To guide us to greatness.
> We believe in the inequality of the races
> And in the right of the Aryans to live
> According to the laws of the folk.

In The Ceremony of Recalling, the Preistess blindfolds the Priest and takes him to each member of the congregation who kiss him. After being lifted on an alter containing "red candles and quartz tetrahedron", the Priest has his robe removed by the Priestess as the others walk around him. After performing a sexual act on the Priest, the Preistess removes the robes of the congregation. Meanwhile, the Mistress, dressed in a white robe, "takes the person she has chosen and indulges herself according to her desire. The congregation consume the consecrated cakes [made from wheat, water, egg, honey, animal fat and marijuana] and wine and take their own pleasures according to their desires."

The ceremony ends with the killing of a chosen one; in a symbolic sacrifice, an animal replaces a person. On the next new moon, the congregation consume cakes containing the sacrificial victim's blood.

Myatt returned to political activity in 1993 even more committed to extra-parliamentary means. "We have to stop dreaming of winning national power by playing the unfair electoral game of our opponents," he contested, "and start being practical. The primary duty of all National Socialists is to change the world. National Socialism means revolution: the overthrow of the existing System and its replacement with a National-Socialist society. Revolution means struggle: it means war. It means certain tactics have to be employed, and a great revolutionary movement organised which is primarily composed of those prepared to fight, prepared to get their hands dirty and perhaps spill some blood. To succeed, such a revolutionary movement needs tough, uncompromising, fanatical individuals."

In the streetfighters and pub brawlers of C18, Myatt saw the raw material from which a revolutionary movement could be formed: men who had discarded the electoral path and were prepared to use violence to achieve their goals. Myatt himself had been to jail twice, describing it later as "an educating experience. It taught me not to be afraid of anything the State could throw at me." Even the indiscriminate violence of Browning and friends was not off-putting; quite the contrary. "I don't see anything inherently wrong with it. It's a question of using that material, of harnessing that in a productively useful way. You are trying to raise people up, to harness their own instincts."

Myatt was particularly interested in the skinhead followers of Blood and Honour. "These mostly young Aryans have the right instincts; they have the right feelings about life. Their often-rowdy behaviour, their tendency to like brawls, is natural and healthy because it is part of the warrior heritage. Indeed, the skinhead cult was and is natural, instinctive Aryan (and working class) rebellion against capitalist bourgeois respectability and the multi-racial society ... To be National Socialists, all such people need is some understanding of National Socialism, and some guidance so that they can use their toughness, their aggressive spirit, in a revolutionary way." Myatt saw his role as the educator, producing material to turn the C18 stormtroopers and Blood and Honour skinheads into fully conscious Aryan warriors. In February 1995, he began publishing *The National Socialist*, a regular newsletter, to "educate people in the fundamental understanding of National Socialism." C18, and the Sargents in particular, had a new guru.

Yet for all the talk of creating the "New Man", Myatt's bizarre political and religious views hinted at the apparent misery in his own life. He wrote such poetry as "Wanderings of a Gentleman", and his Satanic rituals involved spending days alone on hillsides without any clothes. It is easy to detect elements of schizophrenia in Myatt's personality: his role playing, dressing up in uniforms and other strange attire and the rituals performed by the ONA would transform him into a different person. It is impossible to meet Myatt and read his numerous publications without concluding that he had a troubled mind, the product of an unhappy and lonely childhood. In his poems and his political theory he constructed his vision of the perfect family – in the guise of the Aryan race – that he never had.

* * * *

THE RAW AGGRESSION that so impressed Myatt was being felt across the country as NSA foot soldiers took up Charlie Sargent's challenge of inflicting pain and misery on their racial and political opponents. Most of their attacks were cowardly episodes in the middle of the night or with numbers greatly in their favour. Some were serious. In Wales, four Anti-Nazi League members were ambushed as they left a march by four men armed with a club and a sharpened weapon. A woman was struck across the back of the head, and a man hit in the face was lucky not to lose an eye. How these and other actions squared with Myatt's high-flown talk of honour and duty was anybody's guess.

Perhaps the most sickening intimidation was carried out

against Jill Milner, a schoolteacher and ANL activist from Nuneaton, Warwickshire. She had written to her local paper in reply to a letter she believed had condoned racism. Armed with her address, local C18 goons began a systematic campaign of psychological and physical terror over an eighteen-month period. "I received a letter saying 'die by the sword' and it had razor blades stuck in the envelope," says Milner. "Death threats taking different forms. I was sent sympathy cards. I had petrol poured on the doorstep and broken glass pushed through the letterbox. I was often played music down the phone, tapes of women screaming and that sort of thing. It sounded as though they were being chased and attacked. I was also sent piles and piles of junk mail, not just ordinary letters but things that were meant to intimidate me. There were letters about plastic surgery, membership to health care plans, that sort of thing. There were also letters and leaflets about home security, all things to make me think I was at risk."

The first attack came when a car driven by suspected C18 supporters tried to run her down, only narrowly missing her. The next was directed at her home: masked intruders smashed her front window and poured tar into her living room. One of them, who was disturbed by a neighbour, was armed with an axe. If her attackers meant to terrify Milner, they succeeded. Eventually she was driven from her home, her town and her job. "I've actually spent a short time in hospital because of the pressures that I was put under because of this. I felt that I couldn't lead an ordinary life."

Another ANL activist targeted was Elaine Hefferman, an east London teacher who had been prominent in the campaign against BNP councillor Derek Beackon. "The post would arrive and you'd open it up and it would be a lot of BNP newspapers or election leaflets. The next time it was a death threat signed by Combat 18," she later told journalists. Again, the threats soon became real. "I left my car in Stratford shopping centre. When I came back I found a Combat 18 sticker on it. The next day I noticed that my brakes weren't working properly and I almost had a crash. The brake line had been slashed in some way so that the brake fluid was leaking out, quite slowly but enough to cause them to fail eventually."

In the West Midlands, a Race Equality building in Sandwell was set alight – causing over £100,000-worth of damage – as was a cricket pavilion in Walsall used by an Asian team. The office belonging to the Birmingham Racial Attacks Monitoring Unit was ransacked: the raiders got into the Afro-Caribbean Resource Centre, where the office is based, by breaking down part of a wall of the building next door and took a computer hard-drive and confidential files before scrawling fascist graffiti on the walls. In other cases, violence occurred spontaneously. After an NSA meeting at a hotel in Derby in September 1995, the fifty in attendance found themselves caught in a clash between rival Derby and Leicester football hooligans. The Derby crew later attacked the NSA group, believing they were Leicester supporters; they received a shock when the NSA supporters began giving nazi salutes before responding with their fists. Steve Sargent typically legged it, running back inside the hotel foyer and locking the revolving door behind him. "They were fuming at me," he remembers with a broad grin.

Special attention was given to Gerry Gable who, as then-editor of the anti-fascist magazine *Searchlight*, had long endured the wrath of British nazis. Ever since his home address was discovered by the NF in 1988, he had received hate mail and threats. The irony of the NF's revelation, coming in its last-ever edition of *National Front News*, was that Gerry and his wife Sonia had been planning to retire from *Searchlight* and move to Wales when the issue appeared: being the stubborn old man that he is, he decided to stay on so as not to look as though the nazis had driven him out. C18 literature was littered with abusive cartoons, stories and threats directed at Gable. He was "obnoxious", "odious", the "Jew boy", "Gerry Bagle" and "Gerry Fable". His wife, who had once gone undercover in nazi groups, was also slandered. While much of it was unpleasant, even sick, it was testimony to the damage that he, and *Searchlight*, had done to the far-right during forty years of anti-fascism.

In the summer of 1994, C18 obtained Gable's home phone

number and began a telephone campaign that continues to this day. At its peak, Gable and his wife would get between ten and fifteen calls a night, many in the early hours of the morning. A few individuals were particularly keen on ringing. Simon Chadwick enjoyed impersonating comedian Lenny Henry and blowing raspberries down the phone, while his friend, the Romford-based nazi Phil Curzon, was always one of the foulest callers, once telling Gable that he had dug up his mother at Auschwitz and on another occasion claiming that he was going to kill his son. In July 1994, even Harold Covington put in a call, reciting a Shakespearean quote on the answer machine. Rarely would a C18 trip abroad go without the obligatory postcard. Darren Wells, Matthew Osbury and Ian Holloway were regular writers, often sending pictures of concentration camps with the words "Wish you were here, 1942-45" scrawled across. Another regular writer was Jon Hodgins, known within C18 as Doctor Death because of his depraved mind and humour. He was later booted out of his job as an electrician at Windsor College after it was revealed in the *News of the World* that he had access to the wing in which Prince William stayed. Some of the postcards were so vile that the Post Office handed them straight over to the police.

In 1996, while on a trip to Prague, Wells and Hodgins decided to send Gerry Gable a present. They bought an old-fashioned suit from a shop and a pair of small, round glasses, shattered one lens and added some soil and the bones of some Kentucky Fried Chicken they had just consumed. Parcelling the package up, they wrote a personalised note claiming that these belonged to his grandfather. To this day the story causes titters of amusement from members of the group.

In 1995, a rumour swept the Right that Gable was dying of cancer. C18 publications crowed with delight. A few months later, he was sent a bag of hair with an accompanying note saying how C18 had held a collection and had come up with a lampstand, a bar of soap and a shower cap – references to the gas chambers. Very occasionally the threats became violent. Several times C18 supporters drove past his house in the early hours of the morning shouting obscenities and beeping their horns. In late 1994, Gable received a crude letter bomb that was defused by a bomb disposal unit. Though no-one publicly claimed responsibility and the incident received no media attention at the time, it was the topic of a conversation at an NSA meeting in the Midlands a few months later.

Will Browning was to lead one attack on Gable when, in 1996, he and a carload of supporters attempted to throw a petrol bomb through his front window. Arriving at Gable's road in the early hours of the morning, Browning realised that he had forgotten the balaclavas. He decided to continue and the gang went to a nearby garage, bought some plastic bags and cut out eyeholes. They returned to Gable's, where Browning leapt out of the car and lit the device he had made. At that moment, a gust of wind swung the plastic bag round on his head. Unable to see, Browning panicked and hurled the lighted bomb in the general direction of what he thought was the correct house. He pulled the bag from his head only to see the device explode in the next-door neighbour's drive. Even if he had hit the right house it was unlikely to have had the desired effect, as Browning had not realised that to cause maximum damage he needed to pack shrapnel into the device. After a huge blast caused by the petrol igniting, the bomb soon fizzled out.

The most concerted violence outside London occurred in West Yorkshire, where local nazis began a year-long campaign against their opponents. Two weeks after anti-fascists prevented a BNP election meeting in mid-March 1994, a group of Leeds-based nazis attacked a Socialist Workers' Party paper sale in the city centre. A week later the SWP were attacked again. In protest against the growing right-wing violence, an ANL-organised demonstration was held a fortnight later. This too was attacked, with one nazi brandishing a machete. Two more C18 attacks on the SWP came that summer, both after BNP paper sales in Leeds city centre. Kevin Watmough was arrested in one of the attacks: when he appeared in court two days later there was more trouble, with one nazi threatening people with a crowbar he had hidden inside a plastic bag. Two days later, in an apparent act of revenge for Watmough's arrest, a small record shop had its windows smashed. The BNP paper sale three weeks later was another springboard for violence, as eight nazis split off and attacked a university student, having smashed their way into a hall of residence armed with pool cues, bricks and sticks. Over the next week, two more record shops were attacked and their staff threatened.

In July, the house of Ian MacDonald, the secretary of the local Trades Council and a vocal opponent of fascism, was attacked, with windows at the front and back being smashed. He had earlier received phone threats from C18. Following the attack he was rung again and asked, "Have you learnt your lesson?" Three weeks later, C18 smashed the window of the Duchess of York pub following a Chumbawamba gig. The next day a group of men went into the pub and brazenly told the landlady that they could firebomb it at any time. Later that same evening, a crossbow bolt was fired through a second-floor window of a flat that had previously belonged to a local anti-fascist. This was followed minutes later by three masked men wielding baseball bats smashing the front and back windows of a house belonging to an ANL activist in Beeston. "C18" was daubed on the side of the property.

The violence drew the attention of Channel Four's *Dispatches* programme, which was investigating BNP links to C18. On Saturday, August 27, 1994, a week after the Beeston attack, two journalists – one of them this author – travelled to Leeds to secretly film the nazis. Our hidden cameras rolled as twenty mobbed up with an assortment of weapons, including hammers, iron bars and rounders bats. The nazis soon discovered they were being watched and gave chase, and we were forced to take refuge in the local C&A store while the nazis patrolled outside. After slipping out through the staff entrance, we took a taxi to Headingley, where we hoped to sit out the hour until the next train back to London. As we got out of the taxi we realised that we had been followed. Five men, travelling in a red car a short distance behind, began pulling down balaclavas and brandishing baseball bats. Fortunately our taxi driver had stopped in traffic and we jumped back in, much to his excitement – he said it was just like the movies – and fled the area. Later that evening, the nazis firebombed a car belonging to an ANL activist.

Perpetrating much of this violence was Kevin Watmough, the former BM organiser, who distributed C18 material; Kevin Harrison, a local BNP official who collected much of the intelligence; Paul "Floppy" Bennett, who was photographed punching a female ANL supporter in Leeds city centre during one attack; and another man who stole the address book of the radical weekly the *Northern Star*. They were to be named on the *Dispatches* programme, but on the morning the show was to be aired, West Yorkshire Police arrested three of the main protagonists. The programme was due to be critical of the poor police response to the violence and included an interview with a senior officer who claimed that there was no real problem: the timing of the raids, which prevented identification of the individuals, seemed dubious. The following day the three men were released without charge. *Dispatches* did manage to track down Watmough, who had previously been filmed displaying highly-visible nazi patches sewn onto the seat of his jeans. Asked about his involvement in the violence, the race warrior hid behind his mother.

One of those arrested – and arguably the most violent of the group – was a former Klan member with several convictions. He cannot currently be named for legal reasons but I shall refer to him as "Don". In early 1994, having recently come out of prison, he targeted Eric Barnes, a Unison official whose crime was to organise an anti-racist meeting in Scarborough, Don's temporary home. Don posed as a son of a health worker seeking assistance from the union and was given Barnes's home address. Over the next two weeks this was repeatedly visited, with the words "Die SWP" and "slag" painted on the doorframe and nazi stickers plastered on the door. In the meantime, the venue for the meeting, a local library, was daubed with swastikas and C18 slogans. Police installed a panic button and surveillance camera at Barnes's home but Don remained undeterred. On the morning of the event, a brick was thrown through the front window of the house. On his way to the meeting, Barnes saw

Don standing by a phone box, obviously watching people entering the library. When confronted, he claimed he was on his way home. Later that evening, Barnes received a call in the pub he had retired to after the meeting. "I'm going to put you in *Redwatch*, you bastard," Don shouted. "I'm C18. There's a bullet with yer name on it. I'm gonna get you with a baseball bat. I'm laying low at the moment 'cos I've just come out of prison for cutting someone's throat and I'm gonna cut yours." Minutes later, a student who had attended the meeting was bricked as he left the pub.

Barnes was to have the last laugh when he literally bumped into Don at a train station a fortnight later.

"Now then, Don," Barnes said, standing inches from his tormentor.

The startled thug, there with his girlfriend, looked confused. "How do yer know my fucking name?" he demanded.

"We hear these things."

"Do you want a fucking go?" said Don, while at the same time stepping backwards.

"No, Don, not now. We'll decide when and where."

"What yer fucking doing then?"

"Waiting for friends."

Don grabbed his girlfriend's hand and walked briskly away.

★ ★ ★ ★

CHARLIE SARGENT WAS becoming ever more strident. In an interview for the French publication *Terror Elite*, he openly preached what he had long been saying at NSA meetings. "We have to incite the niggers and Arabs. I and others are personally dedicated to declaring war on the system over the coming years. I know that could mean being put to death or life imprisonment, but I hope to light the touchpaper to a fire so powerful that ZOG will never be able to put it out." If people did not follow his lead, he concluded, then "our race is too weak and deserves to die".

Sargent was also beginning to consolidate the group's core. While the NSA was mopping up supporters from across the far-right, Sargent wanted the organise an elite. In the spring of 1995, he wrote the first of several *Brown Letters*, the newsletter of his national socialist cadre. The cadre was hand-picked to act as a "small but fanatical group of men who will act as agents of the underground movement we are trying to build in this country". Believing that the banning of nazi groups was likely in the near future, Sargent added, "From the start the National Socialist cadre will be conducted like an underground and illegal movement, our ultimate goal is to create a National Socialist state via a Revolution. The cadre will we hope bring about this revolution by its attacks upon the system."

Thirty people were initially selected, each paying £5 a month. In issue two of *Brown Letter*, Sargent expanded on his vision:

> Now I feel we will not see the real benefits of the cadre until it has built up in strength, which should be our main aim over the coming year. Hopefully by this time next year we will number over a hundred. A large number of comrades who are really dedicated to the cause like that would enable us to react to things like the recent riot in Bradford by the pakis (i.e. the following day we could be on the streets to protect the whites of Bradford, and showing the whites of England that there is a group willing to stand up and fight). Never forget one hostel attack in Germany a few years back sparked a whole wave of copycat attacks all over the nation, a similar thing could happen here! With us leading the way. Sadly when it did happen in Germany the police crushed the Movement, but with us organising from the start an illegal group it will be much harder for the State to crush us.

He included a four-page document entitled *System Overthrow: The Tactics Required to Create a Revolution*, in which the cadre could read about covert direct action, covert recruitment and the distribution of propaganda. "It needs to be emphasised," the booklet said, "that any means are justified in the struggle to overthrow this System. The means which are necessary include physical violence against individuals; using lethal force against enemies and targeted individuals; and using explosives and incendiary devices against specific physical targets."

The launch of the NSA proved damaging to the BNP. Sargent's fiery rhetoric pulled in the more dangerous elements of Britain's nazis just as the BNP drive for respectability was alienating some of its supporters. By the summer of 1995, C18 boasted that three-quarters of young right-wingers were with them. The euphoria that greeted the BNP election victory in Millwall dissipated as Derek Beackon lost his seat the following May. Though Beackon increased his vote – and the BNP achieved impressive results in neighbouring Newham – many within the party thought that its promised new dawn was greatly overstated. Candidates outside London achieved their usual derisory results. The party's problems were compounded when, without the physical support offered by C18, it found it increasingly risky to operate without fear of attack. Brick Lane had been lost three days after Derek Beackon's victory and, even more disconcertingly, a group of leafleteers were attacked in the run-up to the London-wide elections in May 1994. Several unidentified men, some masked and all armed with sticks and bats, ran through a small group of BNP activists as they distributed leaflets in east London. While most of the BNP members escaped without serious injury, local candidate Michael Davidson lost an eye.

Yet some within the BNP were unwilling to even contemplate a rapprochement with C18. Among them was Michael Newland, the party's press officer, who argued that the party had to lose its thuggish image and skinhead following if it was to ever be electable. He took the message around the country, with mixed results. He was warmly received by those most closely involved in the Beackon election victory but met with intense opposition from many BNP branches, especially outside the East End where electoral success was as remote as ever. Newland became the subject of sniping and verbal abuse, sometimes to his face. At one meeting in south London, his speech on reinventing the BNP was somewhat diluted by C18 literature being sold at the

back of the hall. A short time later, at the BNP's annual rally in
1994, Newland complained to the leadership after seeing
members of the audience openly sporting C18 tee-shirts. Fearful
that any public rebuke would only increase the party's internal
problems, the leadership of Tyndall and Edmonds remained
silent.

Others around the country were content to identify with both
groups. In some areas, the number of nazis was so small and
ineffective that splitting its half-dozen activists into two or three
separate parties was crazy: better to attend BNP meetings and
paper sales, but, if needed, attack their opponents as C18, a
position best demonstrated in Leeds. Gradually, however, the
country did begin to divide. Several BNP branches made a
complete switch to the NSA, among them Dundee, Liverpool,
Oldham, Halifax, Derby and Northampton. In London, home to
much of the BNP leadership and of its only electoral success,
members switched to the NSA in droves. Perhaps this was not
surprising, as only a couple of years before they had regularly
drunk and fought together. In September 1995, eighty nazis met
in Holborn, central London, to hear Sargent and a leading
member of the Danish National Socialist Movement. Sargent
told the crowd that if everyone in C18 killed two people, then
400 would be dead within a week. The police might be able to
catch a few people but the scale of the killings would shock the
nation. It would, he believed, ignite the race war for which they
strived. In the audience were about forty BNP supporters,
including party organisers from Tower Hamlets, Newham,
Camden, West London and Croydon. In fact the only London
BNP organiser absent was Tony Lecomber.

With over half of its London team ignoring orders to have no
contact with C18, the BNP leadership was left angry but
impotent. It threatened to discipline members who attended the
Holborn meeting but knew that such a sanction would destroy
party organisation in the capital. In an effort to save face, a
scapegoat was found when one BNP member gave a nazi salute
at the party rally a few weeks later. Though Tyndall and Edmonds
both told the accused that they thought that the charge was

pathetic, they felt compelled to act because of a complaint from the anti-C18 faction within the leadership. The man was warned not to repeat his behaviour.

However much John Tyndall tried to distance himself from C18, the evidence around the country continued to embarrass him. He floundered on television when confronted by the Channel Four *Dispatches* team. In a highly amusing exchange, Tyndall tried, quite unsuccessfully, to defend his case. "There is no official tie-up at all," claimed the BNP leader. "C18 was formed entirely independently of us." When he was asked to clarify that C18 had never provided any security at BNP meetings, he again resolutely denied any connection. "Not C18 as C18." The screen then switched to a still photograph of Charlie Sargent personally minding the BNP leader in 1992. Next it went to the party's General Election rally in east London in the same year: at the rear of the BNP contingent were a number of men wearing red BNP stewards' armbands, led by Sargent.

Two BNP members interviewed on the programme gave a different story. "BNP members go out leafleting, trying to get support," said one. "They have the respectable image. Then if you get somebody coming out mouthing it, then their name and address is taken down and they're targeted later on. They'll get a visit off C18." The other BNP supporter, from Scotland, offered much the same insight. "We won't admit to having anything to do with [C18], but at the same time, if our policies don't work, it's switched over to them. It's basically the same people, but with a violent side to it."

Faced with the evidence, Tyndall again stumbled in his reply. He claimed that any BNP members who committed violent acts without provocation would be expelled from the organisation, before admitting that this had never happened during the party's twelve-year existence.

★ ★ ★ ★

THE NSA WAS at its peak by the summer of 1995, with well-attended meetings in the West and East Midlands, Blackpool,

Yorkshire and London. By comparison the BNP was divided over strategy and unable to mobilise a street force to defend its activities. On one Saturday in June, the BNP and the NSA both held events in the Midlands. The BNP meeting attracted only twenty-six people; the NSA event, over 100. In the last weekend of July, fifty C18 and NSA supporters drawn largely from the north of the country, though with a few from London and the Midlands, spent a sunny weekend in Blackpool. The gathering brought together the bulk of the Oldham and Rochdale BNP and the BNP's regional organiser for Yorkshire. Its party atmosphere contrasted sharply with a BNP meeting in Leeds over the August Bank Holiday weekend, where former NF leader Nick Griffin was to speak. A group from south London who had spent a couple of days with Griffin in Wales made their way by bus to the re-direction point at Leeds railway station, where they expected to be led to the venue. Unfortunately for those on board, the only company that arrived was the Leeds branch of Anti-Fascist Action. Every window on the coach was smashed as AFA ran amok.

It was a spectacular defeat and had lasting implications for south London BNP. Recriminations flew among those who had been attacked. Some blamed the Leeds organiser who was supposed to meet them, while others blamed C18 for setting them up. One man even claimed that they were attacked in a police Special Branch operation. Within days, south London BNP split, with a group led by Adrian Woods forming the Surrey Border Front (SBF). Believing that the BNP could no longer protect its activities, Woods met Charlie Sargent in an east London pub and agreed to align his breakaway group to the NSA. Like many of the NSA affiliates, the Surrey Border Front was to have little impact on society; aside from the odd leaflet to oppose the building of mosques in south London and Chichester, its followers were largely inactive, except for the social evenings. Guests were plied with alcohol and then proceeded to repeatedly stab papier-mâché models sculptured to represent black faces that had been filled with red paint.

Tyndall and the BNP were on the ropes. Despite their official policy to expel any member with links to C18, modernisers such as Newland, Lecomber and Butler were finding it impossible to enforce. Many members were keen to align themselves with C18 on a street level while some in the leadership remained national socialists at heart. At the same time, the NSA was at its peak. It had been successful in bringing together Britain's nazis, with the exception of the British Movement leadership. With over 500 people attending its events or receiving literature, the NSA had become largest and most active far-right group in Britain.

CHAPTER NINE

The Homeland

BY THE END of 1994, Combat 18 was at its peak. It had taken over the nazi music scene, courted the Loyalists, mobilised the football hooligan gangs, orchestrated a string of attacks on its opponents and successfully set up the National Socialist Alliance. Yet Steve Sargent was in little mood to celebrate the New Year. The gang's increasing activity had sparked a growing clamour for the authorities to act against them. And they still had not begun to achieve any of their political goals. "If you think the inner cities are bad now," Sargent wrote grimly in the first issue of *Putsch* in 1995, "imagine what they will be like in five or ten years time! It's frightening. Big brother mentality is springing up everywhere, CCTV cameras are going up all the time. More immigrants are coming in all the time, more brainwashing media filth is being churned out, more race mixing is taking place, more drugs and violent crime, more lowering of moral standards and more promotion of illnesses like homosexuality. Again this is now, think of how it's going to be in five or ten years time!"

A General Election was fast approaching. With the Conservatives in internal disarray, it was obvious, even to C18, that there was going to be a change in government. Steve Sargent predicted things would get worse for them under Labour. While this might eventually push increasingly disgruntled white youths towards their cause, the more immediate prospects did not look good. "Under a Labour Government, laws will be put into effect to try and banish us once and for all from Liberal society," he wrote. "I feel we have around a year left to lay the groundwork and put into effect our plans for our salvation."

Within a week of the New Year, Sargent's gloom proved well

founded. Police officers raided the homes of Will Browning and Charlie Sargent over issue three of *Combat 18* magazine, with its bomb-making instructions and exhortation to "kill" left-wing activists. For Steve, it was the final proof that they were being victimised for their beliefs. "In the last issue I mentioned how I believed we only had probably this year left to finally sort ourselves out before the ZOG came down on us. No sooner had I uttered these words then it happened!" he wrote in the following issue of *Putsch*. It had been a bad few months for the younger Sargent. He had also been arrested, leaving his brother's Harlow house in the possession of fifty *Combat 18* magazines; this came shortly after he had been prosecuted for threatening the woman near the Chelsea football ground and suffered exposure on the *Dispatches* documentary.

To Sargent, the raids proved that, despite their successes, they couldn't change society from within. Something new was needed.

> You can keep on floundering away in a state of denial, refusing to admit that you are lost, refusing to address the problem until you drown in the mud and sink out of sight OR you can turn around and go back to where you made a wrong turn, however long, weary and painful that journey may be. Comrades, that is the situation we are faced with today. We have been cynically betrayed by men of boundless ego and insatiable greed who have claimed to be our racial leaders. They have failed us and dragged us down into the quagmire with them. We have one option in my view. Leave the ethnics and reds, and the whites not with us, to the inner cities. We must become like the Jews and Asians, build our own communities and then keep our money in our own circle and help each other out ... Now its time for us to knuckle down, we must be for our Volk and sod the rest. An Aryan homeland is our only chance, and from there we will build our base of resistance."

Steve Sargent knew that such a homeland could not be created immediately, yet he believed it was their only hope of salvation.

> By moving in sufficient numbers to such an area we can
> create a real feeling of community, and this will give us, in
> this area, POWER. We will be able to make this area, at
> least, a stronghold of Aryan culture and a 'no-go' area for
> the trash of modern society. Ethnic minorities will not like
> the idea of moving to and living among or near to such a
> strong, aware, White community. As our numbers grow,
> so will our influence. We will shop in stores run by Aryans.
> We will employ and work for Aryans and we will generally
> emulate Jews and Asians in respect of keeping our own
> money circulating among our own people. We will get our
> own people on the school boards, our people into all walks
> of the community and commerce. We will turn the Home-
> land into one that is totally controlled by us. We will no
> longer have to whisper our views over a pint in the local
> pub on a Sunday afternoon, for the whole pub will share
> our opinions and if the landlord does not he would lose his
> trade to someone who does . . . Those already resident in
> the Homeland area will see the benefits of our presence.
> Those that do not will go!

A scheme would assist supporters to move to the area, some to a
building provided by the movement while others would be in
shared rented accommodation. Some people would be put to
work on the lands, while others would develop or utilise existing
skills such as building, carpentry and plumbing. Eventually,
money would become less important as they developed a barter
system, exchanging goods and skills between one another. And
that was only the beginning. Once established, the homeland
would attract converts from across the country who would see
that a right-wing society was possible. Success would breed
success, with the homeland eventually expanding beyond its
initial boundaries as other white people flocked to the area.
Contending with an area under C18 control, ZOG and its agents
in the police would become increasingly wary of interfering in its

internal affairs. The homeland would become increasingly autonomous and separate from society.

A model for what could be achieved came from an unlikely quarter – the IRA. However much they hated the Provos, there was grudging admiration for what they had done in Northern Ireland. A few hundred men with roots deeply-laid in working class Catholic communities had been holding the British Army up for over twenty-five years. Performing an influential role in the lives and communities of Catholic areas, the IRA showed what could be achieved by an anti-establishment, terrorist organisation.

"We must secure the existence of our people and a future for white children," wrote David Lane, serving 190 years for his part in the American terrorist group The Order. The *Fourteen Words*, as they became known, were the catchphrase Sargent used to promote his scheme. Like much of its ideological development, C18's homeland owed much to the political strategies adopted across the Atlantic: white-only compounds have become very much part of the fabric of White Supremacist America.

★　★　★　★

AS STEVE SARGENT put the finishing touches to his homeland issue of *Putsch*, he felt quietly pleased, even, dare he say it, elated. This was uncharted territory, reworking an idea from the American Right for the British situation. Its initial advocate had been John Cato who, since 1992, had been urging other national socialists to leave the urban conurbations for the country. He developed the homeland idea in an irregular newsletter, *Lebensraum* (the German word for living space, used to justify Hitler's invasion of Eastern Europe and the Soviet Union). "Men could pack their bags and their belongings and head home," Cato wrote. "Home to where the White man can still live – rurally and urbanly. Home to where we can establish anew; home to where we can constitution a real Aryan Nation, or at the very least, inaugurate the work to begin one."

At the time, Cato was living in the Kent town of Gravesend. He worked shifts as a semi-skilled machine operator at an engineering firm. His low pay and unsociable hours were only slightly offset by the increased free time made available by the shift work. Though residing just out of London, he shared his city comrades' desire for a new living space: "Home, gone from the scum and slime that is the nigger saturated London, its outreaches and Britain's other major towns and cities. We do not need to concern ourselves with Blacks, Jews and communists. Or anything that they may fancy and do. Leave them to it. We are supposed to be Aryans, we should then begin living as Aryans. As free spirits and men. Then we can reclaim our nation." Within six months, Cato had uprooted his family for the rural tranquillity of an all-white Lincolnshire village. Despite the initial hurdle of moving into rented accommodation without any electricity, Cato found the area clean and friendly. His house was an empty shell, but the challenge only increased his skewed sense of personal and racial survival. He was literally building a new life.

Cato's advocacy of a rural retreat received quite a reaction, little of it positive. In a period when the BNP had achieved its Millwall electoral success, the thought of leaving the city for the countryside seemed perverse. Separation, most right-wingers thought, was an idea that should not even be countenanced. The priority, according to one opponent of Cato, was "to salvage our land, *now.*" Cato wasn't put off, rejecting any notion that he was proposing a hippy commune and arguing for a radically different society. "Aryans must seclude themselves from mainstream degeneracy. And stay segregated. Away from everything that is detrimental to the Aryan function in life. We have done enough living with one foot in the Aryan world and the other sunk in ZOG filth. Move."

The majority in C18 ignored Cato, especially as they actually made up much of the anti-social society that he deplored. Most were preoccupied with street punch-ups and drinking. Yet his writings struck a chord with Steve Sargent. While Sargent had a reputation for violence, earning the nickname "Murphy" for his

Irish-style barroom brawling, he also had a sense of humour. It made his *Putsch* and *Thor Would* occasionally amusing and satirical journals amid a sea of hate. He was also one of the few C18 followers who read the outpourings from Covington, Cato and Myatt. Sargent had spent most of his life in north London, either with his parents at their Barnet council house or, latterly, sharing rented accommodation in nearby Palmers Green. His perception was of a changing capital, one that was beyond salvation. Bill, his oldest brother, had left London twenty years before for the racing town of Newmarket, while Charlie had moved to Harlow following a mysterious fire at his Camberwell flat – fortuitously his furniture had been moved out only days before. By the beginning of 1995, Steve became convinced that for both personal and political reasons, he too needed a new start.

His concept of a homeland differed from Cato's rural retreat. Sargent accepted some realities, principally that most C18 supporters were not farmers. Having been brought up in London, it was fanciful to believe that they would pick up a pitchfork and turn over the land. Rather, he believed, they had to utilise their existing skills and experiences. Targeting a council estate and its working class inhabitants was far more realistic. "The area chosen is the county with the biggest National Socialist support base, it is clean, white, has cheap accommodation, easy access to major towns including London, unemployment isn't too high." Never one to miss the opportunity for a quip, Sargent continued, "and most importantly, I know a barmaid who lives there! (only joking). The question has arisen of having regional homelands, but this just wouldn't work out, as there simply isn't enough of us to make any impact if we was all to split up."

The chosen county was Essex, the home of Essex Man, the aspirant, right-wing leaning, working class male who swept Margaret Thatcher to power in 1979. "You go to any Essex town – Chelmsford, yeah – and they've trebled in size. They're building, building, building in every Essex town and the reason is that the whites are leaving London," Charlie Sargent told the journalist Nick Ryan. "It's always been a bit stronger for racist support, always," says Steve Sargent. "The East End always had its racist support. Them racists that voted for the BNP and NF in the Seventies, most of them now live in Essex."

The evidence seemed to support this view. There had been an almost doubling of the Essex population over forty years, though since 1981 it had been virtually static. The vast bulk of these newcomers were white, which greatly pleased the Sargent brothers. According to the latest census material, less than two per cent of the population are non-white. "In a small town like Chelmsford, people who understand us have already moved there," continued Charlie. "If we tried to set up in Northumberland or Cornwall, it wouldn't mean nothing to them down there. Most London people who moved down there have left because they don't like fuckin' niggers, whether they admit it or not. So, when we come up to them and talk about our views, they understand us, while they wouldn't if we went to Durham or Cornwall."

Charlie Sargent's view of a homeland differed greatly from that of his brother. He said that, once settled in an area, it would be used as a base from which attacks could be launched against ZOG. An absurd proposition, says Steve. "How can something as small as us attack the Government?"

Despite these differences, Steve moved out of London and took up residence in a Chelmsford flat with Charlie, whose common-law wife had moved with their three children into temporary council accommodation in Harlow, claiming they were a single-parent family. The two brothers were soon to be joined by Herve Gutoso, a Marseilles-born Frenchman who was on the run from the authorities across the Channel. A short, powerfully-built skinhead, boosted by steroids, Gutoso was leader of the Charlemagne Hammerskins, a French grouping, and lead singer of the band Assault. He had fled France after an extensive fraud operation was uncovered and, after a couple of years in the United States, arrived in Essex.

Having established a foothold in the county, C18 intended to expand. Chelmsford would be its initial base but the Sargents also had their eye on Witham, a small Essex town on a direct train line to London. Within each area they "occupied", they hoped to exert their influence on the people around them either by discussion or force, creating white enclaves by squeezing the non-white inhabitants out in what they described as "ethnic cleansing". This banal phrase had become popular among the homeland supporters ever since the world's press began reporting such events in the Yugoslavian conflict in the early Nineties. It disguised the personal horror for those on the receiving end, in much the same way that phrases such as "collateral damage" and "strategic targets" sanitised the Gulf War. C18 promised to "cleanse" their chosen land of immigrants, Reds and drug dealers.

Bridging London and Essex, the Harold Hill estate is riven by drugs, youth crime and violence. For three years one family there suffered sustained and despicable persecution at the hands of local C18 supporters, including several convicted drug dealers. A boulder was thrown through their door. When it was repaired, "C18" was sprayed across it. A corrosive liquid was thrown in the wife's face at work. The husband, a taxi driver, had his car wheel nuts loosened. Finally, the family dog was killed and thrown through the front window. The family fled. No-one was ever arrested.

★ ★ ★ ★

THE HOMELAND WAS one aspect of a fundamental shift in C18 thinking, a rejection of the path so forlornly trodden by the BNP and NF. It might have sounded pure fantasy, but they thought it was more realistic than the alternatives. "It may seem that our struggle in Europe is a fight between White nationalists and Black immigrants that have come to live in our nations, but in truth our fight should never be viewed as a simple black v white thing", Steve Sargent wrote in *The Order*. "We must realise that we have an infinitely more dangerous group of people in our midst 'THE WHITE RACE TRAITOR'. In every European country we have White do-gooders, White Political parties that grovel to the ethnics, homosexual loving Church leaders, all of whose aim is to foster upon us a multi racial, One world society."

Even if most white people in Britain came over to their way of thinking, what could be achieved would be very limited. "They," he wrote, referring to the NF and BNP, "play the game the system dictates and then wonder why the state always wins. They dream of a Britain that ceased to exist seventy years ago that ruled the world and had no need for Europe, all the policies put forward echo this thinking. What they fail to see or understand is the mess we are in today is a direct result of such thinking by our grandfathers seventy years ago. Until they understand the problem of this nation is not due to the immigrants, but the people who brought them here, the Tory ministers, the factory owners, the bankers and start fighting them instead of blaming some Asian or Blackie brought here to be used as cheap labour, they will never have a chance of winning any power."

Sargent derided the repatriation policy of the right-wing. "In modern times it is only African countries who have expelled their immigrants. You cannot compare Africa with Britain, how would these African countries have fared if they had no bordering countries to push the immigrants into, and you had to transport them by boat? People have remarked that a policy of repatriation is needed to give Joe Public some hope, and catch his vote. My view is 'Fuck Joe Public'." He was dismayed with what he saw as the ignorance of the majority of white people and knew that hoping that they would flock to his cause was far-fetched. The degenerate society had infected them to the point where they had, initially at least, to be ignored. "The bloke in the pub who thinks our way but likes the black bloke he works with, is he worth fighting for? The pretty girl across the street who spends her money buying black records, is she worth fighting for? How about the postman who's got his hair in dreadlocks, is he worth it?" Steve Sargent deemed it unnecessary even to give an answer.

He viewed the BNP and NF with contempt. It was time to be honest about your politics, he thought, not hide behind the Union Jack only to reveal your true identity after you had come to power. Honesty, Steve Sargent felt, was what was lacking within the Right. "I just don't like them," he declared about black people. "I cannot justify what's in my heart, nor do I feel I should have to. I don't like carrots, but I don't tell people it's due to the way they are shaped or grown, I just don't like them. When you don't like something, you move away from it, you don't sit and worry about how you can get it back into the greengrocer's shop. You leave the carrot and it soon decays and disappears from your life." For once, it seems, he wasn't joking: comparing people to vegetables seemed perfectly reasonable in Steve Sargent's worldview.

Tony was one C18 supporter who was interested in living in the homeland. It was not simply poverty or immigrants that made him angry but the feeling that others were given preferential treatment, making whites second-class citizens in their own land. "You can't have a coffee morning for white ladies only, but for any other denomination, race or creed, it is possible. It is a frustration. We definitely feel that we are treated differently to other sections of society. It would have been ideal to have our own little community where we went and where we were the ones in charge." The homeland plan coincided with a general shift in C18 strategy away from public, street-orientated activities. "It was partly that we began to think more about our ideas" says Tony, "but it was also a question of the law of averages. The early days had been fun, we had the Left on the run and we were all on a high, but we realised that sooner or later things would come on top of us. The authorities were beginning to take a closer look at us and it became increasingly difficult for us to get away with things. Many of the East End lads, who were there from the start, began to get paranoid about it all. They were looking at long stretches if they got caught, and unsurprisingly they didn't want that. People condemn us as being thick, but we weren't. You'd be surprised about how many lads read the literature and were thinking things through."

It was easy to let the imagination run riot; some began to see the homeland as the answer to their own personal and economic problems. Mark Atkinson and his common law wife, Liz Hunt, yearned for what they described as a simpler, "better" life. With three children, and another on the way, Hunt spoke longingly of a homeland with their own shops, schools, businesses and church.

"What's the problem with that?" she asked journalist Nick Ryan. Atkinson even said that he would like to teach his kids at home as many do in America. "That would be my ideal way," agreed Liz excitedly. "I'd absolutely love it." Whether the children would be so grateful to be taught at home by Atkinson is another matter, as he was not one of C18's sharpest minds. When asked by Ryan to explain the term ZOG, the west London C18 leader looked nonplussed. "It's something to do with the Jews, I think. I'm not really sure," he responded, despite having been in C18 for four years and having often used the word in *The Stormer*. Reality merged into romanticism: their problems, and society's, were simply put down to the presence of black people in Britain. With their removal, so the logic went, their problems would disappear. It was this simplistic but comprehensible explanation that fuelled their resentment and bred their contempt.

Gradually, the majority of C18 got behind the homeland idea. It couldn't, they believed, be any less successful than the parliamentary process. And with the NSA becoming the dominant force on the far-right, some truly believed that there was a chance of controlling their own little corner of England. "Everyone was on a general high of wanting to believe that anything was possible, the homeland, an election victory," remembers Tony. "We even thought that in ten years time we would have been marching down Downing Street vying for who was going to be Minister of Repatriation. People wanted to believe in it because they had had so many years that it was not fun being on the Right, everything being against us. You can't go into a pub and openly admit what you are, it doesn't do you any favours jobwise, it's not an overly attractive feature in pulling prospective females into your den, but something like this would be. It was like a false dawn. You look at it and tend to discount the reality because you would want it to happen."

★ ★ ★ ★

ONE MAN FIRMLY behind the homeland was the bearded Satanist David Myatt. He described it as the NSA's overriding task –

other than the general push for a national socialist revolution – and called on the movement's followers to forsake their comforts and take up the idea. "We either make these sacrifices, and find the determination to do such a thing as this in order to benefit our race, or we make excuses, and act like immature, spoiled children, selfishly indulging ourselves with the comforts which the decadent materialistic society can provide. The time for talk and excuses is over, either you believe in Aryan survival or you do not." For Myatt, living in an Aryan enclave was more than a retreat, it was fundamental to his beliefs, as he wrote in his *National Socialist* newsletter. "To be an Aryan now means to be a National Socialist, and to fight the present System which is so detrimental to us, our culture, and our civilisation. National Socialism is a means whereby young Aryans can free themselves from the worthless, materialistic, degenerate System which seeks to make them, and keep them, weak. National Socialism is a means whereby Aryans can live and act like Aryans – and so be strong, and fulfil the purpose of their lives. Anything else is fundamentally irrelevant, and a waste of life and living." Myatt informed the Sargents that he was prepared to invest £30,000 towards the £200,000 he imagined was needed for the project to be a success, the rest to be raised by a combination of contributions from supportive comrades and a bank mortgage.

While Steve Sargent spoke about the project in general terms, the fanatical Myatt was more specific. "The absolute minimum of land required to begin the project is ten acres," he wrote to supporters of the idea. He accepted that the homeland would have to be run on a practical basis, both financially and in the eyes of the law. "We may well bemoan this situation but it is the reality and we cannot, as yet, do anything about it." The priority was to buy an existing farm or agricultural land with buildings suitable for conversion into dwellings. He was quite exact in his requirements; buying land not designated for agriculture or agricultural land with no buildings would only give the authorities an excuse to intervene at an early stage. The other prerequisite was the suitability of the land for crop production. "The aim or ethos is for the farm to be or become as self-sufficient as possible.

The very striving to do these things will hopefully produce a healthy life-style for those working on the farm and their children, as the farm itself will provide, as it expands and becomes established, work for those National Socialists living in the homeland, as well as a place for National Socialists from other areas to meet, attend celebrations and/or come for a holiday. Hopefully, some kind of hostel accommodation can be built to facilitate these things. Given the organic and horse orientated nature of the farm, it will be 'labour intensive'."

Myatt's vision was diametrically-opposed to that of other C18 supporters. Steve Sargent proposed working within a council estate; Myatt perceived a rural retreat. "Our practical aim, apart from using organic methods, is to use horses for heavy tasks, such as ploughing, instead of tractors which have come to dominate modern farms," he wrote. "It needs to be stressed that a lot of hard work and long hours will be necessary. Consequently, those seriously considering the commitment to move should be prepared for such things. They must also be prepared to make at least some material sacrifices for a period of some years, since a high material standard of living – gained by making large profits from the farm – not only cannot be guaranteed, but is contrary to the ethos or spirit of the venture."

Myatt wrote in the isolation of the countryside and his own peculiar lifestyle, and that, coupled with his obvious unease in the company of others, meant that his writings were largely ignored. The theoretical content was well beyond the comprehension of most C18 people. Steve Sargent was one of the few who actually read Myatt's work but even he thought him strange. Days before I was due to have a meeting with Myatt, Sargent warned me that the Satanist was "the crow in the tree outside the pub" and could "turn you into a frog". With his visions of horse pulled organic farming, it is not surprising that Myatt feels continually disappointed with those around him.

★ ★ ★ ★

IN THE END, few outside the Sargents took up the homeland idea.

It is possible that some others would have made the move to Essex had not Charlie and Will Browning been facing prosecution and possible imprisonment for issue three of *Combat 18* and had the organisation not become embroiled in internal and external feuds. Steve Sargent did receive pledges from people, some visited the area to have a look around and others asked for accommodation lists. But it was doomed to failure. "At the time everyone thought it was a good idea," reflects Tony, "but people were reluctant to be the first to move down there. No-one wanted to give up their job or their house to move to somewhere which might fall through. I think everyone was quite keen and wanted to do it and if a few people would have done it, if six families had done it then a lot of people would have followed."

Unfortunately for C18, Britain is not the United States, Essex is not West Belfast and they are certainly not the IRA. Establishing encampments might be feasible in the vast expanses of North America, where the widespread distrust of federal government and the liberal gun laws enable the right-wing to run paramilitary training in relative secrecy. Britain is different. To believe that the police and politicians would allow a nazi community fifty miles from central London was absurd.

The scheme also lacked coherence. Even the Sargents couldn't agree on how to shape it. Despite Charlie's grandiose suggestions that the homeland would be the launchpad for war, the place envisaged by Steve was more of a retreat; he accepted that they were unlikely ever to attract large numbers of white people to their cause. He would have been happy with an area where, as he wrote, "we will no longer have to whisper their views over a pint in the local pub on a Sunday afternoon, for the whole pub will share our opinions." In an interview with this author three years later, he was even more candid. "It's not that I don't believe in things, I just know victory is never going to come for us but that's no reason to give up. Everyone seems to accept now we're fucked, from our political point of view, but that don't mean to say we can't associate. If the right-wing becomes a drinking club amongst ourselves, so what? At least we're together."

CHAPTER TEN

Dublin – A Riot Too Far

AS DAVID KELLY peeled away to celebrate the Irish Republic's first goal, the vast majority of the 45,000 crowd at Lansdowne Road, Dublin, erupted in a roar of approval. The home team were in the lead, against all expectations, and their fans sensed a famous upset.

"You'll never beat the Irish, you'll never beat the Irish," they sang, revelling in the chance to get one over on their English rivals.

The travelling army of England fans glowered back. Almost all were young white males, many wearing baseball caps and balaclavas to hinder identification. Some chanted their standard response: "No surrender, no surrender, no surrender to the IRA." Others began to abuse the Irish supporters in the lower West Stand, caught between English to their side and in the tier above.

"Paddy scum."

"What are you looking at, you Irish bastard?"

Within a couple of minutes of the restart, someone threw a missile. Soon coins, seats and wooden planks rained down indiscriminately on the pitch and innocent Irish fans seated below. David Platt, the England captain, raced over to the West Stand to appeal for calm, but it was too late. Within seconds, a full-scale riot was on as the small group of initial troublemakers were joined by hundreds of their fellow countrymen, out to prove the no-one beats the English. Platt and the other players were forced to retreat as the thugs tore wooden benches from their fixtures and hurled them as improvised spears. The uninterrupted barrage forced those in the lower West Stand –

Irish and English alike – onto the pitch in a desperate attempt to escape injury.

Not everyone was lucky. One English supporter was left fighting for his life after a wooden stake struck him on the side of the head, penetrating his brain. Thirty metres away, a young Irish fan lay unconscious in the goalmouth, another victim of a flying object. "It's a wonder many, many more people weren't hurt," one Irish supporter later told a TV crew, unaware that outside the stadium a man with a history of heart trouble had collapsed and died.

Belatedly, the Irish police moved in with batons drawn. They clubbed English fans at will, only adding to the already extensive injury toll. At 6.45pm, twelve minutes after the first objects had landed on the pitch, an announcement was made that, for the first time in British and Irish history, an international football match had been abandoned through crowd disorder.

On the far side of the pitch, England striker Alan Shearer summed up the feelings of revulsion in the English dressing room. "It's a sad night for football," he told a reporter. "The thugs responsible should be ashamed of themselves. It's a shame for soccer." The respective team bosses, Terry Venables and Jack Charlton, held back tears and anger as they searched for the words to explain their disgust. They failed, not least because they simply didn't understand. There was no remorse, shame or even regret from those involved. There was only joy. Two thousand "boys" hellbent on violence, portraits of pure hatred. In-your-face chaos. Rule Britannia.

* * * *

"DUBLIN WAS UNBELIEVABLE. I've never seen a firm like it, two thousand football yobs. Everyone knew it was going to go off, to get back at the Irish. There were no families there, no normal people, and very few ordinary English supporters. It was simply yob after yob."

Richard is a football hooligan who runs with a northern firm and is a regular follower of England abroad. He has been involved in clashes in Poland, Italy, Germany and Norway, but nothing comes near the experience in Dublin. The Landsdowne Road riot was the pinnacle of his hooligan career. He speaks quickly, eager to relive the memories of that night, his eyes bulging with excitement.

"Everyone had been talking about it for weeks beforehand, but everyone was surprised with how many had actually made the journey. We were all drinking in the pubs together, the atmosphere was electric. There were seven or eight pubs very close together; they were all packed full. We were all on such a buzz, but there was no one to fight with, even when we got to the ground, there were just a load of Irish bums. We left the pubs together and marched down O'Connell Street. By that stage there were six or seven hundred of us. When they played their national anthem, we just went livid. They don't usually play our national anthem but we have to sit there and listen to theirs. We are English, the greatest country on the planet, and they don't play our national anthem. Not only do they blow us up, but they don't play our national anthem because it upsets their fans!"

But this time the British anthem *was* played. It only added to the nationalist fervour of the English contingent. "The atmosphere there was unbelievable. They were singing their Irish songs and we were singing, 'No surrender to the IRA.' You just knew it was going to go off, there was such a firm there. After the goal they were starting to get really saucy. The Irish were singing that they were going to beat the English and that. A couple of chairs got ripped up and thrown. [Black English defender] Sol Campbell came down to the side of the pitch by us and he got a load of racist abuse. Then it became really boisterous. 'No Surrender to the IRA' began to be shouted, louder and louder with every rendition. Then 'Rule Britannia' and 'God Save The Queen.' Everything was just overtaken by emotion. You are English and you've got these Irish bastards who are openly cheering people who are blowing children up. They were singing IRA songs and there were a few IRA flags."

Irish striker David Kelly's goal was the trigger. "We were all together – we were England. We were not going to stand for what these bastards were doing. Years of it were overloading in everyone. It just went off. They couldn't have carried on with the game, the trouble just would have continued.

"The thing was, everyone wanted the game cancelled. That's the mentality. We are the worst of the worst. We are the only team to have a match cancelled by hooliganism. There was such a buzz after the referee stopped the game. Everyone was cheering; it was as if we had just won the World Cup. It was just mental. I've never experienced anything like it. It was so anti-IRA. The following day we were on a right buzz. It was like the morning after shagging your first bird. You couldn't believe it really happened, but it did. We just couldn't wait to get back and tell everyone down the pub. When we arrived back off the ferry, we were all moaning at the press cameras. But really, we loved it all. It was my proudest day. We were singing at the top of our voices. There was a horrible tension if you were a bystander. But if you were part of it, well…"

The next day – as one injured fan fought for his life – the English press reported events in horrified tones. While crowd disorder had become a regular feature of English matches abroad, it had been many years since it had occurred within a stadium – and it had never forced a game to be abandoned. "Back in the gutter again – shame and despair as rioters halt England soccer match," read the front page of the *Daily Mail*. Its leader comment reported "national humiliation" and the "sickening sensation of shame". *The Mirror*, in its own tabloid style, carried a similar message. "Shame Game," said the front-page picture caption. Its editorial reported that "the English thugs' absurd battle cry on what should have been a great sporting night was 'No Surrender'. But they surrendered all decency on the night when they even shamed the human race."

The pictures told an equally depressing story. Scenes of chaos, wreckage and injury dominated every front page: three English hooligans smashing one Irish fan across the head … a policeman being led away with blood gushing from his scalp … the dejected and bewildered England team being ushered off the pitch as the referee abandoned the game ... an unconscious young fan being treated by an emergency crew.

By Friday morning, the indignation had given way to the search for a target to blame. As if somehow co-ordinated, the newspapers were all arriving at the same worrying conclusion. "Far Right football thugs engineered riot over Ulster," screamed the front-page headline in *The Times*. "Nazi group behind night of violence," echoed the *Independent*. From the *Guardian* to the *Daily Telegraph*, *The Sun* to *The Mirror*, the entire British press had discovered the perpetrators to be a shadowy and violent right-wing group. The Dublin football riot, they almost unanimously agreed, was the work of one organisation. Its purpose was to derail the fledgling Northern Ireland peace process.

*   *   *   *

SEVERAL HUNDRED MILES from Dublin, in a grotty but spacious Essex pub, a rotund, rapidly-balding man sat swigging from a bottle of Holstein Pils. With him, buying the drinks, was a reporter from the *Sunday Express*. Charlie Sargent leaned back in his chair and proudly claimed full responsibility for the Dublin riot.

"We didn't care if England won or not," he grunted, in his slightly incoherent, nasal slur. "The lads was only there for a good fight and to teach the IRA bastards a thing or two, and to try to screw up the so-called peace talks." He talked with relish about confronting the Irish, including a group of thirty wearing Celtic tops. "They were asking for it, wearing those Celtic shirts. It was sheer provocation," he sneered, preferring to call them "Fenian bastards" rather than Irish supporters. He gloated at the subsequent attack. "We steamed them. Those who didn't run away went down like sacks of shit. Didn't even put up a proper fight," he added in disgust, as though he and his followers were somehow cheated.

The reporter, onto a scoop, nodded sagely as Sargent went on. As an active Loyalist, said the nazi, the future of Northern

Ireland was important for him, but secondary to the issue of race. He had no concern for the fortunes of the England team; the inclusion of black players in the national side had long since ended his interest. His role was to lead the troops. "I am the guv'nor. I just egged the lads on a bit. After all, that's what they are there for," he said as a slight afterthought, inadvertently exposing the contempt he held for those under him.

"Ours is the politics of the British working man who has been let down by political failures of the last three decades," he continued. "My view is that all the blacks should be killed. These views are common. You've no idea how deep the hatred is running. I and the others are personally dedicated to declaring war on the system over the coming years. I know that could mean being put to death or life imprisonment, but I hope to light the touchpaper to a fire so powerful that ZOG will never be able to put it out. The rest of Europe, particularly the Germans, look up to C18. We will soon be ready for the big social conflict. I believe in Adolf Hitler and his solutions. There is bound to be a racial war in Europe – it is only a matter of time and we in Britain are ready."

He took another gulp of lager. Sargent was pleased with himself. He didn't know that he had just helped sow the seeds of the destruction of Combat 18.

* * * *

C18 ARRIVED ON the England football scene in March 1993, at a home international against Holland. The attractive World Cup qualifier brought a full house to Wembley. The Dutch had a growing hooligan reputation and firms from all over England mobbed up to greet them. C18 ignored the vast bulk of the crowd to concentrate on this hooligan minority. Despite their success at Chelsea, they had found it difficult to recruit amid the inter-club rivalry of the English domestic scene. This was not such a problem at internationals, where nationalism usually superseded parochial disputes. C18's successful Bloody Sunday mobilisation a couple of months earlier had set the hooligan grapevine buzzing, and an IRA bomb in Warrington five days before the Holland game meant that anti-Irish sentiments would be strong, something C18 hoped to exploit. The game itself was a 2-2 draw and passed off fairly peacefully. It was the post-match attack on the Irish bars of Kilburn (see page seventy-three) at which C18 really announced its presence.

Paul fights for the "English Border Front", the hooligan firm that follows Shrewsbury Town. During the early Nineites, the EBF emerged as a prominent force on the hooligan scene with England: in October 1993, forty-five Shrewsbury fans would be deported from the return World Cup qualifier in Holland. Paul has followed England away for twelve years and has seen trends change. "Most hooligans these days want to be seen abroad at international games. This began when the hooligan scene declined with the start of the party [rave] scene. If you want to be a football hooligan of notoriety, you have to excel yourself with England. You're away from home and you haven't got the restrictions that this country brings you. Basically, there's also little chance of being locked up." Following England abroad has become an opportunity for smaller firms to get themselves known and is undoubtedly more exciting than weekly games at Mansfield, Darlington or York.

Ken, the Chelsea hooligan loosely attached to C18, also understands the importance of following England. "It unifies you when you are together abroad. It's totally different. It's a buzz to be abroad. You've got longer distances to travel together, there's more of a laugh, you're fighting for your country. The whole camaraderie is different from domestic games." He offers a simple analogy to prove his point. "It's no different than if you are a player and you get selected to play for England. It's nationalism."

After Holland at Wembley, England played back-to-back games in Poland and Norway. They needed victories from these matches to guarantee reaching the World Cup finals. Some hooligans decided to make a short holiday of both games, while the majority preferred the shorter trip to Norway only. Among both groups were followers of C18. Unlike the NF or BNP, C18 didn't distribute newspapers or leaflets, preferring to spread its message by word of mouth. "There was no actual recruiting," says Ken. "There was no standing upon a soap box to give a speech but sub-consciously we got our message across. Combat 18 wasn't a firm that went out to recruit people but we just started going, even people who normally don't follow football or hadn't been for five or six years."

Paul from Shrewsbury witnessed this. He was among the 250 hooligans who made the round trip to Poland and Norway and remembers C18 using the train journeys to push its politics. While not everyone agreed with what they were saying, few were willing to take a stand against them. "You're sat talking with a bunch of lads, and it's all like, 'We hate blacks' ... 'Yeah, I do as well,' because you are not going to back down to them. A lot of it is the fear factor, because the lads [C18] are well known for being game for it and you don't want to look as though you're pussying out in front of them. It's all about keeping face. You end up sitting down and listening to them."

"We were happy with normal hooligans because it gave us a bigger street force," says Ken. "If we were going out to smash the Reds, then the bigger the firm we've got, the better. The extent of someone's ideological beliefs really wasn't important, as long as they weren't extreme left-wing. Everyone was welcome. C18 was more like a 'boys' firm really. It was an extension of a football firm." In Norway, C18 certainly impressed. Its mob turned up with no more than twenty-five people but ended up leading 300 hooligans in an attack on an Oslo bar, causing £70,000-worth of damage.

The group's link with the Chelsea Headhunters, at the time the main firm on the hooligan scene, helped establish its credibility. Travelling through Germany, C18 supporters talked admiringly of how the German nazis were burning down hostels and attacking immigrants. "They told us that they would soon begin doing that in England," recalls Paul. While most ignored the pseudo-political rhetoric, a few were taken in. "With every twenty or thirty they get hanging around them at matches, two or three are really going to listen," says Paul. "These two or three are going to take it back to their own local club, their own firm, and start preaching it there." In Shrewsbury, the odd C18 graffiti appeared, despite no known local activist. The week-long England tour of Poland and Norway, while proving disastrous on the pitch, firmly established C18 off it.

"They were the firm everyone was talking about," chips in Paul's friend Mike. Their eagerness for fighting and their strong links with the Loyalist paramilitaries proving a strong pull to hooligans obsessed by image. "And what's wrong with supporting the UDA?" says Mike, menacingly.

C18 also looked the part. "When I grew up in football during the Eighties," says Paul, "I always thought of the BNP and NF as being like a bunch of blokes in anoraks and grey suits who looked like a bunch of trainspotters. We didn't really take them seriously; they were just a joke to us. All football clubs have firms, which is their hooligan element – basically young lads between the ages of sixteen and thirty-five. They always dress well and football hooliganism's always been associated with wearing the right clothes; looking the part." This meant wearing the expensive Stone Island label, in particular. C18 fitted in. "They've started to get a bit of a following due to the fact that they look more like a football firm, because they dress well and are keen for the off. When I say off, I mean they're always keen to start a punch-up."

From the moment the Dublin fixture was announced for February 15, 1995, it was obvious that hooligans would travel in numbers. As they were hosting the 1996 European Championships – and so were exempt from having to qualify – England had not played an away fixture since October 1993. Dublin was easily accessible and the trip could also be used by the gangs to settle scores between themselves. Undoubtedly some hooligans did see the match as an opportunity to strike at Republicanism, though generally this was mere bravado. Past experience had shown that the Irish were not a country of football hooligans, and anyone who really believed that they were going to have fights with members of the IRA was simply daft. More realistically, many hooligans remembered England's last adventure across the Irish Sea, in 1990, when those arrested were fined just £1 and sent on their way. With little threat of imprisonment, they eagerly awaited the match.

The British police, under the guise of the National Football Intelligence Unit, become involved at an early stage. Established in 1988 after the high-profile debacles of several failed undercover operations, the NFIU is principally a clearing house for the individual football intelligence officers connected to all ninety-two clubs in England. While there have been a number of clashes between the unit and regional police divisions regarding jurisdiction of domestic games, as was evident during Euro 96, monitoring England's away matches is firmly under its control. Soon after the fixture was announced, the NFIU contacted the Irish police offering assistance. In what is now standard procedure, it began providing the Irish with regular intelligence assessments, the first being sent on January 24. Two weeks later, a more detailed document was dispatched outlining the travel arrangements of "target hooligan groups". It said that Spurs were flying out of Stansted, while Leeds and Oldham were travelling from Manchester. Everton and Liverpool, who, the report claimed, "are mainly thieves," were crossing by ferry from Holyhead. There was even a suggestion that the playing of the English National Anthem prior to the match would be the signal for some sort of disorder. While the Irish garda, who do not have a specialist hooligan unit, were happy to accept the communiqués, they refused the British offer of practical help. The political sensitivity of having English officers on the streets of Dublin overrode security fears.

The English Football Association was given 3,300 tickets for the game, covering three blocks in the lower and upper tiers of the south end of the West Stand. In the event, only 1,776 were sold. Those remaining were sent back to the Irish FA and later put on general sale in Ireland. Stupidly, the English tickets had not been sold in blocks, resulting in the Irish supporters mingling with the English, a bad idea in such a charged atmosphere. To compound the situation, the Irish FA decided on a low-key stewarding policy. It had intended for a double row of experienced stewards to sit between the rival sets of supporters, but the disorganised sale of the English tickets meant that the stewards were seated in a jagged rather than a straight line. Nor were they wearing any form of uniform or badge: the Irish FA hoped that their ordinary appearance would have a calming influence on the supporters. Not for the first time, the authorities greatly underestimated the hooligan zest for violence. Only ninety police officers were stationed within the stadium, and another 196 in the locality. Out of this combined total of 286, sixty were probationers.

On the night, a number of further problems hindered the police. One of the two public order units on duty was summoned away from the stadium to the port of Dun Laoghaire to deal with a group of disorderly English fans arriving on a late ferry. In another incident, stewards initially refused entry to a group of police stationed outside stadium, which meant police reinforcements were held up for several vital minutes. The problems grew as kick-off approached. A large number of English fans who had obtained tickets from touts or other sources began arriving at undesignated areas under little or no police supervision. Perhaps most fatefully, when tensions did begin to rise inside the ground, there was little intervention from the police or stewards. What could have been a few isolated but contained incidents quickly spiralled out of control.

★   ★   ★   ★

THERE WAS A sense of frustration among many C18 supporters in the immediate aftermath of the game. "Everyone in C18 was going round saying, 'Who the fuck was there?'" says Ken. "We felt that we had missed out, that we were the only ones who weren't there. Everyone was really gutted." It quickly became clear that the vast majority of C18 supporters, at least those from the London area, were not in Dublin. So when Charlie Sargent made his boastful appearance in the *Sunday Express* four days after the match, there was uproar. "He wasn't there!" complains Ken. But the myth had already been made.

It seems that Sargent was motivated by ego more than a desire to promote the group. He even posed for a photographer claiming to be pointing himself out in the crowd. Steve Sargent later said his brother claimed responsibility because "they [the media] were going to say it anyway". He also alleged that Charlie was paid for the interview. Whatever, it was all hokum.

It was easy to understand why many observers jumped to the conclusion that C18 was involved. Even putting aside Sargent's newspaper interview, there seemed compelling evidence of its bootprints. "There is an orchestrated plan by a new hard-core group to spread violence at club fixtures and internationals," one Special Branch insider told the *Daily Mirror* two days after the riot. "A network of thugs are travelling around to any game in Britain looking for opportunities to start trouble. They are using the old National Front trick of recruiting disaffected white yobs via the football terraces and then involving them in their racist attacks." To add credibility to its story, the paper also quoted an unidentified hooligan. "What happened in Dublin had been talked about for the past two weeks. They are neo-fascists and connected to Combat 18. They are complete headcases. You would have to do some pretty nasty things to get their confidence. They just want to hurt."

The *Daily Mail* followed suit, claiming, "Police in Dublin were tipped off two weeks ago about plans to stage a violent demonstration against the Ulster peace process. Special Branch and intelligence officers in London and Manchester learned of the plan while monitoring movements of known soccer thugs and animal rights extremists." Quite what involvement animal rights activists had in the great scheme of things wasn't divulged. The Irish authorities were also keen to pin the blame on the extreme-right, though it mistakenly named the NF as the guilty party. One steward spoke of seeing a C18 flag at the back of the stand, while the official inquiry into the riot reported that a significant amount of right-wing literature was found within the stadium. On the morning of the match, British police notified their Irish counterparts of "information about a flight containing twenty supporters wearing badges which were the insignia of the BNP/Combat 18".

Interviews with returning fans in the national press added weight to the belief that Dublin was orchestrated by C18. "It was all political," said a twenty-year-old from Newcastle, between swigs of lager. "They started singing some IRA songs. I mean, we didn't go there to fight, but if there was a chance of it, we were going to go straight in. You've got to show pride in your team. It's fucking pride. I know two blokes who are in Combat 18 because they believe in the English, no black in the Union Jack and all that. I mean, I'm really there for the football, but I do agree with them."

A twenty-one-year-old from Peterborough backed him up. "England once owned three quarters of the world, didn't it. It's fucking pride. I mean, the niggers and the Pakis own a lot of business." Why did he get involved in the fighting? "I hate the Irish." Several others interviewed in a pub expressed their support for the far-right. "I mean, I love the BNP," said a hooligan from the north of England who, like the others, wished to remain anonymous.

Armed with this evidence, it was understandable that the press concluded that C18 were to blame. The Prime Minister and the Home Secretary were demanding explanations and this line suited everyone. However, it was not that simple. While C18 had forged links with a number of firms around the country, they usually hinged on one or two people rather than the loyalty of the entire mob. Even then, the links involved no more than a dozen firms, a small minority of the fifty-plus that made the trip to Dublin. C18 was still essentially a London mob. And though it could mobilise several hundred for a nazi concert, London C18, even at its height, had a core of no more than a 100 people.

In reality, few hooligans are paid-up members of political parties. They are too independent, ill-disciplined and lazy for political organisations. While some might carry sympathy for groups such as C18, this hardly proves that they are convinced national socialists. Peter Chapman, a former senior officer from the Football Intelligence Unit, describes it as "misplaced nationalism". The Shrewsbury Town hooligan agrees. "They're confusing pride in their heritage with fascism," claims Paul. "They think because they're proud to be English that they've got to be fascists as well. A lot of the boys, they're like, sound, normal people – it's when they get together, you know, it's like the sheep brigade, they all follow on. If the one who's shouting loudest is the fascist then they're going to shout with him." That said, he is the first to admit that in 1993, C18 was causing a stir.

It was widely believed that the impetus for the trouble was the issue of Northern Ireland. "It was so anti-IRA. The English firm is always very nationalistic and pro-Loyalist," claims Richard, who enjoyed every minute of the riot. "The anti-IRA stuff is just being proud of being British, therefore you are pro-everything that is English and hate everything that isn't. The IRA declared war on Britain, so we hate them. We gave the Irish a taste of their own medicine – they come and trash our cities, we trash theirs." Even this must be treated with a degree of scepticism. England had last played in Dublin in November 1990, in the qualifying stages of the European Championship, but despite the importance of the game and the fact that there were considerably more English supporters present than in 1995, there was no serious disorder inside the stadium, though after the game there were clashes in the city centre. If the hooligans were chiefly influenced by the political situation in the North, surely this match would have been a significant target.

In 1990, the IRA had just begun to intensify its London bombing campaign and there was a very high-profile row between the two governments over Dublin's refusal to extradite alleged IRA members. In 1995, a ceasefire was not only five months old, but also actively supported by the two main Loyalist paramilitary organisations. While backing for the Loyalist cause perhaps fuelled the English aggression, it certainly was not its trigger. Rather, shambolic and amateurish preparations and policing of the match gave the hooligans an opportunity to cause chaos. Nationalism and Loyalism were added ingredients and later provided a convenient explanation. Justifying their actions, many hooligans simply identified themselves with those groups closely connected with nationalism and Loyalism: C18 and the BNP.

"There were lots of C18 stickers around in Dublin though there were hardly any C18 people there," says Ken. "It emphasises the point that many hooligans attached themselves to C18 without actually being part of it. Many people, I think, did misinterpret C18 as being an English firm rather than a neo-nazi group." To say that there was hardly any C18 present in Dublin is an understatement. Only two C18 supporters from London made the trip; the rest ignored the event. While there were sympathisers among the hooligans of Aston Villa, Wigan and Everton, any organised C18 plot to disrupt the match would undoubtedly have seen the London unit mobilised. Likewise there were few followers of the Headhunters, the gang with most links to C18. With Chelsea still in Europe, they had other things on their minds. "No-one wanted to get nicked before the Chelsea game in Bruges," says Ken. "Bruges was going to be the almighty one, everyone knew that and no-one wanted to miss it."

In the aftermath of Dublin, C18 became a convenient scapegoat. Politicians and the press found it was easier to blame a small, clandestine group than to answer the far more difficult question of why so many young men in England enjoy terrorising others. The problem of Britain's drink-and-fight culture demands a far deeper critical approach than most politicians care to embark on; analysing the nationalism and racist sentiments within many English people cannot be undertaken without querying their history and traditions and, perhaps more significantly, the media and politicians who perpetuate it.

Many hooligans returning from Dublin were appalled to see the extensive coverage given to C18 as the alleged perpetrators of the disorder. As one hooligan from Derby said, almost comically, "Our big day had been taken away from us." The aftermath of Dublin highlighted the fragile relationship between hooligans and C18. Despite its close affinity to the Headhunters, C18 has faced severe difficulties with other gangs. There are few soccer firms with no black "boys" and with the increase in, and popularity of, black players, racism is no longer the issue within British football that it once was.

The nazis also had difficulty overcoming club rivalry. After the BNP won the Millwall by-election, they toured the surrounding pubs hoping to enlist fighters for their racist cause, but were unable to gain a single recruit. Their connection to Chelsea was well known and the Millwall hooligans, however racist, simply did not want to know. Local tribal loyalties mixed with gang animosity proved too strong for the C18 appeal.

Finally, the nationalism of many hooligans often conflicted with the national socialism of C18 ideology. In 1994, England were due to play a friendly against Germany on April 20, the anniversary of the birth of Adolf Hitler. The match was originally scheduled to take place in Nuremberg but, after opposition from the local council, was transferred to the Olympic Stadium in Berlin, the site of Hitler's 1936 Olympic Games. This time there was a public outcry in Britain. The match was finally cancelled, but not before C18 had plotted a riot with its German nazi counterparts. The plan was to mark Hitler's anniversary with a joint British-German attack on a Turkish immigrant march through the centre of Berlin the day before the match. English hooligan leaders were approached to join the proposed attack but their response was cool. The leader of the Headhunters said that while he was quite happy to take on the immigrant demonstration, it would only be done after the Germans had been physically beaten. If there is one country that English hooligans profess to despise, it is Germany. "Two World Wars and One World Cup" and "Bomber Harris" are among the most popular songs enjoyed by English football yobs abroad. More recently, the theme tune to *The Great Escape* has become their unofficial anthem.

★ ★ ★ ★

WILL BROWNING AND Charlie Sargent had been arrested six weeks before the football riot, over *Combat 18* magazine, but both remained at liberty pending trial on charges of conspiring to supply written and recorded material liable to stir up racial hatred. There was certainly no let up in C18 activities. One of the worst attacks during this period was the firebombing of Gravesend

Anti-Nazi League supporter Gill Emerson, a long-time thorn in the side of local nazis. Emerson had played a prominent role in exposing the activities of John Cato and C18 sought revenge. In early 1995, she awoke to find a fire in the entrance to her house. Slogans had been daubed in large letters on the front of the building. C18 was happy to claim responsibility. An international version of the *Combat 18* magazine reproduced a front-page newspaper article relating to the fire, overlaid with the words, "Combat 18: we did it and theirs [sic] plenty more to come." Fortunately, Emerson had installed a fire alarm after receiving a written arson threat, entitled "Fire Warning: We will soon be delivering – quite free of charge – a little extra 'central heating' to keep you warm on those cold winter nights. Unfortunately, pressure of work means that we will have to deliver at around 3am. The method of delivery will be through the front window. Sleep peacefully. We look forward to seeing you in the morgue."

The same arsonist struck again days later, this time attempting to burn out three Asian-owned properties, two of which had families living above. Again C18 slogans were daubed. In Sheffield, thugs threatened the Independent Bookshop with future violence for stocking anti-fascist material and there were a couple of serious assaults on the local Somali community. In Leicester, Asians were sent letters containing razor blades. They were postmarked Bristol, itself the scene of a number of attacks on Asian homes and a Jewish school. Cardiff saw a series of attacks on the Immigration Advisory Service (IMA) office, including shots fired through the window. A hotel where members of staff of the IMA were staying was daubed with C18 graffiti. C18 men were also active in Scotland, where they threatened a Labour election candidate and vandalised his car; other Asian candidates in the city received death threats saying, "Boom, it's as easy as that, Paki." Most of the attacks were cowardly in nature, directed at individuals or unguarded premises. By now C18 had stopped confronting larger anti-racist and left-wing meetings and marches, but that had not diluted their viciousness.

One of their worst attacks was on a group of teachers in a Halifax pub. "It was Comic Relief night," remembers one of the teachers. "We'd all been eating Irish stew because it was also Saint Patrick's Day. We'd all been singing, having a really good time, but all of a sudden there was a pub full of skinheads and they all disappeared upstairs. We went up to have a look what was happening."

The teachers had innocently stumbled across a National Socialist Alliance meeting, booked under the name "White Rose Society".

"One of them turned and said, 'We're fucking cockneys'," says another teacher. "They all had London accents. One of them said, 'Your ethnic friends are not welcome,' at which point they became abusive. He started calling my friend a lesbian, at which we all started laughing, a nervous laugh, but we still laughed. It was so ridiculous. Then one of them said to her, 'I bet she is a fucking Jew with that long nose.'"

"They came out and stood at the top of the stairs," the first teacher says. "They said, 'You lesbians, you think we are just BNP teenagers who you can scare off, but we aren't, we're Combat 18.' And then they hit us. A lot of punches landed on my head. I don't know really what happened. My nose and mouth was bleeding. My friend jumped in to protect me and I heard her nose crunch. It was horrible."

Her friend remembers that night only too vividly. "I got punched twice in the face. I got my nose broken. I don't remember the second punch; I was stunned. My glasses flew off and I just remember this blind panic, absolute panic, as twenty to twenty-five skinheads punched and kicked eight of us down the stairs."

Both women later identified Will Browning and Charlie Sargent as two of their assailants. Sargent, they said, did most of the mouthing off, while Browning led the attack on a male Chinese teacher. Despite their clear recollection of events, no-one was ever caught. The police failed to respond to a 999 call. If they had, they would have found the C18 group just down the road; rather than leaving the area, they simply went to the next pub along the street.

★ ★ ★ ★

CHARLIE SARGENT MAY have viewed the furore surrounding Dublin as a high point for C18 but in fact it was a turning point. At last there was pressure on the Government to act. Only days before the fateful match, Prime Minister John Major had told a delegation from the Jewish community that little could be done about the neo-nazis, but the Government and police line – that C18 provided little real menace – seemed hollow after Dublin. The *Observer,* the *Express* and the *Telegraph* all now reported the establishment of a new police squad to deal with C18, with internal discussions at Scotland Yard taking place at a very senior level. At the same time Anthony Hancock, the nazi printer, finally was raided in connection with issue three of *Combat 18*.

The increased media attention soon reduced C18's ability to operate with anonymity. Shortly before Dublin, the *News of the World* had reproduced a series of photographs taken moments before Browning and Mark Atkinson attacked Ross Fraser on the coach in the Czech Republic. While neither man was named, it was to be Browning's first public exposure. His cover was well and truly blown a few weeks after the Dublin match when he and Atkinson featured prominently in another *World In Action* documentary. Six million viewers saw Browning at his craziest when, confronted by a TV crew in the street, he leapt across a skip and repeatedly struck at the camera. At one point, he half pulled out his favourite weapon, the trusted Browning screwdriver, though he eventually thought better of using it.

"Dublin was definitely a good press day for us," sums up one C18 activist. "After Dublin, I think we found ourselves at the start of the internal problems for Combat 18. It was the beginning of the end. Ever since then it began to implode, we were all attacking each other. Why? I don't know. I suppose it will all come out one day."

CHAPTER ELEVEN

Opposition Grows

DISSENT WAS NOT tolerated; Combat 18 would go to almost any lengths to silence it. So it was that Will Browning led eight followers onto a plane bound for the Danish capital, Copenhagen. Their target was a Swedish skinhead called Pers Johanson, better known as "Pajen" ("The Pie"), a leading figure in the Nordland music empire and a strong critic of C18. Pajen had been at the forefront of a verbal war with C18. Nordland was a rival with C18 in the nazi music business and backed Paul Burnley, giving the English singer a platform to continue after being forced out of London by Browning. When ISD Records gave sole distribution rights in Scandinavia to Nordland's rivals, Ragnarock Records and NS88, Pajen called for a boycott of any Scandinavian group linked to C18. Pajen, a link between Nordland and the highly-influential Gothenburg skins, became the target for C18's wrath. He in turn had little time for C18, dismissing them a bunch of demented football hooligans and Browning as a "steroid pussy", something which seriously annoyed the health-conscious Londoner.

Browning flew with Steve Sargent, Darren Wells, Ian Holloway, Darren Wilkinson, Phil Curzon and three others. Their cover was an England football friendly in Norway which, coming only eight months after Dublin, was causing intense concern to the Norwegian authorities. They were greeted by Thomas Nakaba, a local skinhead Browning had met during a trip that August to the Rudolph Hess demonstration at Roskilde, commemorating the death of Hitler's deputy.

In many ways, Nakaba was the Danish equivalent of Browning, feared but respected throughout the right-wing scene. He was only five feet six inches tall but made up for it in courage and had been in and out of trouble since his early school days. In 1993, when still only twenty-one, he was to serve the first of four prison sentences. His record included convictions for theft, drugs and violence. Yet he seemed a surprising convert to the far-right, given his family background: while his real father was Danish, his mother re-married an American of Japanese descent while he was still young, hence the surname. Their relationship was not to last, with his mother eventually finding happiness with a man of Pakistani origins, with whom she had another child. While there was some confusion to Nakaba's ethnic origins because of his name, there was no mistaking the mixed-parentage of his younger sister. He was, however, strongly protective towards her. "It's a pity about her colour," he would remark with a wry grin.

Nakaba had been incredibly impressed with Browning's exhibition at the Roskilde event where, almost single-handedly, he led a counter charge into a crowd of anti-fascists, an episode caught on local television. It was a startling display of naked aggression. Against heavy odds, the Beast screamed for his fellow nazis to put up a fight, boarding one coach of mainly Swedish nazis and demanding that they get off. He then ran across the street alone to a group of local people and press and began lashing out wildly. A short time later, he was captured on film standing by himself in the middle of a road junction hurling stones at the anti-racists mobbed up fifty metres away. In another incident, TV footage caught Browning coming into frame across the street. The Londoner could be seen to notice the film crew and march menacingly towards them, until, some twenty metres away, he disappeared off the screen. Moments later, the cameraman let out a cry of pain and the camera jerked upwards; Browning had come behind him and dropped a block of concrete on him.

Not all the Britons were so willing to fight that day. With anti-fascists closing in, Charlie Sargent made a dash for a coach but, as he reached the vehicle, relieved that safety was nearby, the door swung shut and the wheels rolled forward. Embarrassingly for the C18 leader, the incident also was captured on local TV. It did little for Sargent's image abroad, while Browning became a hero.

Nakaba was closely connected to the Danish National Socialist Movement (DNSB), run by Jonni Hansen, and it was to their headquarters that the C18 team was brought. Hansen had become a supporter of C18 since meeting Browning and Sargent at a secret conference in Copenhagen in the spring of 1995 to organise the Roskilde march. While the others enjoyed the Copenhagen hospitality, Browning and Wells settled down with Nakaba to prepare the attack. Nakaba knew Pajen well and was pressured not only to join the group but also to act as a Trojan horse, persuading the Swede to open his door for the rest of them to burst in. First through would be the "dog-squad", a two-man team designated to deal with Pajen's fierce rottweiler. They carried long sticks with knives taped to the end. It just so happened that the two Englishmen given this task were out buying "substances" when the group voted on who should do it.

Jonni Hansen listened in horror as Browning divulged his plans. "Pajen's really going to get it," said the Beast, pacing up and down the headquarters. Hansen had a lot of time for Browning but also had a greater liking for himself and his building: while Nordland might not have the confidence to retaliate against Browning in London, they might just seek revenge in Copenhagen.

"We need some weapons," Browning said to Hansen.

"I've only got those with which we protect this place with," replied Hansen in broken English, pointing to a box in the corner of the room. Browning walked over and simply emptied the contents into a bag, which from that moment became known as "the bag of justice".

With time to spare, the English contingent spent Sunday evening relaxing in Copenhagen's red-light area, long a favourite for English hooligans and nazis on their excursions abroad. Browning, ever the puritan, had no intention of joining their sordid tour. His unease at simply being in the area amused the others. Wells was in one bar with a few Danish skinheads when

they got into an argument with some locals. At that moment
Browning walked in and, seeing the commotion, went over to a
man shouting his mouth off and stabbed him in the throat with
his screwdriver. Another Dane, who claimed to be a martial arts
expert, stood up in a fighting position. Wells punched him in the
face. The brawl continued outside, with Wells throwing a bike at
the bar window only for it to rebound and hit him, sending him
flying to the floor.

Eventually Browning persuaded a few of the group to break
from their sex tour to accompany him into what seemed an
ordinary bar, with a restaurant on the first floor and signs
advertising a gym running along the front of the building.
Browning marched in, content that he was escaping the lurid
drop-out dives with their over-aged prostitutes. Sadly, he had
led the group into a gay bar. "Browning's a poof!" they cried in
hysterics as their leader growled and stormed off. (Four years
later, Browning inadvertently took a C18 group into another gay
bar, this time in Belgium. "Repeat offender," mocked one of the
group).

Early on Monday, the gang, with Nakaba in tow, left for
Gothenburg by train, breaking the journey with the short ferry
crossing between Helsingor and Helsingborg. It was a trip that
Steve Sargent was not to forget in a hurry. As they left the boat,
a female customs official, described by one member of the trip as
looking like a Russian shotputter, stepped in their path and
pointed. Nervously averting their eyes, the English nazis ducked
their heads and marched forward, all hoping that the woman's
attention would focus on somebody else. Solidarity was out of
the window; it was every man for himself. Steve Sargent froze.
As the others literally ran through customs, he was last seen
being led into a cubicle by the fearsome-looking official for a
body search. It was not an incident he was allowed to forget:
during his next visit to west London he was greeted by dozens of
marigold gloves.

Once reunited with Sargent, the team continued by train to
Gothenburg. They reached the corner of Pajen's block, situated
on an industrial estate. Browning stopped the group to hand out

the weapons taken from Hansen's fortress. They had bats, hammers and a gas gun. Just as they were readying themselves, Browning looked on in horror as an obviously relieved Pajen sped past them in a transit van. Browning raced round to the Swede's shop, which sold skinhead clothing and nazi memorabilia, to see the "closed" sign still swinging loosely behind the door and a note stuck to it announcing "C18 are in town."

Browning's black mood deteriorated when he managed to get Pajen on the phone.

"You are just a drug dealer and football hooligan," the Swede told him in broken English. "You are just scum, you're not worth bothering about."

Browning was shaking with rage. "How dare he say that I take steroids," he bellowed, coming off the phone. "He even called me fat!"

Pajen's phone was now constantly engaged and some of the British contingent were getting worried that the Swede might be getting a mob of his own together. They checked the timetables and agreed they would stay until the night train, so as to arrive Oslo in plenty of time for the football. While personally prepared to wait as long as necessary, Browning was forced to accept the majority view.

Finally, he got through to Pajen again.

"You come out here, you bastard," Browning yelled into the handset. "Come out and face us, our mob against your mob. We've only got ten, but we've come all this way to your manor, you gutless fucker."

The others had gathered quietly around the phone box, slightly apprehensive at Browning's increasingly venomous challenges.

"If you want, we can make it one on one. Just me and you."

Suddenly the line went dead. Browning furiously smashed the handset into the machine.

There was little they could do except sit and wait. With little appetite for yet more alcohol, the group waited in vain for Pajen and his supporters to turn up. Browning fidgeted noisily while the others sat in silence. He simply could not believe that the Nordland gang would ignore an open challenge to their authority in one of their own cities, but they didn't show. By 10.30pm it was time to head for their train. Browning tried to get the group to wait longer but the thought of the football was increasingly enticing for the others. Privately, most were keen to get out of Gothenburg. Nakaba tried to say goodbye but was talked into continuing with them to Norway.

They were never to reach Oslo. As the gang crossed into Norway, border police boarded the train and picked them out. The Norwegian authorities had been alerted to their presence by the commotion in Gothenburg and were keen to keep them in custody to prevent trouble at the match. Police vans surrounded the train and the group was taken off in pairs and transported to a nearby police station. When the police ask them to identify their bags, one was left unclaimed. No-one wanted to take responsibility for the "bag of justice".

Browning had a hard time in the cells, especially from the cleaner, who took an instant dislike to him and his politics and each day threw the contents of the prisoners' buckets into his cell. He was also starving. Having been denied food for their first day of captivity, the group eagerly awaited their first proper meal in two days. Darren Wilkinson was first to get his, and began laughing.

"What is it?" shouted Browning, in the cell furthest from the wing door. "Is the food good?"

Soon Darren Wells and Ian Holloway, in the cell next to Wilkinson, were laughing too. Then the others joined in.

"What's so funny?" Browning fumed. "You'd better leave some for me."

Finally the strict vegetarian learned why his friends were so amused. He was served with a dish of meatballs. Browning hurled the contents against his cell door.

Browning was equally outraged when forced to endure a body search. Again, there was barely concealed laughter from the other cells as his compatriots foresaw his reaction. 'You want me to do whaaaat?' they heard him shout. 'You fucking homosexual! Do you like looking at men's balls?'

Steve Sargent was resigned to a repeat of his treatment at the airport. 'Oh, no, not again,' he said.

On day three of their captivity, the nazis were deported back to London. Browning had five officers just for himself as he screamed and shouted obscenities to all and sundry.

* * * *

WHILE THE DANISH trip reinforced C18's feelings of invincibility, it further alienated their fellows in the nazi music scene. Sooner or later – especially with both Sargent and Browning facing prison for *Combat 18* magazine – this was bound to backfire. The first public manifestation of the discontent came in the summer of 1995 in the Derbyshire town of Heanor, where fifty skinheads had gathered in a local pub for a BM-organised concert. Performing were Squadron and English Rose, two bands previously involved with Blood and Honour. One by one, people took to the stage to complain about the heavy-handed tactics of C18.

The background to the rift was a dispute between Brad Hollanby, Squadron's guitarist, and the C18 leadership, who alleged that he had ripped off ISD Records. First, they claimed that he had stolen £1,000 sent over by a German CD distributor. Hollanby's integrity was next called into question when ISD brokered a deal with another distributor to produce 1,000 CDs for a German band: the British were allowed to keep 500 to sell through their own outlets, and were to receive £2,500 to cover production costs. It made good commercial sense and Hollanby, who had been helping Browning run ISD Records, was put on the case. While Browning waited for the German disc to be produced, Hollanby brought out a joint album with Steve Jones, lead singer of English Rose, under the new band title Bulldog Breed, despite both men having told C18 that they had no money to produce their own material. When pressed on the origins of their good fortune, both men claimed that they had a financial backer who wished to remain anonymous. Only later, during a routine telephone conversation with the German distributor, did Browning realise what had happened. "It was a pity the German CD couldn't be produced," Browning was told, "but *Bulldog Breed* was selling quite well."

Hollanby, it seemed, had used the initial £1,000 to record his album and then financed its production costs with the £2,500 from the German distributor. Browning went ballistic, demanding not only the return of the £1,000 but also another £1,500 to compensate for the profits that would have been generated by the German CD. At first, Hollanby and Jones refused, both claiming innocence. However, with irrefutable proof that the £2,500 had been sent over, and amid growing threats from Browning, the two men paid up. The fallout from this incident was to have lasting significance. Both Squadron and English Rose vowed to break all links with C18 and ISD Records.

The C18 leadership was in no mood to be charitable. "It should be remembered," wrote Charlie Sargent, "that we pay the bands up front 100 CDs or £1,000 for each thousand we press, as soon as they are available. They get paid for the gigs, most get two or three trips abroad each year free to play gigs. They make money out of the concerts by selling T-shirts, sweat-shirts, etc. Jonesy makes money out of a skinzine he sells at gigs. Surely that's enough money for bands involved in Blood and Honour."

If Jones's defection was an irritation, Hollanby's was un-forgivable. Before long, stories began to circulate in C18 literature that he was an informer. How else, it argued, could he have evaded prosecution for his *Combat, Battle and Burn*, a CD for which Browning and Sargent were being prosecuted. C18 also claimed that police had been seen leaving his house. Others, including some within the group's own ranks, were less con-vinced. "I think the truth is that Brad did have the money and set up his own thing," claims one man who was active within Blood and Honour during this period. "Instead of going to Brad's friends and the British Movement and saying, this is the second time he has stolen money and so he's got to get a slap, Charlie started going over the top, saying that Brad was working for Special Branch. I know that someone did go to his house and some police were coming out, but it happens. Police have been into most people's houses, they come round and say they want to talk, we can have it on the front doorstep or go inside, it does happen. It doesn't mean that they are your mates. Then it became Brad was an informer. Brad loved it, he could just say to the BM, that's not true, you know it's not true."

Hollanby played on the rift, knowing that C18 had no proof to support its allegations. "We have witnessed Combat 18 turn friend against friend, with their constant onslaught of verbal and written lies," he later wrote. "The stories that they tell mutate from malicious gossip into unquestionable guilt for the accused within a matter of weeks. Working on the assumption that if you throw enough shit at someone, eventually some of it will stick, they then constantly embellish their stories until they become pure works of fiction passed off as fact."

Watching events was the British Movement. Coming from the same area of south London as Squadron, it was ready to give the musician's denials a sympathetic ear. More importantly, having been pushed out of Blood and Honour by C18 four years before, it now saw an opportunity to re-enter. The BM sided with Squadron, happy to exploit the situation for its own political ends.

Adding to C18's problems was a concerted attempt by the BNP to recover some of the ground it had lost during the summer. The BNP accused C18 of being nothing other than a state operation. In a five-page article in *Spearhead*, John Tyndall asked his readers why he had been prosecuted under the Public Order Act during the Eighties but no one had yet been held responsible for *Combat 18* magazine – the case seemed to be taking an age to reach the courts. "For myself, I can see no logical reason whatever for this failure to prosecute the C18 people other than it suits the establishment to keep C18 in existence." Tyndall ended by urging his supporters to "shun like the bubonic plague that coterie of big talkers, small doers and fantasy revolutionaries who employ various AKAs but are best known as 'Combat 18'. Whether these people know it or not – and my observation is that most of them are too pea-brained to know it – they are doing the enemies' work." The BNP also dispatched hundreds of copies of *The Blue Book*, an anonymously-authored publication depicting Charlie and Steve

Sargent as either MI5 agents or stupid clowns. Charlie immediately contacted sympathetic BNP branch organisers, urging them not to distribute the booklet. While this was successful in some regions, hundreds were still circulated.

Meanwhile, Tyndall was hardening his own political stance within the BNP in order to compete with the Sargent's NSA. In November 1995, he scored a vital political coup when he brought US nazi leader William Pierce over to London to address the BNP annual rally. Pierce had written *The Turner Diaries* and *Hunter*, was leader of the National Alliance and was popular with the party rank and file, as evidenced during the rally when dozens of BNP supporters began chanting, "The Order," the name of Robert Matthews's gang. At the same time, Tyndall finally allowed Nick Griffin, a former NF leader in the 1980s, to join the BNP after two years of trying. Griffin was popular with several of the more hardline branches in the country, including south London, Scotland and Yorkshire. He was an outspoken Holocaust denier and critic of the modernisers within the party, who he claimed were trying to make the BNP just another Conservative Party. Not everyone was pleased: both Eddie Butler and Michael Newland left the BNP, which in turn solidified Tyndall's position. The results were soon to be seen as a few of the branches that had switched allegiances to the NSA returned.

★   ★   ★   ★

THE BRITISH MOVEMENT leadership was in good spirits. With the support of Squadron and English Rose, they sensed a route back into the music scene, though there were still some logistical difficulties. The capital continued to be too tightly controlled by C18 for the BM to have any chance of staging an event anywhere other than its heartland in south-east London. In the East Midlands, the situation was reversed: it was a traditionally strong area for the BM, English Rose had local support and they had little to fear from C18. The local organiser was Benny Bullman, a former scooterist who combined his role for the BM with running Against All Odds, a mail-order business for skinheads.

In March 1996, word circulated that Bullman was organising another gig in Heanor, Derbyshire. C18 was holding its own concert in Harlow a couple of weeks before the BM event and there was talk of a rival scene. "It was decided that they weren't allowed to go ahead with it," says one C18 activist who was present at the Harlow gig. "We couldn't have a rival scene, they were going to try and destroy the Blood and Honour network." Browning issued a call to arms, phoning supporters around the country.

On the day of the Derbyshire gig, an impressive firm of eighty fighters answered Browning's command. They did not know the exact location of the event and so gathered in a Heanor pub to await instructions. Scouts were occasionally sent out in search of their rivals, to no avail. The group became frustrated and began to dissipate, with many heading back home to London. By the end of the evening, only ten or so were left: a carload from the Black Country, and another, which included the Sargent brothers, from the south. Then, by chance, they stumbled across the BM gig. Impulsively, the small C18 group steamed into a group of skinheads outside the pub, but before long the BM had the upper hand and Charlie Sargent and his supporters backed off. The stand-off was broken when Sargent saw the BM security leader, Micky Lane. The broad-shouldered man in his mid-thirties was a BM old-timer who knew the C18 boss from the early Eighties.

"Hiya Micky, how's it going?" shouted Sargent, moving forward to shake Lane's hand.

"Yeah, all right Charlie," replied an obviously embarrassed Lane. He hated Sargent and, with the odds stacked in his favour, had no intention of befriending him now. He stepped aside to escape the handshake.

Sargent had no option but to turn back to his followers, urging them into the car. "I'll give you a ring next week," he shouted to Lane, before ducking down into the car. As the two vehicles moved off, several BM supporters fell about laughing.

"I'll give you a ring next week," one shouted, mocking the C18 leader.

Browning was furious when he heard what had happened. "You did what?" he shouted over the phone. "It didn't matter if you got battered, you should have at least had a go." Patience and tactics were not two of the Beast's strong points.

Browning felt he had to act. It was all about image. Sargent had, in his eyes, made C18 look stupid and cowardly. Feeling that it was up to him to restore pride, he decided to target the main protagonists, and gathered a few of his trusted people around him. He wasn't talking of the odd punch or doing over; he wanted to take out the leadership of the opposition once and for all. A three-man team travelled by car to Derbyshire with the intention of shooting Benny Bullman. In south London, another C18 "hitman" was given a handgun with which to shoot Brad Hollanby of Squadron. A third team, led by Browning himself, was a few miles away, intending to deal with Jim, Squadron's lead singer.

Predictably, nothing quite went to plan. The trio that travelled to Derbyshire had prepared their operation well. Armed with sawn-off shotguns, they dressed in white boiler suits, wore gloves and masks and even covered their shoes with plastic bags. Bullman lived in a tiny mining village just outside Mansfield and worked at one of the few remaining pits. Two of the men made their way to his front door in the early hours of the morning. With guns loaded and aimed forward, they were just about to kick in the door when a man appeared from a neighbouring house. Without batting an eyelid, he strode past only yards from the two armed men. They froze. The sight of car headlights some distance away determined their actions. Jumping back into their car, they ordered the driver to put his foot down, and tore off their clothes before ditching them out of the window. As they left the tiny village, they passed the vehicle they had seen moments before. It was a police patrol car. They'd had a lucky escape.

There were similar results against the two targets in London. The man given the job of shooting Hollanby seemed to lose his bottle, ditching his gun in a hedge before leaving the area. Browning's mission saw slightly more success. He was accompanied by a keen arsonist who poured petrol through the

Squadron singer's letterbox. But the fire didn't take hold and damage was minimal.

Failure spurred them on. Del O'Connor and his fellow Wigan-based nazi David Tickle were encouraged by Charlie Sargent to throw a hand grenade through Steve Jones's front window. When they declined, Sargent turned to Nigel Bromage of the West Midlands NSA to carry out the job. He too refused. A more successful mission was against Greg Remers, a French skinhead leader who had sided with the anti-C18 wing of the music scene. In August, Browning made a routine call to Celtic Warrior's lead singer, Billy Bartlett, only to find the phone answered by a Frenchman. Browning could not believe his luck. Though not knowing Remers well, he immediately contacted a friend who knew the Frenchman personally and who confirmed Remers' identity. Browning ordered an attack and a four-man team from South Wales was dispatched. Knowing that Remers wouldn't open the door to a group of men, they sent a young skinhead to knock on the door. The boy informed a very shy Remers that he had brought an urgent package for Bartlett up from London. Hesitantly, the Frenchman unchained the door, and the four men burst in. Both Remers and a Dutch skinhead who was staying with Bartlett were given a good beating. A message had been sent out to the BM and other C18 opponents within the music scene that they were no respecters of right-wing solidarity. If anything, they took an even greater relish in attacking their own side.

★ ★ ★ ★

EVENTS WERE MOVING fast. Opposition to C18 was becoming more open, especially on the now widely-available Internet. Co-ordinating this opposition were the British Hammerskins, a new organisation formed as a rival to Blood and Honour. The Hammerskins were skinheads disillusioned with C18; some had already publicly fallen out with the London firm, while others simply wanted to create a scene solely for skinheads rather than for football casuals. "[We] are an organisation run by skinheads

for skinheads," their promotional flyer proclaimed. "There has
never been any group or body, in this country, which has been
purely and exclusively for skinheads. We hope to become the
first." There was also a financial motive. ISD Records had made
others aware of the financial potential in CDs. What started as a
small Browning project had mushroomed into a £100,000-a-
year business, and others wanted a slice.

Behind the Hammerskins were a number of men from the
Home Counties who had previously been active in Blood and
Honour during Neil Parish's reign. Among them were Peter
Illing, a very close friend of Paul Burnley, Kirk Barker, who was
once jailed for three years for an attack on an Asian waiter, and
Mark "Jaffa" Jones, a former BNP thug who had served as a
mercenary in Croatia. Despite their declared independence, the
Hammerskins quickly became a convenient cover for Brad
Hollanby to organise against C18.

The Hammerskins were given public support by Eric George
Hawthorne, publisher of *Resistance* and owner of Resistance
Records, one of the largest nazi music outlets in the world.
Hawthorne had long associated himself with Paul Burnley but
until 1996 had never publicly condemned C18. Now, through
the Internet and his own magazine, he provided a platform for
others to criticise C18. In one document circulated by the
Hammerskins on the Net, Hawthorne wrote the introduction to
what was the most co-ordinated and concerted attack on C18:
"They have succeeded in doing more harm to the English
movement than the Anti-Fascist League [sic] ever has, and the
Reds must hold their bellies laughing at the effectiveness of
C18's efforts at destroying the movement. Good riddance to
Combat 18! May we never again allow such a negative
conglomeration of misfits and hooligans to dominate even one
small corner of our noble movement."

Twenty-five organisations or individuals added their own
criticisms, in an open act of defiance. "C18 has been like a
cancerous tumour the last couple of years it feels good to finally
get rid of it," declared Nordland, prematurely. "Look at their
paper called *Redwatch*," wrote Christopher Range from the

Swedish National Alliance and a former leader of VAM, the Swedish nazi terrorist group active in the early Nineties. "Have a laugh at it, but it is not funny. They act exactly the way the media wants us to be seen; like stupid hooligans and trouble-makers." English Rose also chipped in. "There's no room within our ranks for such pathetic fools, nor for the people who believe their lies and support their actions against racial brothers."

Browning's response, predictably, was to go on the offensive. "When I hear the do-nothings, the money makers and the traitors of the scene slagging C18 off and spreading lies, it makes me mad," he wrote. "It's C18 who have people in jail, it's C18 who are being raided by ZOG, hounded by the press, it's C18 who are being attacked defending their race. C18 are the only group in England doing any good, yet it is C18 who are the victims of some of the worst smear stories I have ever heard."

Though primarily engaged in a struggle for control of the Blood and Honour movement and the rewards that went with it, C18 saw a political dimension to the feud. It perceived its opponents as partygoers rather than political crusaders. Even Hawthorne admitted that some right-wing musicians wanted to focus solely on their music. "The reason why B&H was supposed to remain independent is that when musicians disagree with the tactics used by a particular group, they are not bound to support or condemn those actions. Being independent, they can focus on their artistic act of creating music, and they do not need to fret over how a particular organisation is going about achieving its political goals. The bottom line is that just because someone is gifted with a great voice it does not necessarily make them a great politician or activist. Forcing artists to become activists is in direct conflict with the principles of social specialisation. But that is exactly what C18 have done ... marched into a music scene without being invited, and tried to force conformity."

For Browning, this was not good enough. "Combat 18 are trying to clean up the scene and get rid of the parasites and scum dragging us down," he wrote in response to people he privately condemned as weekend rebels. "C18 expects people to be political and active and obviously this doesn't fit in with the

music movement that Brad, Greg, Pajen and the rest of the no-
things want, you know what I mean: cosy little music, gigs, loads
of penfriends, a chance to make a buck selling merchandise and
never lifting a finger for the REAL cause. We don't need these
scum stabbing REAL activists in the back."

★   ★   ★   ★

OVER IN THE nerve centre of the Aryan Homeland in Cornflower
Drive, Chelmsford, Charlie and Steve Sargent were formulating
their own response to the critics in a number of scurrilous and
often puerile publications. Hawthorne was ridiculed and his
apparent playboy appearance mocked. Herve Gutoso joined in;
in the autumn of 1996, he began producing *WOTAN* (Will of
the Aryan Nation). Only two issues ever appeared, and the
opening lines of the first one set the tone:

> Listening to a White Power CD will NOT save our Race
> despite what George Whorethorne [sic] and all the wankers
> and cowards of his own pathetic kind might say or write.
> Buying a CD will NOT promote White Revolution for the
> simple fact that most of the time, the money spent does not
> go to promote the Cause but directly into the personal
> bank accounts of the many Jew like swindling bastards that
> have been using the movement as the best deal for them to
> live off our folks. If music was the best propaganda, then
> why doesn't the IRA stop its campaign of terror on the
> British people and surrender all its weapons to the British
> government to distribute instead traditional Irish music
> CDs? Music isn't the key to victory. Music is simply the
> key for George Whorethorne, Nordland's Pajen, Viking
> Sounds' Ben Orell, Viking's Greg Remers etc to make a
> buck and promote their own ego as well. Music is simply
> the cowardly way all wankers and wimps of our movement
> have chosen to follow so that they stay out of trouble from
> ZOG's oppression and can have a little cosy life.

WOTAN was littered with petty abuse and infantile humour. Hawthorne was always "Whorethorne"; the British Hammerskins were "a bunch of morons, wankers and other lazy bastards"; Greg Remers was "the notorious French cocksucker" and "dwarf" amd his friend Luc Le Diodic was "asslicker"; and Billy Bartlett, the lead singer of Celtic Warrior, was called "the steroid pussy of Celtic Wanker". It also spread lies: one man named on its numerous "scum lists" was Greg from the Dutch-based Viking Records, who was accused of stealing money, after not having paid ISD for a large quantity of CDs. He responded by reproducing a registered mail receipt that carried the signature of Charlie Sargent.

David Lane, one of the imprisoned American members of The Order, retaliated. He was furious about personal attacks on his family, some printed in *Wotan*, and responded, "Regarding the vile accusations apparently emanating from some members of C18, this is a brief rebuttal to crush filth and slander. I usually ignore all the gossip which plagues the resistance, but some have now gone far past the boundaries of either decency or what can be accepted. For alleged White resisters to use the enemy's tactics is ludicrous and deplorable." Contributing to the British Hammerskins website, Lane went further.

> Those who cause dissension, whether consciously or unconsciously, serve the enemy. They then become the enemy and the enemy of our cause. The leadership of C18 are obviously Zionist agents or they are so ignorant and dangerous that they might as well be. It can no longer be tolerated. For now, the bands will need to provide for their own security. At the appropriate time, the enemy amongst us will face a night of the long knives. Furthermore, the vile, unwarranted, vicious attacks by C18 and their associates against my wife and daughter are baseless, fabricated and self-evident, absolute proof that they are men without honour.

David Lane's public outburst against C18 was highly

damaging; while Nordland and *Resistance* could easily be dismissed as profit-hungry leeches and business rivals, Lane was a nazi idol. The language used by C18 shocked even their supporters. "It was toilet wall abuse," admits one. "It's the sort of stuff you'd find in a children's school. Of course Hawthorne took it and said, 'Here you are David, here's what they are saying about your daughter.' David Lane is banged up doing two hundred years; he doesn't want to hear his fourteen-year-old daughter called that. He went nuts about it and openly came out against us. David Lane is one of the most respected nazis in the world and so you have to ask yourself what was the motive of those who wrote it."

C18 still had recourse to violence. A non-political skinhead concert in Kings Cross brought them onto the streets again. The event was headlined by The Business, a prominent Oi! band of the early Eighties that had recently reformed. It offered C18 the prospect of several targets. Rumours that Hollanby and other members of Squadron might attend the gig would alone have proved tempting, without the added incentive of a possible appearance by Anti-Fascist Action and the news that The Business had played recently at an anti-racist festival in Italy. On the day, a forty-strong C18 mob was out for blood. The intention was to wait for The Business to perform before storming the stage, but one young C18 supporter from south-east London lashed out prematurely at a black punk in the audience and mayhem quickly ensued. The venue was trashed, as was much of the equipment of the support band that was performing at the time. A doorman was seriously beaten up and an Asian punk had a brick thrown through his car windscreen as he fled the area.

The attack on the gig was good for internal morale, but was of little benefit in the ongoing feud. Many of C18's more peripheral supporters were increasingly perturbed by the group's indiscriminate violence. The pendulum swung in favour of its opponents who, by the autumn of 1996, were becoming organised under the Rock Against Communism banner, headed by Billy Bartlett and Steve Jones. A rival scene to Blood and Honour, it attracted several anti-C18 bands, among them Squadron, English Rose, Scottish Standard and The Ovaltinees.

From its apparent dominance just eighteen months before, C18 was suddenly in bad shape. Its problems were of its own making. Sargent's abusive letters, publications and stealing, and Browning's inability to control himself, had alienated a large section of the music scene. Supporters were deserting. The Loyalist link had been severely damaged by arrests and by the progress of the Irish peace process. The media and the police were on the warpath after the Dublin riot. And Browning and Sargent facing trial and almost certain imprisonment for their magazine. The pendulum had swung.

Yet none of this seemed to matter to the small, fanatical team around Browning. They had long dismissed the majority of the fascists as either weekend rebels or greedy profiteers. Stung by the label "Hollywood Nazis", first coined by John Tyndall, this hardcore clique were secretly plotting the day of retribution.

CHAPTER TWELVE

Special Delivery

THE ATTEMPTED HIT on Benny Bullman would prove to be a catalyst for future action. It convinced the group around Will Browning that the time for talking was over. No-one felt this more than Eric Wallis, a Glasgow-based C18 supporter who, by the summer of 1996, was spending an increasing amount of time in the company of Browning, Darren Wells and Mark Atkinson. Wallis, a former serviceman, had been involved in the nazi scene for many years, attending events at home and abroad. Wallis first met C18 during a trip to Duksmuide in August 1994, and then again when he joined them in protecting a Loyalist march in London in April 1995, but it was not until he accompanied a Scottish Blood and Honour contingent to a concert in February 1996 that he became actively involved. He found himself keenly courted, both for his eagerness for direct action and because of his connections to David Lane and other members of The Order. Wallis was fascinated with the U.S. terrorist group, regularly corresponding with its imprisoned members, and had a framed picture of Lane on his mantelpiece. He read everything there was about them and became convinced that a terrorist strategy was needed in Britain.

While Wallis impressed Browning, Atkinson and Wells, he deeply unsettled his fellow nazis in Scotland. One man who was particularly concerned for his state of mind was Steve Cartwright, a former member of the Territorial Army and leader of Scottish Blood and Honour whose support for C18 had begun to wane. He was a close friend of the ostracised Brad Hollanby and was disturbed by the militancy of Wallis. In the spring of 1996, Cartwright told C18 to ditch him or risk losing the rest of their

Scottish support. The C18 leadership was divided. Browning
said there was nothing to discuss: they had to back Wallis over
the moderate wing of the movement. Charlie Sargent was less
convinced. Mindful of the financial repercussions of losing the
Scottish firm and how it would upset the balance of power in the
music scene, he tried to persuade Browning to placate Cartwright.
But the Beast was in no mood to submit to "talkers" within the
movement and his view eventually prevailed. Shunned by his
Scottish comrades, the unemployed Wallis began spending more
time with Browning and Wells. Inspired by *The Silent Brotherhood*,
an account of The Order, and by *The Turner Diaries*, the quartet
of Browning, Wallis, Atkinson and Wells were determined to
drive C18 forward.

* * * *

ACCORDING TO ITS propaganda, C18 was a revolutionary national
socialist organisation that believed the ideal society could only
be achieved by overthrowing of the existing system. It was the
rhetoric of armed struggle that first impressed the nazi-Satanist
Dave Myatt. He had called on C18 and NSA supporters to
channel their energies into a terrorist campaign. "The primary
duty of all National-Socialists," wrote Myatt, "is to change the
world. National-Socialism means revolution: the overthrow of
the existing System and its replacement with a National-Socialist
society. Revolution means struggle: it means war." In *System
Breakdown: A Guide to Disrupting the System*, Myatt called for
terrorism: not a few "wasteful and pointless" attacks on isolated
targets but instead a prolonged attack on society, tantamount
to a strategy of tension. "It means persistent and calculating
pressure applied to the whole structure of everyday life – and it
means that a power base has been built which can supply the
dedicated people needed to mount and sustain such pressure
over a period of many years. Tension within certain communities can be raised by 'direct action'. Members of covert
action groups should infiltrate themselves into organisations,
groups, businesses and other concerns to either (a) sabotage it

from within, or (b) obtain useful hardware. All covert direct action organisations must be prepared – at some time in the future – for armed conflict with the forces which aid and support the system."

Four years on, the race war had not materialised. With the exception of Browning, few within the ranks seemed to show any inclination to go beyond basic street scuffles and intimidation, and even there, the Beast was central to their worst excesses. Now he pondered his next move. The core group of himself, Atkinson, Wells and later Wallis formed a cell within C18. They were prepared to go one stage further. "People had had enough of punch-ups in pubs and paper sales," Wells would tell *World In Action* in 1998. "Some of us in C18 wanted to take a more hardline approach, to actually get out and do what people have been talking about for years. We wanted people to take notice of us, to move onto the next level. Some in C18 wanted to be a proper terrorist organisation."

First they had to contend with more police attention. In late May 1996, officers raided the houses of four men suspected of involvement in *The Stormer* magazine. They included Mark Atkinson and Rob Gray. Among the possessions seized at the house the two shared were several hundred copies of the magazine, some parcelled up ready for posting, and computer discs containing previous editions. Simon Dutton, whose computer was used to produce the magazine, was raided but never charged. Within days, four C18 supporters from Oldham were also arrested and charged with the possession of inflammatory racist material with a view to distribution. Known as the Fitton Hill Crew – after the estate where they lived – the group was led by Jason Wilcox, who recently had been released from prison for his part in attacking a Chinese takeaway owner. Finally the leaders themselves were targeted. Browning and Charlie Sargent, still on bail awaiting trial over *Combat 18*, were arrested in a pub in Mile End as they gathered to travel to Derby for a gig. Sargent was caught in possession of a knife; Browning was frog-marched to his car, where several hundred racist CDs were discovered.

Browning also had to endure further accusations of play-acting levelled by George Hawthorne on the Internet:

> C18 consider themselves 'terrorists' of sorts, and proceed to behave in a manner right out of a bad Hollywood movie about the White Power movement. The only problem is that 'terrorists' that like to talk about how 'terrible' they are never actually do the things they promise. In addition to making errors in judgement worthy of a group of kinder-garten students, C18 feel that it is also their duty to force the entire English movement to also become Hollywood 'terrorists'. But the type of 'terrorism' they actually employ are the juvenile actions atypical of drunken thugs, not the kind of focused warfare that will serve to weaken the system. Brawling at football games may seem like a lot of fun to some people with nothing more productive to do, but it DOES NOT constitute an act of revolution. The only 'terrorism' that I have seen from C18 is directed at members of the racialist community that speak against their lies and treachery.

Browning was furious at this abuse, coming as it did from someone whose only violent act, he claimed, was an attack on a fifteen-year-old anti-fascist girl. Yet he knew there was some truth in it. He privately admitted that few in C18 really had the stomach for the fight. That's why he was so keen to develop a small, committed cell. A dismissive article in a Jewish student's magazine had first motivated him a few years before; now his desire to silence critics from within the right-wing was pushing him towards terrorism.

Barbecue in Rostock was Browning's next response. Even though facing conviction for distributing racist material, he still brought out what was simply the most vile and racist CD ever produced in Europe. Accompanying the album was a Browning-authored newsletter:

> When I hear the do-nothings, the money makers and the

traitors of the scene slagging C18 off and spreading lies, it makes me mad. So it's down to you out there, do you want the scum and the parasites in your movement? If not get rid of them and if you hear them spreading lies about C18 and real National Socialists, send them packing. Don't let scum and traitors stab real fighters in the back.

The lyrics are guaranteed to incite racial hatred, I mean what is the point talking about smashing ZOG if you're too scared to even break the Government's race laws? I'm sure ZOG won't be too pleased with this release. The whole album contains references to the eternal Jew who NO REMORSE blame for all the present conditions facing our folk, it also gives NO REMORSE's solutions to this and many other problems as you will hear. I mean if the Jew is your enemy, then you shouldn't be scared to name him, the same thing goes if you feel, you should shoot them niggers, then you shouldn't be scared to say that either. FUCK THE RACE LAWS!

And, by implication, his critics too.

Browning did cover his tracks by releasing the CD from a Welsh P.O. box run by C18 supporter Leighton Jones. A year later, Jones was jailed for six months for arranging production of the CD at a plant in Gwent. Unlike Browning, who used a false name when getting CDs produced, Jones gave his full personal details, leaving a straightforward trail for the authorities.

★   ★   ★   ★

THE NEW C18 cell was not alone in the quest to do the unthinkable. Across the North Sea, a young Danish skinhead was reaching the same conclusion. Thomas Nakaba was to be the fifth member of the inner circle. Since their initial meeting during the Hess demonstration in August 1995, the friendship between Browning and Nakaba had flourished, cemented by the trip to Gothenburg to deal with Pajen. It was then that Nakaba had first met Wells, sitting next to him on the train when the Norwegian police made their arrests. They shared a police cell together. If anything, the Dane's friendship with Wells was to become even stronger than that with Browning, and Wells began a relationship with the best friend of Nakaba's girlfriend, Anya. The unemployed Nakaba and Anya lived at her mother's flat Copenhagen until Anya discovered she was pregnant, giving them the leverage to secure public housing. They moved to a small newtown, thirty kilometres north of Copenhagen. Nakaba had been a prominent member of Jonni Hansen's Danish National Socialist Party, often acting as the leader's personal bodyguard, but now left and drifted into obscurity. It was a deliberate ploy, on Browning's advice; Nakaba privately remained in contact with only those close and trusted comrades who felt similarly to him. C18 Denmark was born.

In September, Nakaba travelled to Britain and, in the company of Browning, Wells, and Wallis, attended an NSA conclave at a Chelmsford pub to sort out the organisation when – not if – Sargent and Browning went to prison. Though the court case was again postponed, this time until early December, the Sargents decided the meeting should continue. About twenty people had been invited. However, on the day it became impossible to restrict numbers, as many others turned up for a social event later that evening. When the twenty tried to leave the pub to have their meeting in a nearby community centre, the rest quickly followed.

Charlie opened the meeting before dozens of uninvited guests, including many from the Continent. He announced that a twelve-man committee was being established to manage the movement's affairs while he and Browning were incarcerated. This committee would meet monthly and would comprise representatives from C18, Blood and Honour and the NSA. Ian Holloway, a west London activist and leading Headhunter, joined Darren Wells, Mark Atkinson and northern organiser Del O'Connor on the C18 contingent. *British Oi's* Chris Hipkin and Razor's Edge lead singer Andy Nolan represented Blood and Honour along with Mick Dunne of Chingford Attack and Martin Cross, guitarist for Razor's Edge. For the NSA there was Nigel Bromage, Mick

Shore, Kevin Watmough and Jeff Dunn. There was disquiet in
the hall, as some of those named on the committee had never
been asked, while others were upset that their names were read
out so publicly.

Sargent remained oblivious. Continuing, he spoke of the need
to buy an NSA headquarters in the chosen homeland of Essex.
He had been deeply impressed with Jonni Hansen's building in
Copenhagen, equipped as it was with a radio station and spacious
sleeping quarters. He felt £100,000 was needed. Some suggested
a mortgage but Sargent said the bulk would be raised through
ISD Records. In addition, he announced that ISD would be
funding the NSA to the tune of £20,000.

Browning was embarrassed at the mention of money. He was no
bookkeeper. What accounts that did exist were in his head or
written down on scraps of paper littered around his house. He had
never run ISD along formal business lines for others to audit; he
had after all, established it with the intention of funding illegal
activities. However, on the insistence of Charlie, who had already
told NSA activists that the accounts were going to be produced at
the meeting, he had scribbled down a list of ISD assets and debtors.
The latter included Marcel Schilf, who owed over £20,000. Charlie
proceeded to read out the list, against Browning's express wishes.
Worse still, he went on to thank those responsible for attacking
Greg Remers, before telling the audience that Browning was
planning to travel to Sweden within the next few weeks to kill Pajen.

The Beast, sitting impassively at the back of the hall with
Nakaba, Wells and Wallis, was incensed. But that was nothing to
his anger when Charlie began outlining NSA short-term priorities.
Eighteen months earlier, the squat C18 leader had boldly told
audiences around the country about their imminent terrorist
campaign; now he listed their objectives as regular paper sales.
Hardly anyone will turn up, somebody said. Charlie responded
triumphantly. "We'll make the paper sale a direction point for a
gig, then people will have to turn up." Browning disconsolately
walked out of the meeting. Having split from the BNP to follow
a more confrontational path, C18 seemed to be backtracking.
Sargent's priorities seemed absurd to Browning and his close

followers. They had established ISD to fund terrorist operations, not pay for newspapers and public meetings.

It was clear that the two men at the top of C18, so different in temperament and character, were heading in different directions. Sargent, ten years the older, had once been able to manipulate Browning, but no more. Reconvening back in London, Browning's inner circle discussed their alternative agenda. In an atmosphere of vitriol, the Danish Plan was hatched.

The plan was simple. While continuing to use the name C18, the five men were going to act autonomously, with occasional help from a small group of others willing to go beyond talk. ISD Records would fund them: Browning was going to keep the money away from Sargent and the NSA. They would follow Nakaba's example, moving out of the city and gradually dropping out of public activity; then, after a period of silence, they would begin to strike at selected targets.

It was Nakaba who first suggested Denmark as a base. It had, he told them, everything they wanted. It was suitably remote yet easily accessible to central Europe and Scandinavia – an ideal country in which to disappear. With its liberal laws, virtually everything was permissible, in sharp contrast to Britain, a nation of CCTV cameras, busybodies and telephone hotlines. Denmark, and Scandinavia as a whole, also had a far more militant right-wing tradition from which they could draw support and recruits. Nakaba talked excitedly of the opportunities. They could rob banks with ease, he said, describing how few had the security of their British equivalents. A close political friend of Nakaba's worked in a security company which had fitted the alarm systems to many of Denmark's military arms dumps scattered around the countryside. Many were unmanned and easily accessible.

There was agreement. Denmark offered opportunities that were unavailable in Britain. Media exposure had increased the group's UK profile and they could no longer operate anonymously. It was decided to move to Denmark after Browning had served his impending prison sentence. The intervening period was to be used to raise money and buy weapons. Browning and his little squad were planning to wash their hands of Britain.

★ ★ ★ ★

CHARLIE SARGENT'S CHELMSFORD speech revealed his differences with Browning. And his reaction to an incident a few weeks later proved to be a defining moment in their relationship between the two men. Browning had unfinished business with Benny Bullman, the East Midlands BM organiser he had plotted to kill. Bullman had mocked C18 for not stopping a BM-organised concert in Derbyshire in late September, claiming this was evidence of their decline. Browning now travelled north with Wells, Atkinson and another man armed with at least one gun. They arrived to find Bullman had already left for work on an early shift. They decided to wait for his return and spent the day in coffee shops and pubs in nearby Nottingham.

Meanwhile Sargent, who knew nothing of their mission, was trying to locate his C18 colleagues. He had been told by Liz Hunt, Atkinson's partner, that he was visiting his mother in Northamptonshire but, on ringing her, discovered Atkinson was not even expected there. In the meantime, Hunt told Atkinson about Sargent's attempts to locate them. Deciding to determine the reason for Sargent's frantic calls, Atkinson rang the C18 leader, only to be met with a tirade of abuse against Browning. He held the phone up so Browning could secretly listen in. This was the first time Browning heard at first hand Sargent's accusation that he had stolen ISD funds. He listened in with growing rage. When the call was over, he aborted the mission in favour of confronting Sargent, but by the time the quartet arrived in Essex their quarry was gone.

Browning and Wells set off for Denmark early on Saturday, October 26, leaving behind a storm over the *Barbecue in Rostock* CD. A *Searchlight* exposé of its content, in a special issue on the nazi music business, signalled the beginning of a concerted effort to shut down the C18 music empire. First the *Guardian* and then a host of newspapers and radio stations across the country took up the story. Nimbus (UK), the company that pressed the CD, handed documents over to the police. It was obvious the authorities were going to take action. However,

Browning had already decided to move ISD to Scandinavia, to keep it away from Sargent and others when he went to prison.

Their first appointment was with Marcel Schilf, the owner of NS88, a nazi video and CD company closely aligned to C18. A German national, Schilf moved to Denmark as a teenager and, though still only in his early twenties, had a long record in nazi politics. He had been involved with the Nordland music empire but in 1994 had moved away to form his own operation. Schilf was a man of action. He came to prominence at the age of fourteen as a computer wizard and before long was a leading member of Cronics, a group specialising in computer hacking, telephone fraud, explosives and bombs. In 1991, he teamed up with another right-wing extremist, Peter Simonsen, who had manufactured five litres of acetone peroxide, a liquid used to produce explosives. Schilf and Simonsen used some of it to make bombs and sold the rest to nazi friends at a New Year's party in Berlin. The following year, the police raided Schilf's house the day after a letter bomb had killed Henrik Christensen, a tweny-nine-year-old left-winger in Copenhagen. They found a powerful home-made bomb, around a dozen smaller bombs and bomb-making materials. Schilf was arrested along with Simonsen, who had just been excluded from technical college for distributing material from the National Socialist German Workers' Party. However, British experts from Scotland Yard, called into help, were unable to link the deadly arsenal found at Schilf's flat with the device that killed Christensen. In 1993, he was suspected of involvement in a series of letter bombs sent to people in Vienna, Austria. The Austrian police suspected that Danish nazis had helped their German counterparts to make the bombs – but again Schilf was not charged.

Browning and Wells travelled from Denmark to Helsingborg, a busy Swedish coastal port twenty-five minutes from Denmark. Passing the pastiche facades of the high, beach-front houses, they found Schilf in a warehouse converted into a nazi haven. Club Valhalla was a jointly-owned enterprise with Erik Blücher, a Norwegian nazi involved in the printing and music scene. There was much for the men to discuss. Schilf had built up a

large debt to ISD, something Browning was keen to collect
before he went to prison. Schilf also wanted to re-press a number
of ISD albums for sale through NS88 and agreed to pay Browning
£2,000 for each title. This was a risk-free way of making £20,000,
two-thirds of the amount Browning thought he needed to relocate
to Denmark. At the same time, Browning was keen to release a
number of new CDs on ISD Denmark, a new Scandinavian arm
of his music empire.

While Schilf agreed to front ISD's Scandinavian operation,
Thomas Nakaba was to be its initial beneficiary. He was to
establish a separate bank account into which Schilf would make
regular payments. Nakaba would be able to draw on it to purchase
weapons and other necessities, though the bulk of it would be
Browning's ultimate disposal. Having concluded their business
to everyone's satisfaction, Browning, Wells and Schilf returned
by ferry to Denmark. A half-hour journey brought them to the
small town of Pivo, Nakaba's new home. There the four men
rehashed the arrangements agreed in Sweden and toasted their
deal. Marcel Schilf was now fully aware of their plan: to send
lethal parcel bombs to their enemies.

Pivo was the product of 1970s Danish planning, when concern
over dispersed local communities led to a policy of bringing
isolated hamlets together. It was home to fewer than 8,000
people, most of whom commuted the forty minutes to Copenhagen or north to Helsingor. Cheap, basic accommodation had
transformed a once-wealthy commuter suburb into a dumping
ground for the poor. Unemployment was way above the national
average and immigrants made up twelve per cent of the
population. At the centre of a spider's web of housing estates
was a covered concrete shopping centre, and at its heart was an
open square, bordered by the town's library and two small
supermarkets. On another side was the shopping centre's only
pub, nestling next to Tony's Pizzeria, one of only two restaurants
in the town. It was to the pizzeria that Nakaba, Browning and
Wells retired after Schilf had returned to Sweden. The weather
was unusually cold for the time of year, the snow already a few
inches deep.

The three men discussed their plot between mouthfuls of pizza. Nakaba produced some sticks of dynamite. Browning revealed a block of plastic explosives that he, Wells and Schilf had brought across from Sweden earlier that day. There were giggles as they fingered the deadly hardware, their nervous excitement overcoming any anxiety. Their laughter suddenly stopped when Nakaba said the dynamite was at least ten years old and so was highly volatile in extreme changes of temperature. Browning looked at the freezing weather outside, before glancing back at the dynamite. They quickly agreed that the dynamite had to be disposed of, but not before Browning had finished his pizza.

Snow was still falling as the three returned to Nakaba's two-bedroom flat with its wooden parquet floors. It was cramped but better than nothing. According to a statement later given to police, Nakaba said he was worried about having the explosives in his flat. Browning reassured him that they were completely safe. To illustrate his point, he tore off a section of explosive and threw it to Nakaba. Nakaba threw the block on to Wells, beginning a game of catch. Browning grabbed the block back. "It's not a toy," he shouted. There was silence. The seriousness of their situation began to sink in.

★　★　★　★

THEY HAD ORIGINALLY intended to launch their attacks after Browning came out of prison but the obtaining of explosives now proved too great a temptation. The world would be left with a little reminder while the Beast was away that C18 was very much alive. Detractors within the movement would be silenced and the authorities given a deadly taste of things to come.

The final preparations were made in December when Nakaba, using ISD money, came to London for three days. A new list of targets was drawn up, a refined version of what had been provisionally agreed. It had five names: the London address for Anti-Fascist Action; BM street leader Micky Lane; *Searchlight* magazine; the mail address for the British Hammerskins; and the former Olympic swimmer Sharron Davies, now a TV presenter. Davies was selected purely because she was married to the black athlete Derek Redmond. Browning also handed Nakaba a design to make a detonator, a rudimentary drawing copied from a guerrilla warfare manual. Armed with his instructions, Nakaba returned to Denmark. There he was left to his own devices, with a rough timetable of mid-January, 1997, for posting the bombs.

Browning had agreed not to speak about the devices over the telephone, but became frustrated when, after several weeks, nothing had happened. After several failed attempts, he finally got Nakaba on the phone at 10.38pm on the evening of January 16.

"Have you sent me the messages yet?" asked Browning, using the agreed code.

"Yes," replied Nakaba, with a slight hesitation in his voice. His English was okay but he often found the London accent of Browning hard to follow.

"You promise?"

"Yes."

"You promise?" Browning repeated. He wanted to believe Nakaba but suspected he was stalling.

"Yes, I told you." Nakaba was irritated by Browning's questioning. *It's okay for him*, he thought, *he's not the one having to post them*.

"Fucking brilliant," said Browning. "There's only a few of us, the rest of them are wimps, they're wankers. When we've done this then we'll go on and do the more important stuff."

Nakaba mumbled a response but Browning did not wait to find out what he had said. He was on a roll. After all the talking, the war was about to begin.

"Was the concert you went to in Sweden?" asked Browning, a coded reference to the country the bombs were to be posted from. He was asking too much but excitement was getting the better of him. He wanted to know and, anyway, if the packages had been sent, it was too late for the authorities to stop them.

Nakaba was again hesitant. "Yes," he answered, somewhat sheepishly.

"You did remember to wear gloves, didn't you?"

"Yes," said Nakaba, wishing the conversation would end.

Satisfied that the job had been completed, a jubilant Browning moved the conversation on. "Are you coming over for the gig?" he asked, a reference to a concert in London the following week.

"I would, but I haven't got the money. I have to bring Anya, but it's too expensive."

"Hasn't Marcel given you any money?" inquired Browning. Schilf had paid an initial sum of £3,000 to ISD but had already lapsed on his debt repayments agreed in October. "He should be paying £4,000 and then another £2,000. I'll speak to him about that."

After a couple of minutes more of irrelevant chitchat, the line went dead. Nakaba slumped back in his chair. He had not sent the packages, and before long Browning would know it. He felt trapped. He looked across the living room and saw Anya cradling their baby. He faced a stark choice: the threat of being caught and going to jail, or the wrath of the Beast. After a pause, Nakaba decided that the more immediate and certainly more painful threat came from the Englishman. He picked up the phone and dialled his brother-in-law. Michael Volder was at home as usual. It was late in the evening and he and his flatmate Nikky Steengaard lay on the sitting room floor, out of their brains on weed. Nakaba spoke briefly, checking that the pair of them would be at home the following day. He was coming round to sort out some business, he said. He hung up without giving his brother-in-law time to reply.

★ ★ ★ ★

NAKABA SLEPT BADLY. He was not the only person awake that night. Just twenty metres from the entrance to his flat, two sombre-looking men sat in a parked car. They were Danish police officers.

British police had learned of the bombing plot and on January 14 had contacted the Danes. "C18 are entering their bombing phase," the message read. "Browning has brought explosives and a gun into the country." The Danes had to act quickly. Their intelligence service made an official request for total surveillance on Nakaba, including the tapping of his telephone. The Danish Interior Minister immediately gave the go-ahead. Within hours of receiving the British message, Thomas Nakaba was being watched.

On January 15, officers had listened in when Reno Peterson, a Copenhagen right-winger, rang Nakaba with the news that he had obtained "what you asked me to get – half-second delay and seventeen of them, at eighty kroners each." They were listening again the following night when Browning rang the Dane. Browning's amateurish attempts to code his conversation were not difficult for the trained eavesdroppers to decipher. References to "messages" were obviously the bombs; the query as to the whether the gig was in Sweden gave an indication of where they would be posted. Browning's insistence on Nakaba wearing gloves left little to the imagination.

Nakaba did not notice the watching detectives when, shortly after 9.30 on the morning of the January 17, he left the house with Anya and their baby. Anya had rung the college where Nakaba was attending a construction course to say he was ill. Nakaba carried a holdall containing a screwdriver and some solding equipment, while Anya cuddled the baby. They strolled along the underpass, passing the library and the shopping centre until they reached the train station. The bulk of commuters had already left for Copenhagen, so the train was fairly empty for the thirty-minute journey. Anya knew what was happening but had learnt to say nothing. She had desperately wanted to speak her mind – if only for their baby's sake – but knew it would make matters worse. For her husband, the cause came first.

Copenhagen Station was busy with long-distance travellers carrying bulging multi-coloured rucksacks and suburbanites streaming out of the commuter trains. Loitering around the benches, a few drunks had started early, hoping to drive the winter chill from their bodies. Nakaba kissed Anya goodbye. It was a long embrace. He told her that he would be back before midnight; if he was not, she knew what to do. Nakaba stroked the face of his little daughter; her arrival had slightly softened his attitude to life but not enough to stop him from his mission that day. They went their separate ways: Anya to see her mother and Nakaba in the direction of the shops.

Video cassettes, masking tape, motorcycle light bulbs and a pair of rubber gloves were on his shopping list as he passed the twenty-four-hour sex cinemas and peep shows that dotted the neighbourhood. This was one of the least desirable areas of Copenhagen, where prostitutes mixed with heroin addicts, voyeurs and down-and-outs. Armed with what he needed, Nakaba continued his journey by train to the suburb of Enghave. Waiting at their flat along Ingerslevsgade were Michael Volder and Nikky Steengaard, his two closest friends. Volder was four years his junior and completely loyal to the cause. Steengaard, while not a true believer, was co-operative.

Nakaba was clearly in charge as he barked orders to his slightly bewildered and not-so-able assistants. He asked Steengaard to fetch the explosives he had been storing in the basement of his father's house ever since Nakaba had handed the book-size block over just before Christmas. Steengaard did as he was told. He always did as he was told. A bright young man, he liked the hashish too much for his own good. His flatmate Volder was his supplier and, in return for free smoke, Steengaard acted as the house butler, washing the clothes, shopping and cooking. He had dutifully agreed to store the plastic explosives.

Nakaba pulled out a folded piece of paper from his pocket. It looked like a cooking recipe, with small diagrams accompanied by instructions. It was a basic manual to make a detonator, which he had been given on his flying visit to London six weeks before. He fiddled about with the light bulbs he had just bought but had great difficulty in piercing the glass without shattering it. Before long, the remnants of four bulbs littered the floor.

"This is impossible," screamed Nakaba. He ordered the other two to get up. He had tried to save money by making the detonators himself but couldn't. "We're going to Peterson's house," he barked.

Peter Peterson was another believer in the cause. A tall, lanky skinhead, he lived within walking distance of the others and was considerably more reliable. Reaching his house shortly before 2pm, Nakaba was resigned to parting with some money. Peter's brother, Reno, had rung a couple of days before to say he had seventeen detonators to sell. Nakaba had hoped not to spend any more of his meagre resources but now had no choice.

While Nakaba negotiated the purchase of the detonators, Volder and Steengaard occupied their time admiring the cuddly animals scattered around the flat. Despite the importance of the day the pair couldn't resist a smoke; perhaps this explained their amused interest in a large furry turtle in Peterson's bedroom. Nakaba, meanwhile, was in the kitchen haggling over the price. "How do I know they are going to work?" he demanded.

Nakaba wanted proof of the detonators' effectiveness, so they departed for a nearby cemetery. Crouching down behind some headstones to hide, Peterson detonated two devices. "They work," cried Nakaba. He bought four and raced back to his brother-in-law's apartment, his two assistants following a pace or two behind. Nakaba needed only three detonators for the job and so decided to test one more for good measure. Leaning out of the kitchen window, he blew the spare device. It worked beautifully. Now it was time to get on with the job.

The flat was cheap and messy. Steengaard obviously had not been doing his job that well recently, as washing up was stacked high in the kitchen and dirty clothes littered the floor. With both men on welfare and partial to dope, there was little left over for life's luxuries. Nakaba was also feeling the financial pinch. Moving house and the arrival of the baby had finally convinced him to train for work, a prerequisite for any building job in Denmark. Pushing thoughts of his family to the back of his mind, he ordered Steengaard to buy their final requirements, a pack of padded envelopes and a couple more bulbs to replace those shattered. By 6pm, Nakaba was almost ready. His two companions were now fairly out of their minds but their job was done. The rest was down to Nakaba.

Leaving the flat, he stopped at a telephone box to ring Anya one last time. She seemed restless, having just received a call from someone purporting to be from the Red Front, an extreme left-wing group. There was no direct threat; they just rang to let her know that they knew her number and address. Nakaba was puzzled: he had never heard of any such group. "Go to your brother's, I'll pick you up from there," he told her. With a reminder of what she had to do if he wasn't back by midnight, he hung up. He was now alone.

It was early evening and the temperature had dropped fast to three degrees below freezing. Nakaba zipped up his jacket to protect against the biting cold and to hide his highly-visible nazi tattoos from public show. He caught the bus into town; from there it was a quick dash across the city centre to Havnegade, where the hydrofoil left for Sweden every half-hour. Commuters rushed out of their offices, clutching their bags tightly as they ran for their own transport. There was no time for conversation; people were more concerned with getting home and into warmth. That suited Nakaba fine. He was jumpy and in no mood for exchanging pleasantries.

Arriving at the hydrofoil terminal, Nakaba was shocked to find it closed for business. The bitterly cold weather had frozen up the river. He was told that the ferry from Dragor, to the south of Copenhagen, was operating a shuttle service. This would add a couple of hours to his trip but there was little he could do. He had agreed that the packages had to be sent from Sweden. He boarded a packed bus laid on by the hydrofoil company and made his way across the city.

Dragor is usually a quiet port in winter. The absence of tourists with their camper vans and trailers leaves the terminal relatively empty for several months of the year. This evening was different: the cancellation had caused a scrum as commuters and shoppers sought to board the remaining boats. Nakaba paid his thirty-kroner fare and slipped aboard for the fifty-five minute journey. The trip was uneventful but Nakaba could not relax. Adrenalin pumped through his body and his forehead was wet with sweat.

He had been involved in extreme right-wing politics at school but over the years had become disenchanted with party leaders, who he believed were too busy inflating their egos. He was a man of action, always had been. Ever since school he had been in and out of trouble and had even been connected to the fringes of the ultra-violent Danish Hells Angels movement. It was his chance meeting with the English of C18 that had finally focussed his energies. He knew deep down that he was not going to see the society he yearned for but felt he had nothing to lose. Trying was better than not. By completing the job in hand, he was sending several messages. The enemies of his race would be taught fear. Sympathisers would see the way forward. And those within his own movement who ridiculed the likes of him as "Hollywood Nazis" were going to learn a lesson. *There are only a few of us. The rest are wimps, they're wankers. Once we've done a good job here, we can go on and do more the important stuff.* That was what Will Browning had promised.

Either way, people were going to take notice. And this was only the start.

★ ★ ★ ★

NAKABA DISEMBARKED AT the ferry terminal and made his way into Linhamn. In summer its sandy beaches attracted residents of nearby Malmo, but in winter it is a depressing place. Its once great concrete factory now lies derelict, a depressing epitaph to a prosperous time long forgotten. The architect behind those heady days was Fredryk Berg, owner of the international construction and engineering giant Skansen, whose love of building churches earned him the nickname "the Concrete Jesus". The evening darkness had long set in and most sensible people were indoors. Ice formed on the pavements, making walking hazardous. Mindful of his step, the young skinhead walked past the letterbox and continued up the street, stopping at a shop window to check there was no-one following.

Nakaba thought about his family: his drug-dependent American father of Japanese descent, with whom he had long broken all ties; his Danish mother, who hated her son's politics but hoped one day he would change; his little sister, who still lived with their mother in Copenhagen, the mixed-race child of a Pakistani father who had long since disappeared. Despite the hatred he held towards every black person on earth – a loathing for which he was prepared to kill – she was his little sister and he was strongly protective of her.

He walked back towards the post box. The street was empty and the air was bitingly cold. Nakaba had not been involved in the Dublin football riot or any of C18's street attacks, yet he was becoming an integral part of its history. Reaching inside his shoulder bag, he pulled out three identical padded envelopes. He would have smirked there and then, but the freezing weather contracted his muscles to a tight rigidity. Each parcel contained a video cassette, each cassette a small piece of wiring that would be triggered when the package was opened. A connection would be made, the detonator igniting a small piece of plastic explosive that had been inserted inside the video casing. The rest would be history.

He took one final look at the envelopes. Anya and Tanya and his little sister were pictured in his mind, as were those who had conspired with him a couple of months before. He had been instructed to carry out a job, now it was being done. He sorted the packages and put them in the slot: Anti-Fascist Action, a left-wing organisation, they deserved everything they got; Michael and Leigh, two leaders of a rival right-wing group, the British Movement, serves them right; Sharron Davies, Olympic swimmer turned TV presenter, married to a black man, the cardinal sin. "She's a race-mixer and should be taught a lesson," the English-man had told Nakaba when the plan was hatched. In they all went. Nakaba took in a cold, deep breath, shivered for a moment, and walked briskly away.

The plainclothes officers had been following him all day. They had watched Peter Peterson demonstrate the detonators in the cemetery. They had seen Nakaba test another one from a kitchen window. They had even overheard his conversation with Anya from a public callbox – an officer was in the next cubicle. The only scare of the day was when the surveillance team lost him in the ferry terminal, but he was soon picked up again in desolate Linhamn. Finally they watched him drop three packages into the postbox. As some officers followed Nakaba back to Pivo, others isolated the postbox until the bomb squad could arrive. The green light was given for Nakaba and his team to be picked up.

Danish officers kicked down Nakaba's front door at five o'clock the following morning. The startled nazi grabbed a gun and let off a single shot, hitting one officer in the groin. He was swiftly overwhelmed. The bombing campaign was over before it had begun.

★   ★   ★   ★

THE ARREST OF Nakaba hit the headlines early that Saturday morning. Browning and Wells were on their way to Chelmsford in search of Charlie Sargent when they heard it on the car radio. Aborting their mission, they returned to London to find the phone ringing constantly.

Also on the case was Danish TV. Furnished with Mark Atkinson's mobile number by *Searchlight*, they contacted the C18 man for a comment. Wells was instructed to accompany him to speak to the press. "I've been authorised today to make a statement on behalf of Combat 18 claiming full responsibility for the events in Denmark over the weekend," said Wells, his face shaded by his Reebok sports cap. The irony of a nazi waging war on what he perceived as a Jewish-controlled government while wearing a cap from a Jewish-run company was obviously lost on the C18 man. "We are not prepared to discuss any members in Denmark that may or may not have been involved. I am prepared to say that they were known associates, but I'm not prepared to say whether they were members of Combat 18. Whatever they did, or whoever they did it for, we will send them our full support and they are heroes to our movement."

Atkinson nodded in agreement as Wells continued in a tense voice. "I certainly wouldn't admit to being involved in any violence, but if people feel that's the only way to get across their feelings then I certainly understand that." The anxiety of the last few days showed through his nervousness and unshaven stubble. But the message was still uncompromising. "To destroy the enemy," chipped in Atkinson.

When quizzed as to the enemy, Wells stepped back in. He was more coherent than his friend. "Every enemy of the white race in whatever form they might take. Namely the Zionists who want to take over the world at the expense of the white race. We will always be here until the last man to combat that. The military campaign against ZOG will continue. All units have been put on full standby across Europe and we will continue from here. Nothing has changed."

CHAPTER THIRTEEN

A Casualty of War

WILL BROWNING'S TRIP to Denmark had given Charlie Sargent time to organise. The chubby, balding co-leader of C18 did not know where Browning had gone but guessed it was another foreign jaunt on ISD money. The National Socialist Alliance meeting the previous month had opened a split at the top of C18 that had rapidly become a chasm. Sargent was bitter about the running of ISD Records, which he never imagined would produce such large profits. He wanted a slice and so did others. Around the country, leading NSA activists also wanted greater accountability and collective decision-making. The formation of a twelve-man inner council was seen as the first step to more democratic leadership. The NSA, firmly controlled by Charlie and Steve Sargent, had long been promised some of the proceeds of ISD, in addition to the funds assigned for the homeland scheme, but nothing had materialised.

An NSA meeting set for the first Saturday in November 1996 was seen as an opportunity to resolve the financial issues. Midlands and northern activists gathered in a small hotel room in Derby. Charlie and Steve Sargent drove up from Essex with Martin Cross, recently appointed to the NSA council. Conspicuous by his absence was Browning. He had returned from Denmark and almost immediately left for Jersey, where he was spending a few days with his girlfriend celebrating their recent engagement. He knew of the meeting but had no inclination to curtail his holiday to sit around discussing paper sales or how much money he should hand over from ISD funds. The internal affairs of the NSA were becoming irrelevant for a man who had turned terrorist. He had heard rumours of the discontent over funds but was unaware that this was set to be the main topic at the Derby meeting. Even if he had known, he may still not have made the trip: to him, the NSA had always been the Sargents' baby. The meeting was also without many of Browning's close supporters. Darren Wells was house-sitting for Browning, Mark Atkinson got the date mixed up and Mick Dunne made the journey but claimed to have been told the wrong place by Charlie.

The conclave began amid unhappiness at the lack of NSA autonomy. Despite the formation of the inner council, the NSA was still perceived by those outside London as being run by the Sargents. The issue of money, about which many in attendance felt deeply aggrieved, was symptomatic of this. Charlie claimed that funds would liberate the NSA and blamed the lack of money solely on Browning. "I asked him to provide me with accounts," he told the audience, "but he's only given me a scrap of paper with the names of a few people who owe money." Charlie was pacing up and down, occasionally glancing at his watch. "I don't know where he is," he continued, feigning perplexity. "I told him he had to come and bring the books." He was calculated in his actions, knowing full well that Browning was not coming. "He has repeatedly been asked to produce accounts, but has continually refused," he added. Sargent was implying that, by his absence, Browning had something to hide, even slipping into the conversation a rumour that Browning was holidaying in Florida.

It was a defining moment: the backstabber supreme was now knifing his only serious rival for the leadership of C18. There was considerable confusion amongst the audience. Most of those present seemed to accept Sargent's version of events, though they thought that he must have benefited somewhere along the line. For a man who had no obvious means of income, his expensive designer clothes and plentiful beer money raised eyebrows.

Browning soon got to hear about the meeting. He was furious, and ordered the Sargents to a meeting in east London. His tactic of slowly withdrawing from the public eye went straight out of the window; Browning was once again acting on impulse.

On the night arranged, Mark Atkinson was first to arrive at the Firkin pub, a spacious drinking hole situated next to Mile End Underground station. Atkinson still hoped that a sensible compromise could be reached. Before long he was joined by the Sargents, Martin Cross and the No Remorse drummer Jean-Charles Tanzi, known as "JC", who was only present because the Sargents had asked him for a lift. Finally, Browning arrived outside with Wells and Eric Wallis. He sent the Scotsman in to order Charlie out.

"No, I'm not going," said Sargent. "If he wants to talk to me then he'll have to come in here."

"He wants a one-to-one outside," said Wallis.

Charlie panicked. He hadn't wanted to go to the pub in the first place.

"Tell him, Mark," said Charlie, gripping Atkinson's arm. "Tell him I won't go out."

Wallis turned and walked out. Minutes later, Browning, flanked by Wells and Wallis, entered the pub. He stood, head slightly tilted, looking down at the seated Sargent.

"Outside," he ordered.

"I'm not going anywhere," Sargent replied nervously. He had rehearsed his statement but, with Browning looming over him in a new puffa jacket, quickly forgot his lines. His mind was racing. His attention focused on what he thought was a bulge in Browning's jacket, which he took to be a gun.

"What the fuck are all these people doing here?" Browning said, looking at Cross and JC. "I told Steve, just you and him."

"Hang on, Will," said JC, in heavily-accented English, "Just calm down, don't take it out on me." Everyone was feeling the discomfort, none more so that the little Frenchman.

"I just want to talk to him," responded Browning, his eyes fixed on Charlie. "Alone."

Close to tears, Sargent finally agreed to leave the pub if Browning proved he had no gun. Browning opened up his jacket for inspection and Sargent reluctantly got up. The others sat and watched uneasily as the two men headed outside. Small talk could not disguise the anxiety. After twenty minutes, they had had enough and, led by Wells, they too left the pub to see what was occurring outside.

Much to everyone's surprise, Sargent and Browning were deep in conversation. Sargent claimed that he had been mis-interpreted at the Derby meeting: far from calling Browning a thief, he was merely saying that they had to get their accounts in order before their trial. He did, however, admit to being put out by Browning and Wells's recent disappearance, especially as he had a CD order to fill and no plastic covers. While Browning seemed placated over the Derby meeting, he remained annoyed that Sargent was so worked up over CD cases.

"While you complain about CD covers," he told Sargent pointedly, "some of us have been risking our necks."

At that, and against his better judgement, he told Sargent about the trip to Denmark. "We brought explosives in from Poland," he said excitedly.

It was then that the others came out. It became a general free-for-all; everyone had a suggestion as to who might receive a "package", their euphemism for a bomb. Tellingly, most of their suggested targets were fellow fascists. JC walked off to ensure he had no further involvement. The meeting eventually broke up. While nothing had been resolved on the issue of the ISD money, the talk of bombs diverted everyone's attention and, in an atmosphere of conciliation, they parted company as friends.

The peace was short. Within hours of returning home, Browning heard via the Frenchman that Sargent had been badmouthing him again on the way home. "Who does he think he is?" JC told Browning, reciting Sargent's words. "He came out with all this bullshit but I mugged him off and he still hasn't come up with the ISD money!"

Browning's reaction was predictable. Angry with himself for being lenient, he was out of the house at 5.30 the next morning, accompanied by Wells. The streets were clear as the two men drove out of London. As they approached Sargent's Essex flat just before seven, Browning was almost uncontrollable. He banged on the door.

Sargent's flat, which he shared with his brother, was small and untidy. Clothes were scattered across the floor and the living room was strewn with magazines and newspaper cuttings. Herve Gutoso had been bedding down on the settee for some time, his presence adding to the general untidiness. Charlie answered the door in a pair of boxer shorts. Having just woken, he found Browning's aggressive growl quite disorientating. Steve was still in his bedroom, while Herve lay motionless on the settee. The peace of Cornflower Drive was shattered as Browning and Wells barged in.

"What the fuck is going on?" Browning bawled.

"What do you mean?" asked Charlie innocently.

"I know what you've been saying. JC told me that you were slagging me last night. What's your game?" Browning was actually shaking with fury. Turning to the now-awoken Herve, he snapped, "Do you wan' it?"

Gutoso, propped up on one shoulder to watch the argument, ducked down once more in an appearance of submission. By now Steve had been stirred by the commotion and was also in the room. Charlie tried to pacify Browning but it cut little ice.

"We're through," said Browning. "I don't know what you're up to, but I don't want to be any part of it any more. You do your thing and we'll do ours."

"You've got it all wrong. I haven't been slagging you off. It's just a misunderstanding."

"You're just causing trouble. You're badmouthing me to everyone in the movement and I want it to stop." Browning paced the room, attempting to keep some degree of self-control. Wells and Steve sat on the sofa; despite their contrasting allegiances, they sat together in silence. Gutoso disappeared into the kitchen.

"Just forget it all," said Browning. "While you've been moaning to people we've actually been getting stuff done. We've got the explosives while you've sat on your fat arse."

"Yeah, but…"

"No buts. We've been to Poland and brought plastic explosives over the border into Denmark. What the fuck have you been doing?"

"Yeah, but it'll bring it on top for my tee-shirts," whined Charlie, with his trademark shoulder-shrug, his hands out-stretched. Almost instantly, he realised how stupid that must have sounded.

Browning's mind was made up. "I've finished with you," he repeated as he got up to leave. "I don't want to see you again."

He walked out of the flat, followed by Wells. Combat 18 was irreconcilably split.

★ ★ ★ ★

THE TWO MEN did not meet again until a gig in Newmarket just before Christmas. The atmosphere was electric. Browning, knowing a fight was possible, had made plans, discussing them with Wells a couple of days before the gig using a new set of codewords.

"Don't forget it's the little girl's birthday on Saturday," said Browning.

"Yeah, yeah. I haven't forgotten," his trusted sidekick replied.

"Have you got her a present?"

"Yeah."

"You got her the bicycle?"

Wells nodded silently. Despite telling everyone to be careful about what they said on the phone, Browning was once again breaking the rules himself.

"You definitely got a bike?" Browning persisted.

"Yes, I told you."

"You sure?"

"For fuck's sake, yes."

"So, er," Browning paused to clear his throat. His deep cough mid-sentence had become infamous. "You're going to keep it in your pocket then?"

After a moment, Browning broke the silence. "Yeah man. If it turns nasty you can get it out and let him have it."

The "bicycle" remained in Wells's pocket throughout the evening as Sargent kept well away. News of the split had spread throughout the movement, with the majority either remaining neutral or believing it was a personal rather than political dispute. Most tried to keep their distance from both men.

The two sides began producing literature against the other. In *Come Clean About the Funds Now*, Steve Sargent – his authorship hidden – accused Browning of stealing. "Now Charlie has called on Will to hand over the £20,000 as promised and show the NSA proof of ISD Records funds. Will responded first by saying that there was only £5,000, the rest was owed and produced a scrap of paper with figures wrote out on who owes money (very nice but not proof). I will hearby again call on Will to give a full account of ISD and hand over the funds. If he is not profiting from it as he claims, why should he object? So far all he has shown is £5,000 and a list of debts scribbled on paper. As for lifestyles, again Will lives in a £80,000 town house, while Charlie's kids live in a homeless people's unit, and he sleeps on a settee at his brother's flat." Charlie claimed Browning had personally profited by almost £100,000.

The Browning camp was slow to respond, though they eventually brought out a number of their own publications. In *C18 – A Few Tonnes Lighter, but the Future Looks Brighter*, Browning had his say about Sargent:

> At the small gig in Bury St Edmonds before Christmas, he earnt £800 from his T-shirt stall alone. And it was only a small gig, not including the £10 entrance fee (yeah ten quid). Now there were only about 200 people there so we'll give Sargent the benefit of the doubt and say that 50 people didn't pay. That's still £1500. He then also did the beer, selling it from kegs at more than it costs in a pub, £2.10 a pint to be exact. So let's say everyone had between 5-10 pints, some more, some less. Work it out for yourselves. Have we been mugged off or what? Now at the gig Sargent was meant to give the proceeds to Biggsy but sadly all he walked away with was £30. Don't laugh too hard, there's more! Atki went up to Sargent and asked for £20 for a wreath for a comrade that had just died. Charlie five chins said, "Sorry mate, I haven't got it."

Fuck me the cunt's pockets were ready to burst!!!

After four years of trading by Sargent incorporated there is not one penny in the Blood and Honour account! I kid you not. And this is down to Sargent, no-one else controlled any of the money, so where is it? It's vanished! And this is down to the man who called Tyndall a thief."

The document went on to list £25,000 ISD had contributed to the movement, from recording equipment to legal fees. "Then there are the illegal things which were bought and stashed, you don't need to be a brain surgeon to know what we are talking about." Coming so soon after Denmark, everyone knew what he was referring to. With £50,000 of stock left unsold, Browning's camp claimed that everything was in order.

Supporters divided along regional lines. Browning gained backing in west London, the north of England and South Wales. Especially important was Del O'Connor, the C18 leader in Wigan and a member of the NSA inner council. A formidable fighter, he had been head of Skrewdriver Security and Ian Stuart Donaldson's best friend, and was an influential figure in the north-west. His support was keenly sought.

Born to an Irishwoman in Wimbledon in 1959, O'Connor had spent most of his youth in Streatham. Like several other C18 activists, he had an unhappy childhood. He never knew his father, was not particularly close to his mother and was bullied at school, though he later turned the tables by filling himself out at the gym. He became a punk, then shaved his head after hearing some early Oi! music at the Brixton Apollo in the late Seventies. Captivated, he knew that this was "his music". In 1979 he joined the BM, though within three years he had left, believing that the group was too money-orientated. He remained within the skinhead scene, becoming particularly close to Chris "Chubby" Henderson, BM Leader Guard organiser Nicky Crane – one of the most feared nazis in Britain during the Eighties – and Ian Donaldson. He joined the Ku Klux Klan in 1990 along with several other leading Blood and Honour supporters, rising to become head of security, but left after eighteen months, feeling it was too Americanised for the British scene.

O'Connor was never far from trouble. In 1993, after finding his wife was having an affair with her boss, he went berserk and put the man in hospital. The assault earned him a three-year jail sentence. He was released in 1995 and, having known Charlie Sargent through the skinhead scene, became involved in C18. O'Connor established the White Wolves as a means of giving northern C18 supporters their own identity. He also began producing his own magazine, *The Wolf*, a small photocopied hatesheet that reached ten issues before another prison sentence put an end to it.

Despite his obvious aggression, O'Connor was one of the more intelligent and committed C18 supporters. He was never a simple racial antagonist and often saw black people as just as much victims as working class whites. Nor was he a thoughtless subscriber to the Jewish conspiracy theories that dominate the nazis. "I think the politicians are puppets," he told *World In Action* in an interview that was never broadcast. "They aren't the real people in power. I think that these are the people with money. I wouldn't say it's exclusively Jewish, but I think when you have money, which many of them do, it puts you in a different category."

O'Connor found a close political ally and friend in another Wigan-based nazi, Dave Tickle. They worked on club doors together, went shooting together and even built crude explosive devices together, which they detonated on a nearby farm. Both men at the time were committed to the war that C18 promised. "Somebody has got to be the first person to stand up and say I'll do it," said O'Connor. "I don't want to go to prison. No-one wants to go to prison, but you have to put yourself at risk sometimes for what you believe in. If you are not willing to risk your own freedom you are not going to change anything. If you're not, how can you expect anyone else to do the same? I have absolutely nothing to lose." It was only a matter of time before O'Connor and Browning came together. Following the Newmarket gig – where Browning revealed Sargent's treachery and his own desire for terrorism – the pair became allies.

The Sargents, meanwhile, were supported by NSA units in the West Midlands, Essex and Scotland, as well as individual older nazis such as David Myatt and Tony Williams. In mid-January, 1997, Charlie accepted an invitation to address the West Midlands NSA to put across his version of events. The meeting, in a Birmingham hotel, attracted thirty people. Just over half were from the Aston Villa soccer mob, a white-only firm with strong links to Loyalist paramilitary organisations. The lead singer of Razor's Edge brought six supporters from the Black Country, while the remainder of the audience were from Coventry and Leicester. Sargent was escorted up by his brother Steve and Tony Williams, who no doubt hoped that his appearance would add weight to the Sargent case. However, Williams's presence unnerved several people at the meeting, who were suspicious of his laid-back attitude, well-spoken accent and aloofness.

The floor was given over to Sargent. His line was the same one he had pushed at the Derby meeting a few months before. ISD Records, he told the audience, was established to provide money for C18 and the NSA, but neither had seen a single penny. Now, Browning was trying to use threats to stay involved in the movement. "He must be expelled," concluded Sargent, enthused by his reception.

A less receptive audience gathered in west London a week later. The southern division of Blood and Honour was hosting a concert headlined by the American band The People Haters. At first Charlie and Steve thought that it would be a chance to explain their case to the all-important west London group, the largest single contingent within C18, but they were told in no uncertain terms that they would not be welcome. It had been a week since news of Nakaba's arrest and, though precise details were hard to come by, it was the principal topic of conversation that evening. There was a feeling of militancy at the gig and the arrival of riot police halfway through the evening added to the siege mentality. Neither Browning nor Wells publicly admitted involvement in the Danish plot, but few present were left in any doubt that they had some role in the affair. Most expressed their support. To audiences of one or two, Browning and his team systematically explained that Charlie had been expelled from C18 for trying to divide the movement and force out the militants. The money, the Browning camp told people that night, was carefully hidden and accounted for.

Yet Sargent's presence was still felt. Like Browning, he had spent the previous fortnight canvassing support by phone and in person. Some spoke to him out of friendship, while others met him out of curiosity or obligation. During one conversation with Stuart Glass, Charlie announced his contempt for Darren Wells, claiming that he hid behind Browning's skirt. "I'm going to knife him," bragged the deposed leader. In the highly-charged atmosphere, such a threat was not to remain secret for long. Glass met Wells at the gig and joked that he was surprised to see him, duly informing him of the threat. Wells was furious. Breaching all security considerations, he left a message on Sargent's answer phone challenging him to a fight. Later that evening, Wallis left another message saying that if Charlie was not careful he would find himself face down in a ditch.

Wells's mood was no more conciliatory by the Monday morning. He, Browning and Wallis travelled up to Harlow to confront Sargent at the mobile home park where his partner Maxine and their children lived. Though one of the stipulations for her living at the site for homeless families was that she was a single parent, Charlie was regularly there. However, that day he was nowhere to be seen. They continued on to Chelmsford, where they kicked in Steve Sargent's front door and found Gutoso in the living room.

"Where is he?" Browning demanded, offering the Frenchman out for a fight.

"I don't know," replied Gutoso, terrified.

Wells and Wallis searched the flat. They knew their way around: only weeks before, Wells, Atkinson, Browning, and Chris Castle, a C18 supporter from Catford, south London, had been in the flat, taking or stealing – depending on who is telling the story – a screenprinting machine. Browning claimed it belonged to C18 while Sargent unsuccessfully argued it was his, having been given the money to buy it by a Chelsea hooligan.

The frustrated trio returned to Harlow. They collected the Chingford Attack lead singer Mick Dunne, who was staying with the Kevin and Roy Johnson, two local activists who had previously controlled Skrewdriver Services, before continuing their search. There was still no sign of Sargent and they again linked up with the Johnsons, who had gone to visit their mother close to the Harlow mobile home park. After a brief chat, they headed back down to London. Dunne left with Roy, and Kev Johnson was just about to depart when, from out of nowhere, several marked and unmarked police vehicles screeched up and surrounded his car. He was hauled out and forced to lie on the floor at gunpoint. Officers from the Tactical Firearm Unit demanded to know what weapons Browning had at his disposal and any information about his intentions.

Browning, oblivious to what was happening to Kev Johnson, decided to abort the search for Sargent. As he, Wells and Wallis left Harlow, they realised they were being followed. The Beast dodged and weaved through traffic, slowing down and then speeding up, but the following car stuck to his tail, so he decided to have some fun, repeatedly circling a roundabout to the clear annoyance of the following driver. However, as Browning turned onto the M11 in the direction for London, the tailing car was joined by two other cars, which then boxed him in and chaperoned him back towards the capital. Once Harlow was far behind, the unmarked police cars pulled away, leaving an annoyed Browning free to make his way home.

He found his girlfriend contorted with worry. While they had been out, Steve Sargent had called, screaming about Browning's behaviour. "You've gone too far this time," he had shouted, "you're well out of order."

Unsure what had happened, she feared the worst. Browning had only just finished putting her mind at rest when Kev Johnson rang and recounted the incident involving the armed police. Things were getting out of hand. The three men decided to grab a meal at the local McDonalds. As they left the house, they saw a middle-aged man parked just up the road, within clear sight of Browning's front door. The C18 leader approached the vehicle, demanding to know its driver's business. "Just waiting for a friend," came the reply, but Browning wasn't convinced. When they returned from McDonalds the car was gone but a neighbour told Browning that there had been a lot of coming and going by unknown men in the flats opposite his house.

Back indoors, there was no disguising the anxiety that hung in the air. Everyone believed the police were finally making a move, something they had been expecting since Nakaba's arrest nine days before.

Kathleen Wallis was impatient. She had always intended to catch the last train back to Scotland, and the day's events only reinforced her desire to leave. Eric went with her; he had also had enough. With the moment of reckoning seemingly so close, his departure was a bitter blow for Browning. He was left with just Wells for support.

Later that night, Browning and Wells went out in the car to buy the first editions of the morning papers. They realised they were still being followed. Browning, consumed with a mixture of rage and tiredness, forgot about the newspapers and instead drove his clapped out E-reg Orion into a dilapidated industrial estate on the outskirts of Wapping. With few streetlights to guide their journey, the car and its tail meandered through empty, derelict streets. Browning eventually turning into a dead end. Slamming his foot hard on the brakes, he spun the car round until it faced the other vehicle head-on over the brow of a bridge. Their stalkers stopped their own vehicle thirty yards away and hit the headlights full on. Browning and Wells sat there, exhausted, for what seemed like an eternity. Browning suggested they get out and approach the other car.

"We'll just see what happens," he said, his voice betraying his exhaustion.

Wells was not so keen. "I think we'd better leave," he said. They drove back home.

Once inside the house, both men armed themselves with handguns. There was no disguising the gravity of the situation.

At any minute they expected police to come through the door. Browning and Wells had been through so much together: the street fights, ISD Records, the Danish plot. It had been nine days since Nakaba had made the trip to Sweden; nine long days of stress and tension. Now was Judgement Day.

For all the talk of the white race, the Aryan army and leaderless resistance, it had come down to three people in a two-bedroom house in south-east London. Will Browning, the C18 co-leader, who had been central to almost all its violence since its inception some six years before; his girlfriend, who had long rejected the Right but had stayed loyal to him; and best friend Darren Wells, surprisingly articulate and affable for a man committed to nazi politics. So this was what their lives had come to, thought Browning, as he waited for the inevitable. He turned his armchair around to face the front door and kitchen window. If anyone was going to come in it would, he guessed, be from that direction. He rested a high-powered crossbow on one arm and held a fully-loaded pistol in the other. Upstairs his girlfriend and Wells flitted from room to room, peering behind curtains, hoping to see movement outside.

Browning was prepared for the worst. There was a strange calmness about him, a contentment that was perverse given the situation. The man who carried so much hatred inside seemed at last to be at ease. First arrested at the age of ten; sent to a secure school at eleven; thrown off Jersey at fifteen; sentenced to three years prison by the age of nineteen; skinhead, race-hater, terrorist, thug. Suddenly his life had a purpose. He fully intended to use his weapons, to go out in a blaze of glory. He would be remembered when others were forgotten.

He shuffled in his chair to find a more comfortable position, his index finger still resting lightly on the trigger of the gun. He seemed to smile as he fell asleep.

CHAPTER FOURTEEN

Seeking Justice

THE CRASH THROUGH the door never came. By morning, it was clear that there was to be no raid. But news of the previous day's events spread fast throughout the grapevine. The situation was clearly out of control. Some slipped out of the movement altogether; others stayed well clear of both Browning and Sargent. Even those who had been part of the feud, such as Eric Wallis, kept their heads down. Wallis claimed he was receiving attention from Special Branch.

Yet with both sides unwilling to compromise, a violent conclusion seemed inevitable. The Sargents were quietly confident that they could muster enough muscle to win any physical confrontation between the two groups, as Steve asserted in a letter to Kevin Watmough in early February. Deriding Browning as a "bully boy wanker," Sargent vowed revenge for the attack on his flat the week before. "I went up to Brum Sunday for a NSM meeting, all of the Brums have come out with us, the only region to actually take a stand on either side, to their credit," he wrote. "We're a firm now of probably 50 from Essex, Romford, East End. Beast is oblivious to it, also Crossy has a party Saturday, some of the Chelsea are coming down, so I think its fair to say we're going to win! By this week's end, all going well, Beast and co will be out of the game, the long knives are out!"

Within days, his prediction had proved eerily accurate.

On Monday, February 10, Browning and his friend Chris Castle drove up to Harlow. They had in their possession Charlie Sargent's plastering tools, taken previously from his flat. They had agreed to exchange them in return for Blood and Honour and C18 subscription lists and £1,000 in cash that they claimed was owing. Castle parked at the entrance to Sherrards House, a mobile home park, and made his way up the alley to number seven, the home of Maxine Durrant. Browning had agreed to stay in the car so as not to cause trouble.

Several minutes went by. Suddenly, Castle re-emerged, clutching his chest. Browning ran over and took a cursory look under his friend's jacket; he could see no obvious wound and concluded Castle had been hit and winded. He leaned him against a gatepost and went to get the car, but encountered Sargent and another man with a knife, both clearly agitated.

"What the fuck have you done?" said Browning. By now, Castle had collapsed in the mud. Browning could see blood on his back and realised his friend had been stabbed. "Go and get a fucking ambulance or he'll die."

"Fuck him," replied Sargent. "Let him rot."

Unable to find the car keys, Browning dragged his friend back to the park entrance and hailed a taxi. It took them on a desperate race to the nearest hospital, with Browning exerting pressure on his friend's wound to reduce the flow of blood. It was no use. Chris Castle was pronounced dead on arrival, the result of a single stab wound to his back.

Back at Sherrards House, Charlie Sargent and his friend Martin Cross awaited the arrival of the police. Sargent instructed a neighbour to tell the police that he had seen a man with a gun, while Cross went into a field to dispose of the knife. It took officers the best part of an hour to reach Sherrards House. With prior intelligence suggesting that Sargent's home might come under armed attack, and the emergency call making reference to the presence of a gun, they had to hold back for an armed response unit. Heading the investigation was Detective Superintendent Steve Reynolds. It was his first case since being promoted the previous week. With Charlie Sargent, Martin Cross, Kelly Cross and Maxine Durrant on hand to give their version of events, Reynolds quickly formed the view that Browning and Castle had been the aggressors. "That was just the perception at that stage, I think given to us by just one or two witnesses," he later said. It was supported by police intelligence that had been passed to Reynolds only minutes into the investigation. "I think it's fair to say that Sargent and Cross and their wives wanted to speak to us, in fact they were quite keen to speak to us."

Cross was first to give a statement. He claimed that he and his wife, who also played in the band Razor's Edge, had decided to go over to Harlow to visit Sargent and Maxine Durrant. While the women went into town shopping, the men stayed in the mobile home discussing Sargent's forthcoming move. The women had not been back long when Cross, who had gone into the kitchen to dry his hands, heard a noise from the hallway.

> I was standing in the kitchen and the kids and my wife and Maxine were in the living room. Just like out the blue I heard a bang and there was all commotion and the kids were screaming and my wife was screaming. This all happened in seconds. Then I saw an altercation, people beating up on Charlie and I recognised these people, I knew them instantly. It was an irrational situation but I knew because of who those people were, these people had come to kill Charlie and me. In that instant I picked a knife up from the kitchen and er…it was all, it all happened in seconds, and I lunged towards one of the people and then that person and the other person that was there, they ran off."

The second attacker, he told police, was Will Browning. It took thirty-three hours before Sargent was willing to make a statement to police, and only then after having learnt what others had said. He played heavily on the intimidation and threats made by Browning's supporters in the preceding weeks. "It started with phone calls and then we had paint thrown at me house. The car was done on Saturday." Turning to Castle's murder, he claimed that he was first alerted to the presence of others by a bang on the door:

> I called to one of the kids, "Someone at the front." I said,

"Who is it?" They said, "There's someone there," so I opened the door and he [Chris Castle] was standing there with the tools that they'd stole.

He said, "Oh I've got your tools here." So I took the tools. I recognised him but I couldn't put a name to the face, you know. He stepped in and I put the tools down and I looked in.

He said, "Have you got the subscription list still?" I said, "Don't fuck me about, where's the screen printing stuff?" They stole some screen printing stuff off me. I said, "Where the fuck's the rest of my tools, there's only like a hawk and a trowel now."

With saying that, I got clumped to the head and he hit me. I reckoned there was someone behind him but I didn't get a look, you know. I sort of got him, he sort of flew back against the door of the bedroom. I hit him a couple of times then and then he sort of run and whoever else was in the doorway have gone as well and he run and he started screaming. So I just went out of the door after him. As I ran I see someone else there, I believe there's another one run in front of him, so I thought there were three men. I see the third come round the corner and what I thought he was doing was pointing a gun out of the bag.

Reynolds was aware of a number of discrepancies between the two accounts. Sargent said Castle had knocked on the door with a bag of tools; Cross, that the door had been kicked open. While Cross told police that he definitely saw Browning entering the house behind Castle, Sargent was insistent that the mysterious second person was not Browning and he could not even be certain that there was someone else there at all. Cross initially said that he acted in self-defence for fear of his own life but later claimed that he was saving Sargent, who was under attack. "He obviously had some difficulty in justifying why it [the stabbing] was in the back," remembers Reynolds. Why, thought the policeman, if they were acting in self-defence, did Cross attempt to hide the knife in a nearby field? Further doubts arose after the pathologist delivered his report, which found a twenty-two-centimetre-deep wound despite the blade being only twenty centimetres long, indicating the use of considerable force. Reynolds decided that this was not compatible with self-defence, especially as Castle had been wearing a thick leather jacket.

Reynolds's search for the truth was hampered by the reluctance of Browning to give a statement. He had been arrested at Harlow Hospital, minutes after being told that Castle had died. Clearly agitated, he was subsequently charged with aggravated burglary and assault and was held in custody. He was hostile, particularly when told Sargent had been released. However, a breakthrough came four days into the investigation when Mark Atkinson came forward to give a statement that contradicted Sargent's. Rather than Castle appearing unannounced, as Sargent had claimed, Atkinson said he was delivering the tools in an exchange arranged between himself and Sargent.

Armed with Atkinson's statement, Det Supt Reynolds again tried to get the co-operation of Browning. He was initially unsuccessful, especially after Browning was remanded in jail for another seven days. However, the custody sergeant reported that Browning seemed to have a quite different memory of events than that offered by Sargent. Reynolds was helped by Castle's widow, Tanya, who was exasperated by Browning's silence and, through his partner, pleaded with him to change his mind. Some of Castle's closest friends also visited Browning in Chelmsford Prison and pressed him to co-operate. Only that way, they told him, could justice for their friend be properly achieved. Browning's inclination was to inflict his own form of justice on Sargent, but the moral pressure became intense and, following his release on police bail ten days after Castle's death, he made a statement a further ten days later.

He told police that he had accompanied Castle to Sherrards House but decided to stay out of sight while the tools-for-money swap was conducted. He admitted exchanging words with Cross and Sargent but was adamant that it never came to blows. He also flatly denied entering the mobile home. The police were now armed with Browning and Atkinson's statements, the

pathologist's report, and forensics tests which found no evidence
of anyone accompanying Castle into the house. Cross and
Sargent were charged with murder.

★   ★   ★   ★

AFTER THE INITIAL shock, the propaganda war between the two
factions was resumed. C18 – which now meant Browning –
produced a number of bulletins vilifying Sargent and his
supporters. Witness statements were reproduced, documents
highlighted, and key sentences circled, all in a bid to demonise
the Sargent brothers. In *A Chelsea Fan Speaks Out*, the football-
hating Browning wrote anonymously, "As a Chelsea fan I just
want to put the record straight about a fat little mug called
Charlie Sargent, someone has just shown me a letter written by
him claiming that we i.e. Chelsea, etc, support him and we are
with him. For the record this is absolutely bollocks, most of us
have thought for a long time that he was a police informer and
definitely a dodgy cunt." Mick Dunne and Del O'Connor both
appeared in a video attacking Sargent and insisting that C18
would continue stronger and more militant than before.

Steve Sargent co-ordinated the response. In a sombre three-
page letter circulated to supporters ten days after the murder, he
set the stabbing of Chris Castle against the backdrop of months
of badmouthing, threats and acts of violence against the Sargent
household. "Stories are now circulating that Martin & Charlie
ambushed the deceased man, and Browning was down the road
alone unaware of what was going on. I suggest you people make
up your own minds by reading the enclosed press cuttings and
thinking for yourself what a man 'down the road' would be doing
getting remanded for 'aggravated burglary'. Stop listening to the
bullshitters, and stop acting like cowards. I am not of the belief
that these people went to Charlie's for a cup of tea, considering
what they have been mouthing off to the country what they were
going to do to Charlie."

With a realism that was absent from Browning's propaganda,
Sargent went on, "The movement here is now in tatters, no one

can deny this, the NSA will continue in two autonomous regions, West Midlands and London/Essex. It is up to the individuals if they wish to align to either of these autonomous groupings. The very thought of the 'race war' is so laughable when so many in the Movement have shown just what wankers they really are over this matter. Many will now drop out, and good riddance too, those of us in London/Essex NSA will start again from scratch and try and build up a Movement again, to give up and let a small bunch of parasitical would be bullies win would be too much."

This new movement referred to in Sargent's letter was the National Socialist Movement, launched in the summer of 1998 with David Myatt as its leader. "The flag of the NSM is the swastika, and the NSM proudly and unashamedly upholds the political creed of *National-Socialism*," declared its *Aims, Strategies and Tactics*. It aims were "To make known the truth about National-Socialism – its noble idealism, and its principles of honour, loyalty and duty; To encourage Aryans to live in an Aryan way by them striving to uphold the National-Socialist values of honour, loyalty and duty; To encourage the creation of an Aryan homeland as a practical alternative to the decadent anti-Aryan society of our times, so enabling Aryans to live freely and healthily in accord with their natural and healthy customs; To build the foundations for a National Socialist revolution and thus create a National-Socialist State."

It was the same old Myatt nonsense; race hate dressed up in pompous words. Regions, or "active service units", would "further the cause by overt and legal local activities, gain local influence and support; and implement NS ideals at local levels." Or so Myatt dreamt. In reality, the NSM remained little more than a paper organisation, albeit one churning out a considerable amount of rubbish. Past subscribers of C18 publications now received unsolicited NSM material: *The National-Socialist, The Racist Times* and the *Information Bulletin*, while Steve Sargent continued producing *The Order* as well as establishing *The White Dragon*. In November 1997, Tony Williams brought out the first of four issues of *Column 88*, a thick, theoretical journal printed out on his home computer. Lacking street support, the NSM used its publications to reach out to nazis across the country. Within eight months, Steve Sargent had sixty subscribers to *White Dragon*, and the NSM as a whole boasted eighty supporters, though fewer than twenty were fully paid-up members. Its fortunes were not helped by the collapse of those NSA groups which had sided with Sargent during the feud with Browning.

Myatt saw the C18 dispute as a test of his personal code. Replying to the charges levelled against Sargent and Cross, he wrote, "I have ignored, and do ignore, all such allegations and rumours simply because of loyalty and honour. Some time ago I gave my loyalty to certain people and as an honourable National-Socialist I have kept this absolute loyalty. Because of this, I take no heed of what anyone says or writes about the people I am loyal to."

Some time later, Myatt expanded on his theme:

> Anyone who aids the State – our enemy – is a traitor to our Aryan cause, a traitor who has betrayed those fighting for freedom. Even if – as in this case – someone 'on our side' is killed in a scuffle or a fight between two rival Aryan racialist groups or factions, we do not help our common enemy. Thus, we do not give statements to the Police, as we do not give evidence in Court, which might convict fellow Aryan racialists, whatever they have done or alleged to have done. Instead we stay silent – and sort it out among ourselves in an Aryan way. In this case, this should have involved Browning – if he really wanted to act like an Aryan and a real National-Socialist and so champion his friend, Chris Castle, who was killed – challenging Charlie Sargent and/or Martin Cross to a fair fight or a duel. This and this alone would have been real Aryan justice.

Five weeks after the murder, Sargent, Cross and Browning were forced to stand together at the Old Bailey for the long-awaited *Combat 18* magazine trial. They were flanked by burly warders. Sargent and Cross had changed their pleas to guilty, pinning the blame on Browning. There was little the new C18 leader could do but admit the charge at the beginning of the trial. The judge, however, took into account the obvious collusion between Cross and Sargent in attempting to blame Browning. He imprisoned the pair for seventeen months, and Browning for twelve. Browning supporters in the public gallery had massed in anticipation of a clash with Sargent's people but, with the exception of Kelly Cross, there were none to be seen.

A confrontation did appear likely, however, when the two sets of supporters squared up three months later in Harlow Magistrates Court at the murder committal hearing for Cross and Sargent. Supporting the accused were Steve Sargent, Herve Gutoso, Bill Sargent, David Myatt and Phil Curzon. Backing Browning, who was brought in from HMP Brixton to give evidence, were Mark and Liz Atkinson, Mick Dunne, Eric Wallis, Del O'Connor and Matt and Brett Keown, two young skinheads from east London. Abuse began outside the court and continued inside, with O'Connor threatening both Bill Sargent and Myatt. There were repeated interruptions to quell the gallery and Curzon had to be led away by police. The defendants were committed to trial.

C18 soldiered on with Browning in jail. Wells was responsible for much of the anti-Sargent propaganda but it was the brutish O'Connor who emerged as its most powerful figure, taking over the CD operation and becoming the linkman with the Scandinavians. Atkinson tried to perform a similar role in the south but, without the intelligence of Wells or the international contacts of O'Connor, his influence was mainly confined to west London and the Blood and Honour scene, where he continued to run security. Even this was limited, due to a bad-tempered falling out with former friend Rob Gray. The pair had been charged with producing *The Stormer* and Gray, who had only recently come out of jail for violence, believed Atkinson should accept sole responsibility. Wells tried to keep things together in east London as best he could but, without the physical presence of O'Connor or Atkinson, had to rely on Mick Dunne for muscle. A former amateur boxer, Dunne had been a skinhead

Browning (second from left) and the C18 team in Copenhagen on their way to Gothenburg in October 1995 to attack a rival nazi.

Thomas Nakaba, who took the rap for the Danish bombing plot, pictured at the demo in Roskilde in 1995. He first met Browning on this march.

Wigan-based Del O'Connor (left), poses with guns with David Tickle.
Inset: O'Connor in the late 1980s when he led Skrewdriver Security.

Paul 'Floppy' Bennett attacks a female left-wing paperseller in Leeds
city centre in 1994.

The outlandish David Myatt is confronted by a BBC journalist. Myatt's bizarre theories provided some of the ideological basis for C18. © *BBC TV*

American white supremacist Harold Covington exposed on the cover of *Searchlight* magazine in 1992.

Steve Sargent (left), Charlie's younger brother, walks to court with Adam Butler.

A turning point: England fans riot in Dublin in 1995. Charlie Sargent claimed credit for orchestrating the trouble even though he wasn't there. It made C18 a priority target for the British police. © *Empics*

C18 supporters gather to oppose the 1999 Bloody Sunday demonstration in central London. They include, circled from left to right: Warren Glass, Martin Fielding, Matthew Osbury and Andy Frain.

Prominent Loyalist Volunteer Force member Ian Thompson (second from left) at a gig in Wigan in 1998 with Darren Wells (far left) and Will Browning (third from left).

An assortment of C18 and related magazines. The far-right churned out a plethora of extremist scandal sheets.

Mark Atkinson (right) was imprisoned for *The Stormer* mag.

Rob Gray was also jailed for *The Stormer* and fell out with Atkinson.

© David Hoffman

Chris Castle, with his common-law wife Tanya, shortly before he was murdered by Charlie Sargent and Martin Cross in Harlow in 1997.

Sargent's supporters leave a court hearing in Harlow in June 1997

Loyalist killer Steve Irwin (white cap) on a National Front Remembrance Sunday demo in November 2000

Erik Blücher, owner of Ragnarock
Records and a key C18 figure.

Robert Vesterlund, the influencial
editor of *Info-14!*

A Swedish C18 supporter at a nazi
demonstration in Stockholm.

The late Marcel Schilf, who owned
NS88 and NS Records.

Oldham activist Martin Fielding, centre, with northern C18 at a gig in Coventry in 1998. Second from left is pub bouncer David Tickle.

The night of May 26, 2001, and the streets of Oldham burn as hundreds of Asian youths run amok. It was Britain's worst race riot for fifteen years.
© *Press Association*

since his early teens. After a spell as casual, he returned, in boots and braces, to the nazi scene. He was involved in a number of violent incidents, including a fight in Germany which saw him arrested and a clash with a group of Asians in a motorway service station when he threw someone on a hot-plate. Wells and Dunne became inseparable, especially after they set up an East End flat for two German women they were seeing.

Browning, though incarcerated, was never far removed from events. He secured a job in the prison kitchen and used his extra privileges almost exclusively in phonecards. "When he was out it was unbearable, no-one thought it was going to be worse when he was inside, but it was," says one friend of Browning. "Working in the kitchen meant he was up very early and had a cell to himself. He would make ten calls a day, sometimes he would ring Jackie at seven in the evening and say it was his last call, only to spend the next hour ringing us up giving out orders. I just felt sorry for the other inmates who had to endure his endless discussions about Charlie Sargent."

In late August, with Browning due out of prison in a matter of weeks, Thomas Nakaba appeared in a Copenhagen court with his two accomplices, Michael Volder and Nicky Steensgaard. He had been held in solitary for two months and had had no contact with Browning or Wells since his capture. He was at breaking point. Presented with the evidence of the police surveillance, the fingerprints his friends left on the packages, a stash of plastic explosives found in his apartment and the handwritten hitlist of five names he had disposed of in the communal bin, Nakaba finally admitted his part in the bombing plot. He attempted to shift the blame onto Browning, claiming that he had been threatened into sending the packages. "The English kept calling me up to remind me what I needed to do," he testified, before the taped phone conversation with Browning was played to the jury. He did, however, try to save his co-defendants, telling the court that neither man was responsible, but with their fingerprints on the bombs all three were found guilty. Nakaba was sentenced to eight years in prison while Volder and Steensgaard got three years apiece. Little of the case was reported in the British press.

It turned out to be a good fortnight for Browning. Not only had he escaped justice in Denmark, but he was released from Brixton jail. Less fortunate were Atkinson and Wells, who were both convicted within weeks of their leader's homecoming. Atkinson's trial for *The Stormer* received considerable media attention, due largely to the presence of boxer Frank Bruno's mother as a prosecution witness; she had been harassed after her address appeared in the magazine. Computer disks containing previous issues and hundreds of copies of the magazine had been found in the flat Atkinson and Gray shared. Atkinson pleaded guilty but Gray continued to protest his innocence to an unconvinced jury. Judge George Bathurst-Norman took no prisoners in his sentencing: "In thirty-seven years in the law I have never encountered such vile outpourings of hatred and incitement to violence as recorded in these magazines. The purpose was clearly aimed at stirring up racial hatred and violence not only against racial, ethnic and religious minorities and their supporters, but also targeting and naming specific individuals within these sections of our society. It may be that Parliament should look again at the activities of such as you and reconsider whether the maximum sentence is sufficient – because in my view it is not." Atkinson and Gray were imprisoned for twenty-one and seventeen months respectively.

Darren Wells, meanwhile, pleaded guilty before Glasgow magistrates to possession of an offensive weapon and was sentenced to six months imprisonment. He had previous convictions violence and fraud and had been arrested outside the house of a BNP rival armed with a knife.

Given the heat, any sensible person would have kept his head down. Not Browning. Once out of prison, he continued his campaign against the Sargents. One opportunity came in a request from *World In Action* to discuss the murder and possible Security Service involvement. Browning was keen for the true story of Chris Castle to be told but was reluctant to meet the TV journalists, believing that many on the Right would see this as informing. To cover his back, he raised the matter at a C18 meeting in east London. Agreement was secured and he got

Mick Dunne and Wells to act as intermediaries, with Wells eventually appearing on the programme.

Unbeknown to the Browning camp, a dramatic development was unfolding that could not only have influenced the outcome of the murder case but possibly even led to his arrest. In late November, lawyers acting for Martin Cross approached the trial judge asking for the case to be postponed while negotiations with Thomas Nakaba's lawyers took place over his possible testimony in the murder trial. While the judge was reluctant to delay the trial date further, he was notified that Scotland Yard detectives were being dispatched to Copenhagen to take a statement from Nakaba and were prepared to plan the best method for the Dane to appear, be it in person or by video link. Nakaba's willingness to talk to Cross's lawyers was partly fuelled by resentment that he had been imprisoned for something Browning had masterminded. His legal team had also initiated appeal proceedings against his eight-year sentence and encouraged Nakaba to show remorse. This he did in an interview with the Danish tabloid *BT*.

"Of course I regret it today," he said. "My friends – those who weren't national socialists – have distanced themselves from me today. They feel that I am completely mad, and some have advised my girlfriend to leave me after they read about my case in the papers, which portrayed me as a psychopathic thug. I do understand that they find my deeds stupid, but they shouldn't have swallowed all the shit written about me. I don't want visits from others than my girlfriend and our little daughter, my closest family. This is without doubt the worst thing about the situation: that you can't be with the people you love, and this is the main reason I regret. I have been too naïve and have believed in something that can't work out. The goal of the national socialists is actually all right. To create a Denmark for Danes and a Europe for the white race, but you just can't fight the system, the government, the police and so on. This I realise today. We were convinced that we would win one day. It was sheer bullshit. national socialists can't change a thing. This I know today. The only thing I have achieved by being fanatical is ending up in prison."

Nakaba was most bitter towards Browning. "He has co-operated with the police and named me in order to save his skin. The information that the police has can only have come from him and that is the only reason that the police have let him off in this case. In the beginning of my imprisonment I was full of revenge and wanted to kill him, but these feelings have declined some since." Assisting Sargent and Cross was one way to get his own back.

Eventually, Nakaba refused to help either Cross or Sargent, or the English police. Browning did not know about the attempts to have Nakaba testify, but he was told the contents of the *BT* article. He suddenly became concerned about the welfare of Nakaba's girlfriend, who C18 had promised to look after during his absence. Discovering that no-one in the C18 Scandinavian network had made contact with her for months, a frantic Browning ordered Marcel Schilf to send her money and get word to Nakaba that he was not the informer. His swift intervention seemed to placate the Dane, at least temporarily. For Sargent and Cross, Nakaba's change of heart was a bitter blow but there was little they could do.

★   ★   ★   ★

CHELMSFORD CROWN COURT was the venue for the murder trial. Tensions ran high on the opening day and the police put on a show of force which included armed back-up. Browning had issued a three-line whip to his supporters to attend. From the north-west came David Tickle, Del O'Connor's loyal sidekick, and soldier Carl Wilson. Three more came from South Wales. From Yorkshire came Kevin Watmough and Adrian Marsden and from the north-east, Simon Biggs and Dave Draper. The London contingent consisted of Darren Wells, Matthew and Brett Keown and John Henderson; driving the hired van was paratrooper Darren Theron. It was a smaller turnout that Browning hoped for but was sufficient to intimidate the accused, especially as their own supporters stayed away from the opening day. The C18 contingent packed into the small public gallery, only feet from the defendants' box. Beside them were the family of Chris Castle – his widow, who would be present throughout the trial, and his father – and a group of friends, many of whom were former C18 activists, including Phil "The Thug" Edwards. For a brief moment, control was almost lost with the arrival of Sargent and Cross in the dock. The C18 contingent snarled and shouted, while Castle's widow broke down. Sargent exuded an air of smug defiance. "You're going down for the bombs," he mouthed from the dock to Wells.

Proceedings began with the prosecution and defence openings. For the prosecution it was a straightforward case of premeditated murder; for the defence, Cross was defending himself and his friends in the face of a brutal attack. It was clear that the testimony of Browning was going to be vital. So when he stepped into the box, dressed in blue jeans and a blue sweatshirt, there was a tangible air of expectation. Browning told the court how he and Castle had gone to Harlow with the sole intention of returning Sargent's tools, which had been in C18 possession ever since he had left them at the house of Kev Johnson after doing some work on the bathroom. After falling out with the former C18 leader, Johnson refused to hand back the tools directly to Sargent but instead gave them to Atkinson, who had agreed to pass them on. However, after arranging to deliver the tools himself, Atkinson's car broke down, so he allowed Browning to collect them on behalf of Castle, who in turn would bring them to Harlow in exchange for the C18 subscription list and £1,000 that was owed.

"I just went to keep Chris company. I didn't want to see Sargent," Browning told the jury. "It would have been a bad atmosphere if I went to the house."

Browning recounted how, deciding to stay out of sight, he wandered up the main road until screams brought him back to the car park, where he saw Castle. Some distance behind were Sargent and Cross. "Chris was holding his chest but I didn't see any wound," Browning told the jury.

He rested Castle by a gatepost at the entrance to the mobile home park and went to get his friend's car. He came across

Cross brandishing a long knife and Sargent with a crossbow.

"What the fuck have you done?" Browning shouted.

"He's a casualty of war," said Cross.

"Go and get a fucking ambulance or he'll die."

"Fuck him. Let him rot," was Sargent's reply, Browning testified.

Browning told the court that Castle tried to follow him back up the path but collapsed in the mud. Unable to find Castle's car keys, Browning dragged his friend back to the park entrance, where he flagged down a taxi and took him to hospital. It was only then that the extent of Castle's injury became apparent.

Before disputing his testimony, the defence barristers were keen to paint a picture of Browning as a psychopath ready and willing to injure or even kill those he disliked. They implied their clients were justified in fearing for their lives. After getting Browning to admit his three-year sentence in 1989, they repeatedly questioned him about his access to guns.

"Did you have a handgun at the Firkin pub in Mile End last year?"

"No," said Browning.

"Did you turn up in Chelmsford with a gun in your waistband in November, Mr Browning?"

"No."

"Is it not also true that you had a rifle in the boot of your car?"

"No."

"Is it true that when you were arrested, police raided your house and found magazines and books on guns and weapons?"

"No."

"Is it not true that you told Mr Sargent that, 'If you want a war, you'll get a fucking war'?"

"No!"

After lunch, the trial was to reconvene in another courtroom, where a video player had been set up. Browning spent an anxious hour pacing the courthouse, trying to elicit the nature of the video from police, journalists and court officials. He was unsuccessful and entered the courtroom with some trepidation. Had they secured Nakaba's testimony after all? His worries were ill-founded: the court was instead shown extracts from the 1995

World In Action programme when he attacked the camera crew armed with a screwdriver.

Asked if he often carried a screwdriver, a relieved Browning replied dryly, "Deptford is a violence place."

Asked how a screwdriver would defend him, he replied, "Well, unfortunately I don't have a tank, so a screwdriver is better than nothing." It was one of several answers that brought a titter from the gallery.

Browning was quizzed about why he refused to give a statement to police, with the implication that this was because he had something to hide. He said it was C18 policy to give "no comment" replies. The key questioning was over his relationship with Steve Vogel, another crucial prosecution witness, who Browning claimed not to know well. The defence produced phone records showing a total of seven calls made by Browning to Vogel in the week before Vogel made his statement. The C18 leader lamely claimed that Vogel wanted protection because his house was under attack from Sargent supporters and that at no time did they discuss the murder.

Vogel appeared in the witness box the following morning but not before rumours circulated of an altercation in the nearby shopping centre. Nine C18 supporters making their way from the multi-storey car park to the court had come across Sargent's friend Herve Gutoso on his way to work as a chef in a local pub. He was pulled off his bike and attacked by Browning. The entire C18 contingent was arrested, with Browning and Wells being held well into the night. The ramifications for the case were huge, as Gutoso was due to give evidence for the defence. Detectives leading the murder case flitted in and out of the court in a state of near-panic as Sargent sat smugly in the box. The police anger at Browning was nothing to the reception he received back at home from his girlfriend. She accused him of ruining the entire case and threatened to end their relationship.

Vogel's evidence was a blow for the defence. The jury heard how he had been out with ten other C18 activists loyal to Sargent to celebrate Cross's birthday in a pub in Gallywood, Chelmsford, the Saturday before the murder. Much of the night was taken up with talk of the feud, with both Sargent and Cross slating Browning and his group. Sargent told Vogel that he was going to sort this out "physically" and that he would "teach Browning a lesson for thieving money". Cross told Vogel that "Wilf's a cunt, I don't care who the fuck he is. He's a mug." Vogel claimed that Sargent was actively recruiting people in the pub to take on Browning and that he had been asked to make himself available. He told that court that Sargent agreed to use a code when he rang him the following evening, that he would ask him whether he was "up for football", which meant whether he was up for trouble. He claimed Sargent did indeed ring him on the Sunday evening, asking him if he was "up for football" the following morning, but Vogel declined the invitation, using the excuse that he was working. Vogel then testified that the following weekend he went to a pub in Romford where Sargent boasted about the killing of Castle. "He was just a skinhead and he weren't worth a flying fuck," said Vogel, reciting Sargent's words to the court. Unsurprisingly, the defence contested this version of events, claiming it was an account devised in collusion with Browning.

A number of other prosecution witnesses corroborated Browning's story. Taxi driver Clifford Lewis told how he took Browning and Castle to hospital and at no time did either throw anything out of the windows, thus supporting his C18 man's statement that he had no weapon. Geoffrey James told the court how he was walking his parent's dog when he heard "heated and aggressive" voices coming from Sherrards House, but again confirmed that there was no sight of a gun. So did Valerie Hull, who had helped Browning lift Castle into the taxi. Mark Atkinson told the court how his plans to return the tools were aborted when his car broke down, so at seven that Saturday evening he left a message on Sargent's answer phone telling him that Castle would be making the drop. The prosecution produced Atkinson's phone records, undermining Sargent's claim to have had no prior knowledge of the arrangement. Another witness testified that he had seen the altercation following the murder and how Sargent had told him to tell police that Browning had a gun. He then told the court that he "knew there was no gun because if he had a gun he would have used it." This was a telling comment and one the prosecution repeatedly returned to during the trial. The more the defence played up Browning's violence and his access to weapons, the more the jury seemed to believe that he would have used a gun if he had had one available.

The final prosecution witness was Michael John Heath, the pathologist who examined Castle's body. He told the court that Castle died from a single stab wound to the lower left of the back. The knife wound was two centimetres deeper than the actual blade length. That, coupled with Castle's leather jacket and the fact that there was no distortion to the wound, led him to conclude that "severe force was required to cause such an injury". Heath also found that the blade was thrust upwards into the back, consistent with an attack from behind, which contradicted Cross's claim that he thrust the knife in a downwards direction as Castle punched Sargent on the ground.

The defence began its case with Cross claiming that he was not involved in C18, a position already contradicted by Sargent's statement naming him as a member of the NSA council. He admitted he had been friends with Sargent for over twenty years and knew of the feud but insisted Browning was its instigator. "He was going to kill Charlie Sargent," Cross told the court, "he was going to shoot him. He repeated this on dozens and dozens of occasions. There was one incident when Will Browning and Darren Wells came to my flat in Chelmsford. They said they'd been round to Charlie's flat and said they were going to kill him. Browning said Charlie was lucky he wasn't there because they were going to shoot him. Browning then said, 'I'm going to kill that fat bastard, that grass.' It was all common knowledge."

Cross claimed that he was in the kitchen when he heard a commotion, a loud bang and then the children crying. "When I heard the bang I went straight to the door in the hallway. I saw Chris Castle, Will Browning and Charlie Sargent. Charlie was on the floor with Chris Castle over him. I recognised Chris immediately. Browning was standing behind Chris, in between the door. It all happened in a split second. Because of the threats that Browning had been giving, I knew what he was there for.

There was no other reason for him to be there. He was there to kill Charlie and myself. I took a step back and picked up a knife. I went forward towards the door with the knife and stabbed Chris. It was a reaction to their action. I didn't consciously pick up a knife. I froze and then went outside. I saw Will Browning and shouted, 'It's Wilf, he's got a fucking gun.' I thought it was a gun but I didn't see a gun."

Defence barristers produced several witnesses who claimed to have seen Browning with weapons. Herve Gutoso told the court how Browning had smashed his way into his Chelmsford flat but his testimony backfired when he claimed that Browning was scared of Cross. Mark Skyner, from Liverpool, said Browning had threatened to kill Sargent at two skinhead gigs, while Gavin Hockley, a Romford-based C18 supporter, told the court how, returning from a gig in the Midlands, he witnessed Browning hit a man because he was wearing an Anti-Nazi League sticker. He also claimed that Browning carried a crowbar "and I think a hammer" to a gig in Nottingham and said he had seen Browning with a gun at a gathering in the Firkin pub next to Mile End Tube.

The final witness to take the stand was Charlie Sargent. Dressed in a blazer and trousers, with dark-rimmed glasses and shoulder-length hair, he cut a sad and lonely figure. Gone was the arrogance that had accompanied his five-year reign as leader of C18. Gone was the swagger and "up yours" demeanour that he carried towards journalists and the Establishment. Stripped to the bare, Sargent exemplified a loser who sought importance through crude nazi politics. He spoke meekly when quizzed, occasionally stammering. Watching from the public gallery were nine NSM supporters, including the outlandish Myatt, who carried a white glove with which he intended to strike Browning across the face to initiate a duel.

Sargent presented himself as a right-winger committed to a political strategy while Browning wanted terrorism. He even claimed that because of his impending court case for the *Combat 18* magazine, he had already decided to quit the movement. He claimed not to have heard Atkinson's phone message yet proved unable to explain how it had been wiped. He said that Castle had thrown the first punch and he was merely acting in self-defence. However, his talk of landing several good punches on Castle appeared boastful and did little to win the sympathy of the jury. He said that he was aware of another person with Castle but could not recognise who it was. It was only in the car park that he could confirm that he saw Browning. "He was pointing a gun at me, he said that he was going to kill me. I could see this little gun and a bag. I know what I was seeing." Only then, said Sargent, did he realise that Castle had been stabbed.

The jury was sent out shortly before noon on the sixth day of the trial. It was to prove a tense, almost unbearable wait for all concerned. Natalie Durrant and Kelly Cross visited the accused in the cells, while their supporters, numbering as many as fifteen, consumed beer and cocaine in the pub across the road. Friends and police helped Chris Castle's widow as she again broke down with anxiety, while Browning and his mob, now down to eight, remained in the building at the wishes of the police, who were keen to avoid a clash between the rival groups.

At 2.20pm, the jury delivered its verdict on both Cross and Sargent. Guilty. It released a year of tension and anger. Tanya broke down again, screaming abuse at the defendants. Through the cheering C18 camp, Browning's could be seen to well up. The defendants took the decision calmly. Sargent allowed himself one last smirk at the public gallery before they were both taken away.

CHAPTER FIFTEEN

The Search for Mr Orange

MISTER PINK PACED the room. "So who's the rat this time? Mr Blue? Mr Blonde? Joe? It's Joe's show, he set this whole thing up. Maybe set it up to set it up."

"I don't buy it," answered Mr White, shaking his head. "Me and Joe go back a long time. I can tell ya straight up, Joe definitely didn't have anything to do with this."

Mr Pink was not convinced. "Oh, you and Joe go back a long time. I known Joe since I was a kid. But me saying Joe definitely didn't do it is ridiculous. I can say I definitely didn't do it, 'cause I know what I did or didn't do. But I can't definitely say that about anybody else. For all I know, you're the rat."

Mr White looked up. "For all I know, you're the rat."

"Now you're using your head," Pink replied, smiling. "For all we know, he's the rat."

"That kid in there is dying from a fuckin' bullet that I saw him take. So don't be calling him a rat."

"Look asshole, I'm right! Somebody's a fuckin' rat. How many times do I hafta say it before it sinks in your skull."

This scene from the Quentin Tarantino film *Reservoir Dogs* was a fitting analogy to C18 as it descended into accusation and counter-accusation about who was an informer within its ranks. The film was a favourite of Steve Sargent, who decided to codename leading figures in C18 by colour. That there was an informant at the top seemed certain: the question "who?" was what occupied their thoughts. Predictably, the Sargents accused Browning and vice versa.

Questions had first been asked about possible police involvement in the group back in 1995. It seemed incomprehensible that so little had been done to curtail C18 activities despite the severity of many of its attacks. No-one was ever convicted for the Brick Lane assault on the Socialist Workers' Party, nor when C18 supporters ran through the same street smashing windows days before the Millwall election victory. No-one was ever questioned for any of the firebombings and attempted arson attacks in south and east London, nor for the Finborough Arms attack, despite two of the victims being able to identify – from photographs – several of their assailants. Indeed, it was a full two weeks before the police even came to take statements off some of the victims, only to later tell them that the case was "now being handed over to Special Branch". In Halifax, six months later, the police failed to respond to an emergency call when a group of teachers were attacked after they stumbled across an NSA meeting. If they had arrived promptly they would have been able to apprehend the attackers at a pub down the road. When Channel Four's *Dispatches* programme was due to criticise the lack of police action against the nazi thugs behind a nine-month spree of racist violence in West Yorkshire, the authorities responded by arresting three of the main protagonists on the morning of transmission, thus making identification sub-judice, only to release them without charge the following day. Then there were the people targeted by C18 for attack but not warned by police. The authorities did not even inform some of the intended recipients of Nakaba's letter bombs.

While none of this proved a sinister plot by the Security Services – it could simply have shown the lack of interest and low priority given to nazi violence during this period – it certainly gave rise to unease. In the summer of 1995, *Searchlight* mooted the possibility that C18 was either a creation of the state or had been allowed to develop unhindered, either to use as a vehicle through which MI5 could spy on other organisations or to destabilise the right-wing generally through its divisive nature. This is not as preposterous as it may appear. The British Security Services had funded and directed the nazi group Column 88 as a state-sponsored honey trap. Formed in the Sixties by a former Special Forces officer, school master Ian Souter Clarence,

Column 88 exploited an old pals network amongst Royal Marine and other military units. Recruits were pulled in from various far-right groups. It formed the British section of the stay-behind operation Gladio, a NATO-sponsored network of groups to provide resistance in the event of a Soviet invasion or communist revolution. Members of Column 88 were told they were the first line of defence when the Russians invaded and part of their activities would be to eliminate possible collaborators, including trade union leaders and Members of Parliament. Souter Clarence was joined by Leslie Vaughan, the former security officer for Colin Jordan's National Socialist Movement and himself a former Royal Marine. Vaughan carried the rank of captain in the Army Cadets until he was exposed for running paramilitary exercises that matched members of the Territorial Army and Cadets against members of Column 88 in field operations. The Labour Government had denied in Parliament that the group even existed but were forced to back down after the media disclosures. Years later, Souter Clarence was to shelter German nazi terrorists wanted for bombing US bases and Vaughan was exposed in the *Observer* for trying to "fit up" members of a New Age convoy with offers of weapons. Souter Clarence died in disgrace after his liking for very young men was exposed. Vaughan earns his living as an up-market private detective.

The idea that C18 was a front to disrupt the right-wing was endorsed by the BNP, which had suspicions as early as 1995. As BNP support haemorrhaged to the NSA, John Tyndall went on the offensive in a five-page article in his magazine *Spearhead*. He attacked C18 for its assaults on fellow nazis and its call for armed insurrection, "a prescription so crazy in its remoteness from reality that it champions qualify only to be consigned to mental institutions." He also sensed a deeper plot.

> I believe that what we are dealing with today is a strategy employed by the establishment to divide the nationalist movement, and therefore neutralise it, in exactly the same way that it was done in the 1970s. The tactics to some degree differ – in those days they attacked my supporters

> and me for being 'too extreme', while this time we are
> being attacked for being 'not extreme enough' – but the
> end being pursued is identical in all essentials. Meanwhile
> the time-honoured methods of lie, smear and malicious
> rumour are alive and kicking. I know these kind of people,
> and I know their game.

The launch of C18 coincided, he contended, with the rise of the
BNP, and its fallout with the party came shortly after the first
council seat was gained in Millwall. Was this coincidence? For
Tyndall, there was no other way to explain the C18 actions.
It also explained why, up to that time, there had been no
prosecutions for C18 literature, much of it inciting violence,
while he and John Morse had been imprisoned in 1986 for far
less contentious material. Citing the *Combat 18* magazine
specifically, Tyndall concluded, "I can see no logical reason
whatever for this failure to prosecute the C18 people other than
that it suits the establishment to keep C18 in existence. And why
should it do so – other than to enable C18 to be used as a
weapon for damaging, and if possible destroying, the British
National Party."

Tyndall was right in thinking that the authorities were
concerned about the growing influence of the BNP in parts of
London. In the early Nineties, it was the only nazi organisation
systematically monitored by M15, the Security Service that
deals with domestic subversion. MI5 had fifteen informants
within the BNP. Other groups were watched by local Special
Branch officers, though this owed more to local priorities and
sources of information rather than a co-ordinated central
directive. Tyndall did not accuse specific C18 leaders of being
police spies, believing that few were capable of fulfilling such a
role.

> For my knowledge of them I rely on the intellectual content
> of their publications – which beggars description – and the
> personal assessments of some of my friends and colleagues,
> who know them a bit better than I do. From this information

the profile that forms is one of people of very meagre intelligence, albeit equipped with a certain destructively low cunning. It is difficult for me to believe that such people are capable of masterminding such a complex operation as the one in which I suspect they are now engaged. It seems much more likely that they are just small-time gang leaders, class warriors with huge chips on their shoulders, ambitious to build their own little back-street empires and resentful of others who seem to stand in their way. This alone could not account for all of the activities in which they have been involved. Somewhere there has to be a directing brain, much superior to theirs, able to manipulate them to purposes which they would scarcely begin to understand.

Tyndall – whose description of core C18 members was remarkably accurate – thought this man was Harold Covington, long suspected of being a police informant by many American white supremacists. He had presided over the collapse of several organisations and constantly attacked fellow racists, which many thought only served their opponents. In 1979, he played a role in the arrest of several National Socialist Party of America activists after an undercover agent claiming to be a mercenary approached him offering to supply automatic weapons, carry out assassinations for $20,000 a time and hide out nazis with friends in South America. The approach had all the hallmarks of a police undercover operation, but while Covington told the agent he was not interested, he did give him the name of Frank Braswell, another activist. When the agent contacted Braswell, Covington was asked for a reference for the agent, which he duly provided. Over the ensuing months agent Michael Swain, of the Bureau of Alcohol, Firearms and Tobacco, gathered evidence of a plot to avenge the Greensboro trial (see Chapter Three). Six of Covington's closest supporters were subsequently jailed. Five days before they were sentenced, Covington fled the country. The FBI claimed to be hunting him but the big man always seemed one step ahead, first going to

South Africa, then Canada before returning to the U.S.

Suspicion was aroused by Covington's arrival in Britain in 1991. He told Steve Sargent and John Cato that he was studying at a local further education college. Quite why a middle-aged American, who by his own admission had been previously working for $4 a hour in North Carolina, flew into London to study for a City and Guilds qualification remains a mystery. Once in the UK, he sought contacts and information from groups across Europe but was never keen to meet anyone, preferring to operate behind a Post Office box and the telephone. His arrival coincided with an upsurge in racist violence across Europe, particularly in Germany, where nazis were unleashing a wave of terror following reunification, and in Sweden, where the White Aryan Resistance was trying to replicate The Order.

While there are many justified suspicions about Harold Covington, it seems impossible for him to have conducted the operation Tyndall alleged. He did have a considerable influence on the Sargent brothers at the start of C18 but there was no evidence that he contributed to the fallout with the BNP. What influence he did have seemed to be on the wane at the time the split emerged. Certainly by 1995, when the NSA was attracting activists, Covington's role was negligible. The C18 mole had to be closer to home.

Tyndall said was not in a position to name names but others in the BNP were less constrained. The anonymous author of the *Blue Book* wrote:

> Let's face it, these days, the BNP is Nationalism. So why should anyone want to harm the BNP? The answer is no one – apart from the enemies of Nationalism. Jews, niggers, reds and the establishment and their paid tools. Everyone knows C18 began from stewarding meetings for the BNP and Irving and involved most of the London BNP stewarding group. At around this time, C18 was formed and Hitchcock was often to be heard boasting how through security, C18 would control the BNP and get the BNP to do what they they wanted. When that failed, Charlie and

Steve Sargent and Gary Hitchcock decided to wreck the
BNP from the outside.

While the author accepted that Steve and Charlie Sargent could
be "just poisonous shit-stirrers and completely fucking stupid",
he concluded that Hitchcock was a state agent, who "more or
less blew his cover back in January 1994" when he demanded to
know the venue for a Blood and Honour concert in East London;
hours later it had been cancelled by the police. His absence from
the first *World In Action* documentary in 1993 was put down to
the Establishment sacrificing Sargent to protect Hitchcock, a
more important agent. With Hitchcock definitely a State agent,
and the Sargent brothers likely contenders, the author instructed
readers to boycott C18. "Having an MI5 agent right at the top of
C18 is more than just embarrassing, it's a disaster. The whole of
C18 is compromised."

In April 1998, *World In Action* suggested another possible
reason behind Security Service interest in C18: its links to the
Loyalist paramilitaries. The exposure of UDA intelligence officer
Brian Nelson as a British police spy, coupled with the revelation
by ITV's *The Cook Report* that some Loyalist leaders were
racketeering, led to a younger and more militant leadership
emerging. The inner council, which had run the UDA by
committee, was disbanded and the organisation was broken
down into regional brigades. While the pre-1990 UDA had been
heavily infiltrated by the security forces, the new leadership was
more shadowy and far more hostile to British intentions in the
province, at a time when the IRA was secretly in peace discussions
with Westminster. Pressure increased on the intelligence services
to gather new sources of information, especially as Loyalist
violence grew in the early 1990s. Special Branch began to take a
greater interest in the UDA on the mainland, with its role in
collecting money and arms and talk of targeting opponents in
London and in the Irish community in England.

Here C18 provided the authorities with a unique opportunity,
given its closeness to the UDA. There were also those linked to
C18 who owed their allegiances to the rival Loyalist group, the

Ulster Volunteer Force. The UVF's mainland bombmaker and his girlfriend were both known to operate in the C18 orbit: she attended the 1995 Apprentice Boys of Derry march in London in its company when C18 was providing security.

Starting in 1995, there seemed to be a more determined effort on the part of the police to curtail the excesses of C18. With certain exceptions, the group's ability to operate without the fear of legal repercussions was drastically reduced. The police also increased their intelligence on the group, something lacking in its early days. When Browning was raided in relation to *Combat 18*, police missed vital DAT tapes which would have clearly tied him in with the production of specific CDs. They returned a few days later to collect them, obviously having been told by a source or through a telephone tap that the DATs remained in his house.

It was the events surrounding the Danish bombing campaign that proved there was a mole in C18. British police were able to alert their Danish counterparts. Attempts were then made to camouflage the source of the information, with the press initially being told that it was received through an "intelligence clearing house in Germany". The truth eventually emerged that it emanated from London. During Nakaba's trial, the court heard how British police had contacted the Danes three days before the devices were dispatched with the message that "C18 are entering their bombing phase". Simultaneously, the British police notified the Post Office to watch out for explosive devices being sent to nazis hidden in video cassettes. The *Opflash*, a Post Office security warning, was circulated to sorting offices around the country dated January 15, two days before Nakaba built and posted his packages.

A few months later the Metropolitan Police Special Branch, which has the primary task of monitoring the extreme-right in the capital, took credit for the operation in a quarterly assessment of political extremism distributed to police forces around the country. However, despite the success of the operation and the jailing of three C18 supporters, the British authorities were keen to play down Special Branch involvement. Considering how they have basked in the publicity following other foiled terrorist campaigns, this reticence was surprising. It added to the suspicion that they were keen to protect a secret source.

During the civil war which engulfed C18 in 1997, both sides accused the other of working for the police. Such accusations are customary in internal nazi disputes, driven as they are by the paranoia, inflated self-importance and persecution complexes so prevalent throughout the Right. But this time the evidence did suggest that information was leaking out of the higher levels of C18.

World in Action named the leak as deposed leader Charlie Sargent. It alleged that he had been recruited some time after the inception of C18 primarily to provide information to the Security Services on the Loyalist paramilitaries. In the course of researching the programme, its investigators uncovered considerable evidence to support the theory that he was an informer and was the source of police information about the Danish bomb plan. While Browning's side did tell Sargent the basic outlines of the plan during the meeting at Mile End, not everything he was told was correct. Browning told Sargent that he had brought in the explosives from Poland. When the *Daily Mail* covered the Nakaba trial, it reported, "In October last year he [Browning] and a third member of Combat 18 travelled to Poland and handed explosives to Nakaba." When *World in Action* spoke to Arne Stevens, the Deputy Commissioner of Copenhagen Police, he too stated the explosives had been brought in from Poland. Yet it was not true. The explosives had come from Scandinavia.

Nakaba was arrested in the early hours of Saturday, January 18. The news broke in England during the late morning. However, it was of no surprise to Steve Cartwright, the editor of the Scottish magazine *Highlander*, who had fallen out with C18 during the split in Blood and Honour in 1996. Three days earlier, he had been contacted by Strathclyde Police and told that a suspect video package addressed to him had been intercepted by police but had turned out to be a false alarm, even though the sorting office was sealed off and bomb disposal were experts called in to carry out a controlled explosion. Within three hours of intercepting the suspicious package in Glasgow, the Post Office issued its *Opflash* warning to all sorting offices to look out for suspect packages emanating from Sweden or Denmark. It gave a list of possible targets, none of whom were eventually to receive a bomb. Cartwright had actually been warned of a potential bomb a few weeks before. "Sometime in mid-December, through a third party, Charlie Sargent informed me that I was to watch my mail coming from Denmark or Sweden," Cartwright said. Sargent thought that Cartwright was an intended target; so did the *Opflash*.

It was also surprising that Sargent did not make more of the Danish bombs in his murder trial. It remains a mystery why the devices were only referred to in his barrister's summing up, and then only in a passing reference to Sargent being a target, which he was not. Surely any reference to the bombings would have added to the impression that Browning was a dangerous psychopath, a man whom Sargent and Cross were right to fear? When *World In Action* asked a police officer involved in the case why there was so little mention of Denmark, he replied, "It would have alluded to his other role you have inferred to." This was a reference to the journalist's belief that Sargent was an informer.

It was also strange that Steve Sargent, Maxine Durrant and Kelly Cross were not called as witnesses for the defence. Whilst it is true that calling Steve Sargent would have brought up his letter to Kevin Watmough – in which he wrote, "By this week's end, all going well, Beast & Co will be out of the game, the long knives are out!" – Steve could surely have thrown more light on Browning's harassment of the Sargent family. Maxine Durrant could have described how her house and car were attacked and her children menaced by phone calls. Her testimony would surely have been far more powerful than Charlie, Cross and Gutoso relaying these events. Instead the jury had little sympathy for what seemed to be two gangs of thugs.

It also emerged during the trial that armed police were mobilised on two occasions in Harlow in the weeks leading up to the murder, both times to prevent Browning and his friends from reaching Durrant's mobile home. If, in either case, those under attack had alerted the police, this would have been logged, and could have been used in the trial. However, only the verbal testimony of Sargent, Cross and Gutoso was presented, with no supporting call logs. There is the suspicion that police were operating from intelligence received as opposed to an emergency call from the public. Sargent's legal team seemed reluctant to subpoena police officers and intelligence to support his claims against Browning, something which surely could have had an important influence on the jury. Was Sargent unwilling to go down that road because of what else might have been revealed?

The evidence points to at least one informer among the residents of 8 Cornflower Drive, Chelmsford – then the home of the Sargent brothers and Gutoso. If the information about the threats to the Sargents had come from a source in the Browning camp, the police would have been morally bound to inform the Sargents. After all, such a warning was given to Mick Dunne shortly after Castle's death, when police learnt that some Romford nazis were planning to attack his house. If the police had warned the Sargents, this should have been a major issue in the trial. That it did not come up during the court case suggests that such a warning was not given, indicating either police irresponsibility or that the information had come from the Sargent camp in the first place.

When Browning's lawyer arrived at Harlow police station shortly after his arrest, an Essex detective told her that they had intelligence to support the theory that her client had been trying to attack Sargent. Det Supt Reynolds later made reference to this "intelligence" in his interview with *World in Action*, though he refused to elaborate. Browning's lawyer was also told that there was intelligence against her client in relation to the conspiracy allegation, but the policeman refused to say more than "there was intelligence and Special Branch involvement". A tape of the conversation was replayed on the television programme. At an early court hearing on behalf of Browning, the lawyer, from the large City firm Kingsley Napley, asked the prosecution for details of the "intelligence on her client" and of Special Branch's involvement with Charlie Sargent. An embarrassed prosecutor, after conferring with the police and Crown Prosecution Service, refused this request point-blank. The Sargent camp could hardly claim they were unaware of the existence of this intelligence. Browning had made reference to it in several *C18 Information Bulletins* that he circulated against Sargent before and after the trial. But again, the information was not subpoenaed or utilised in the court case.

During a meeting with *World In Action* shortly after the conclusion of the murder trial, an Essex police officer confirmed that Special Branch officers had been to see Charlie Sargent after his arrest on the day of Castle's murder. While the officer refused to elaborate, it was yet another indication of an unspecified, clandestine operation. The Metropolitan Police refused to confirm or deny the allegations, a standard policy relating to informants.

Sargent always denied being an informer. However, he did admit to once being approached to work for the police. In the days following Castle's death – but before he was charged – Sargent told a leading member of Blood and Honour that he had once been offered £500 a week by the police to inform on C18. He denied accepting the offer. While there is no reason to believe that Sargent would have made up the story – as even admitting he had been approached would play into the hands of his detractors – it is questionable whether he would have refused such an offer. He was, after all, a man with no job who had happily boasted of taking money off the *Sunday Express* for lying about the Dublin football riots and also sold a picture of former flatmate Ian Stuart Donaldson to *The Sun* for £500. It had also been proven that he stole £3,000 off a Dutch nazi after claiming that a payment for CDs had never arrived. The Dutchman later reproduced a Post Office form, signed by Sargent, acknowledging receipt of the money.

The revelation that Sargent was an informant throws an interesting light on his activities in the nine months preceding his arrest for murder. He was one of the most vociferous critics of some within the music scene at home and abroad and did much to antagonise the group's opponents. Much of this was done through the production of childishly abusive publications produced in co-operation with his brother and the French nazi staying with them in Chelmsford, raising the possibility that Charlie was not alone in passing information to the police. Along with spoof copies of *Resistance* and *WOTAN*, the three men produced *Focus Eighteen*, *Zigger Zigger* and *The Melbourne Citizen*. All of these widened and personalised the split within the music scene.

Some of the abuse came in personal letters. In late 1996, with the music rivalry becoming intense, a letter sent to Billy Bartlett did much to turn him against C18. Browning had heard that Bartlett wanted to split off and form his own CD label. He wrote to him asking him to reconsider, making the point that he did not want to fall out over the issue. It was only when Browning received a reply from Bartlett complaining about threats that the C18 man realised something was wrong. Bartlett, it appeared, had received a second typed letter from London, carrying the name Will Browning, making threats against his family if he failed to show open support for C18. The letter, coupled with the attack on Greg Remers in Bartlett's flat, persuaded him to throw his support behind the Squadron/ English Rose camp. Browning denied sending the letter. A clue to the author's true identity came a few months later when Charlie and Steve Sargent drove to Birmingham to address an NSA meeting about the split with Browning. On arrival, Steve Sargent asked where he could find a postbox, later slipping out of the room to post some letters. The following day Billy Bartlett received a written death threat from the "inner council of Kaotica – Birmingham KKK", a group attached to the NSA. It carried a Birmingham postmark, dated the day the Sargents were in the city.

Steve Sargent was to write two further letters in the name of Will Browning. The first, written sometime before Castle's murder, was addressed to Pinnochio, the nickname of a leading member of Berlin Blood and Honour. In Sargent's unmistakable handwriting, it claimed that C18 was going to hit the German "on his Jewish nose". A second threatening letter, again supposedly signed by Browning, was set to Thorsten Heise,

Browning's close friend in Germany, after Castle's death. Again it was in Steve Sargent's hand.

It was also suspicious that neither of the Sargents was prosecuted for *Scorpion* magazine, produced just before Christmas 1996. At a time when the police were trying everything to close down C18, the magazine was overlooked. Yet it was clearly actionable: not only did it carry the usual death threats against opponents, but also bomb-making instructions, information about credit card fraud and advice about chemical weapons. This contrasted sharply with the treatment of Darren Wells for possession of a small knife: in the summer of 1997 he was apprehended in east London, handcuffed, and flown to Glasgow to be charged.

Charlie Sargent often encouraged others to use violence in the internal dispute. In 1996, he tried to persuade Del O'Connor and David Tickle to throw a home-made grenade through the window of English Rose singer Steve Jones. When they refused, he turned to the organisers of the Phoenix Society in the West Midlands with the same request, but they too turned him down. In another strange request, Charlie asked O'Connor to supply fifty grenades and said he wanted him to collect them from a motorway service station. While a few were delivered – though what happened to them remains a mystery – O'Connor became concerned and pulled out of the deal.

In Will Browning, Sargent at first had a willing and gullible enforcer. "Browning wasn't difficult to wind up," Darren Wells told *World in Action*, "and Sargent did it repeatedly. He would go on and on about someone, often telling lies about what they were supposed to have said or done, knowing full well that Browning would resort to violence against them. Sargent was a very manipulative person. He was at the heart of virtually all of the disputes within the music scene and all this did great damage to C18. The question remains, what was his motive for doing all this?"

There seems little doubt that Sargent was, at the very least, passing information over to the police in the months leading up to Castle's murder. He was a man out for himself, and himself only. Perhaps it was the lure of money or perhaps it was a hedge to escape prison. When he set up the murder of Castle, he may well have hoped to receive police protection and escape justice. If so, he was wrong. Special Branch visited him shortly after his arrest, but there was little even they could, or would, do to help him directly. Even so, there were obvious tensions between Special Branch and the Essex police leading the murder enquiry. One officer told Castle's widow how Special Branch were constantly looking over the case.

Unable to escape a murder charge, Sargent pinned his hopes on persuading Nakaba to testify to Browning's part in the bombing plot. It looked initially as though the Dane was willing to cooperate, which could have not only seen Sargent and Cross walk free but also led to Browning's own arrest. Nakaba contemplated testifying because he initially believed Browning had set him up. However in a letter to the new C18 leader some months later, he explained his reasons further. Nakaba claimed that during his time in solitary confinement, Danish police had presented him with statements that they claimed had been made by Browning. With all mail being withheld, Nakaba believed that the silence from C18 in England was proof that he had been set up. He also added that during negotiations with the lawyer representing Martin Cross, British police tried to get a statement from him implicating Browning for the bombing campaign. Nakaba ended his letter by apologising for thinking the worst of his friend.

Charlie Sargent bitterly denied the *World In Action* allegations and lodged a complaint with Broadcasting Complaints Commission. After a thorough investigation, in which the journalists presenting their information before the Commission, including signed statements that had not been shown on TV, the complaint was rejected.

There was an interesting footnote to the allegations. The Sargents' key international supporter aside from Harold Covington was the German nazi Carsten Sczcepanski. In the autumn of 2000, Sczcepanski admitted to being a police informer, having been recruited by the internal security service when on remand for the attempted murder of a Nigerian immigrant. During the C18 split, Sczcepanski, codenamed Piato, distributed pro-Sargent material amongst German nazis. He was later to form the National Revolutionary Cells, a proto-terrorist group that openly advocated violence.

CHAPTER SIXTEEN

The War Spreads North

"THESE BOMBS ARE good for business," Marcel Schilf told Will Browning in the wake of Thomas Nakaba's arrest. "The C18 tee-shirts are going like hot cakes." While Browning and Darren Wells were expecting to be arrested at any time, Schilf was exploiting the situation to the full. A hastily-arranged batch of C18 merchandise was rushed through production and snapped up on the streets. The attempted parcel bombing, however amateurish, had captivated Scandinavian nazis, assisted by the propaganda machine that Schilf had built up over the preceding three years. Nakaba was elevated to the hero status reserved for a prisoner of war, and Scandinavian C18, under Schilf's guiding control, flourished.

Schilf had formed a close relationship with Browning in 1995, when the two men began collaborating through their respective music companies. By the time Browning attended the Hess march at Roskilde, Schilf was identifying himself with C18. He supplied information and photographs of Danish anti-racists to an international version of the *Combat 18* magazine. He was a doer, and in C18 he saw a group that was prepared to carry out what he had long preached and done. The respect and trust was mutual. It was from Schilf that Browning obtained the gun with which he hoped to persuade Nakaba to join him in killing Pajen. It was with Schilf that Browning collected plastic explosives and brought them into Denmark. It was to Schilf that Browning handed over ISD Records when he faced prison for *Combat 18*.

Schilf was assisted in his political work by Erik Blücher, a veteran nazi of Norwegian descent. The two men could not have been more different. Blücher was in his forties, an intellectual, tall and balding. Schilf was young, a skinhead, very thin and a street activist. Yet both shared an unwavering commitment to nazism. Blücher emerged as leader of the militant Norwegian Front in the Seventies but was forced to dissolve the group following a much publicised bomb attack on a trade union May Day parade in Oslo. He moved to England in 1982, where he took up residence in Brighton with the printer Anthony Hancock and became the international liaison officer for the League of Saint George. His stay was to be short-lived: within a year he was deported. By the late Eighties, he had moved to Helsingborg, in southern Sweden, where he changed his name to Erik Nilsen and set up a string of mail order businesses selling nazi videos, books and CDs. Another enterprise was Ragnarock Records which, typically, he got others to front. Despite his attempts to disguise his involvement, he was prosecuted for producing racist music through Ragnarock in 1996.

Blücher liked to stay in the shadows. He knew of the Nakaba bomb plot, having met with Browning and Schilf during the Englishman's trip to Sweden in October 1996, yet took no active part in its implementation. Six months later, he walked in on Niclas Lofdahl preparing a bomb in a flat belonging to his girlfriend, an employee of Ragnarock Records. When Lofdahl explained what he was doing, Blücher walked out of the room, saying that he did not want to be involved. Yet he was not averse to being in the company of terrorists: he had arrived at the flat with an Austrian nazi who was on the run for his part in a series of letter bombs sent to anti-racists and politicians in Vienna in 1994.

Blücher's organisational skills complemented Schilf's activism. "He's been around for thirty years," says Stieg Larsson of the anti-fascist organisation Expo. "He's been an activist since his early teens. He's been building legal parties, companies, informal structures and he has handled European relations for the League of Saint George. He is a leader of forces without any force to lead and this has been his problem. He hasn't had a party under him in the last fifteen years, not since he left Norway in the early 1980s. On one hand Blücher is making a living out of his activities, selling mail order, Second World War memorabilia, etcetera. On the other hand he is a very political leader. He's not an idiot, he is well-educated and he has a distinctive political ideology of wanting to build a white Aryan homeland in the north. Even way back in the Seventies, he was with the most extreme circles that were pro-terrorist. That goes back to Norway where his sidekick got arrested for bombing a mosque in Oslo. When he came to Sweden in 1983 he put out a magazine, called *Nordic Order*, where he described the skinhead movement which was just developing in Scandinavia at the time as a 'pro-Nordic army' and then went on to say that although they were unruly and undisciplined, they were the Aryan warriors of the future. So already he was promoting paramilitary, para-illegal activities on the streets, and he was the only one who was really promoting skinheads as a vehicle for the revolution back in those days."

In a statement on his Blood and Honour website, Blücher called for armed struggle by a so-called "international white resistance", whose role model, he declared, should be the Waffen-SS. "The concept of the Waffen-SS contains all those principles, together with the true spirit of our conviction in its purest form, from which we must draw our inspiration to organise a new legion of Aryan gladiators." The article, he noted, was for those who "want to act rather than talk". He named ZOG as the number one target for attack. The components of ZOG – the police, state employees, politicians, journalists and judges – would be "made to pay heavily for their work". He concluded, "The time for chat is over. We have reached the stage of moving beyond inactivity…we have to leave our writing desks and destroy the multikulti [sic], multicriminal ZOG inferno."

Browning was able to tap into Schilf's existing militant network in Sweden, which included the Aryan Brotherhood, a prison organisation that brought together a mixture of criminals and nazis. While not overtly political, it was very strong inside the prison network and was closely linked to The Brotherhood, a Hells Angels biker federation considered by many to be the most dangerous criminal group in Sweden. The leader of The Brotherhood is believed to be a strong nazi supporter and a close personal friend of several in the Schilf/Blücher network. Within its ranks, the Aryan Brotherhood included some of the most ferocious racists in the country.

It was led by Niclas Lofdahl, who was first arrested at the age of thirteen. In 1995, he was caught for burgling the offices of an anti-racist organisation in Gothenburg and in the same year for stabbing a man. Four months after Nakaba's arrest – and while on day-release from prison – Lofdahl sent a bomb to the Swedish Justice Minister with a letter demanding the release of two jailed members of the Aryan Brotherhood. The back of the envelope carried the name of Combat 18. Other Aryan Brotherhood supporters include Goran Gullvang and Daniel Karlsson: in 1990 the two men were convicted for vandalising a church and then, in August of that year, stabbed a gay man sixty times with a bayonet. Despite being found guilty of murder, they received sentences of only three-and-a-half and four years respectively. Karlsson was later arrested for another murder of a gay man. He admitted being present when the man was killed but a court acquitted him of murder. Another Aryan Brotherhood supporter was a nineteen-year-old nazi who was part of a four-strong group who tortured to death a fourteen-year-old boy in 1995. Lofdahl admitted to the close connections between the group and Blücher and in 1997 wrote a message of support to C18 that was reproduced in *Strikeforce* magazine.

Also connected to Schilf was the newsletter *Info-14!* It was similar to *Redwatch*, carrying information on its political opponents, and was part of a wider anti-antifa (anti-anti-fascist) campaign that took in Britain, Denmark and Germany. *Info-14!* was edited by Robert Vesterlund, who began his political career as a young skinhead in the Swedish Democrats. Like many of the others within this orbit, a period of steroid-taking built Vesterlund up and coincided with his move into more extreme politics. Much of the early content of *Info-14!* supported the harassment of *Searchlight*'s sister publication in Sweden, *Expo*. The magazine's printers and shop owners who sold it were targeted.

With C18 deeply embroiled in its dispute with Nordland, it

was not long before Schilf and Blücher became involved. In 1996, Nordland demanded that NS88 break links with C18 over its continuing mistreatment of Paul Burnley and threats towards people such as Pajen. When Schilf refused, Nordland turned to Blücher's Ragnarock Records with the same request. It was a ludicrous demand, as Blücher and Schilf were in business together, and was rejected. The dispute owed more to the domination of the Scandinavian music scene than to the Browning/Burnley split: Blücher and Schilf accusing Nordland of trying to monopolise the scene. Bands who failed to produce their music through Nordland faced negative reviews in its magazine, if they achieved any attention at all.

Schilf and Blücher saw Nordland as nothing more than a money-making venture. "A through and through capitalist outfit disguised as a 'national revolutionary magazine of White Power and Unity'," wrote Blücher in a publication dedicated to attacking "Nerdland", as he called it. "The conflict between Resistance/ Nordland and Blood and Honour/Ragnarock is not purely about money as the media wants to present it. It's about a political outlook, it is about which way the Movement is heading. Do we really want to end up as disco-warriors surrounded by pop-stars and groupies who believe that our leaders should be pop-stars and our ideology pop-lyrics?"

As in Britain, the feud occasionally descended into violence, with both sides attacking key players in the opposing group. At one concert, Vesterlund was attacked by a Gothenburg skinhead wielding an iron bar. In another incident, the Nordland-aligned Midgaard bookstore in Gothenburg was firebombed. The volatile Niclas Lofdahl was at the forefront. He had worked in Pajen's shop before the two fell out over claims that the Nordland man insulted his girlfriend. This personal dispute was carried over into the bigger C18/Nordland political clash. In 1997, Lofdahl sent a letter bomb to Pajen. It exploded in the sorting office before it reached its target. Pajen later told journalists that Lofdahl rang him from prison to say how sorry he was that the device never arrived.

The war with Nordland coincided with the arrival of Del

O'Connor in Scandinavia. He had been dispatched by Browning to maintain the links with NS88 in the spring and summer of 1997 and quickly forged a close friendship with Schilf, splitting his time between Helsingborg and Gothenburg. O'Connor was to leave a lasting mark on the Swedish nazi scene.

He set about publicising C18 and trying to establish local groups. Most of his time was spent in Sweden but he also took advantage of Schilf and Blücher's network to link up with like-minded people in Denmark and Norway. He was helped when he began a relationship with a Norwegian skingirl who had previously been a Satanist and close comrade of "Count" Vikernes, who masterminded a series of church burnings in Norway in the mid-Nineties. However, it was in Sweden that he most made his mark. "Many Swedish nazis were impressed by O'Connor" says journalist Stieg Larsson. "He came here and began fighting with people. He headbutted people; he stabbed people. He attacked their opponents in a way that many local nazis had not done before." In Helsingborg he left an anti-fascist unconscious after repeatedly hitting him with a knuckle-duster.

O'Connor revelled in the violence, though he was to fall foul of the law on several occasions. In Gothenburg, he openly challenged Pajen's close supporters to fights, which they refused, and on one occasion even got word that to Pajen that he planned to kill him. On May 17, he was arrested at Oslo central station after hitting an anti-racist with an ashtray following a political clash on Norway's National Day. O'Connor was released without charge, but a short time later was arrested in Helsingborg for butting a bar doorman; this time was held on remand for two weeks. When the case came to court, both the doorman and his manager had changed their statements and were unable to identify O'Connor. It seemed that in the intervening period a group of Swedish nazis had visited both men and threatened retribution against them and the bar if they testified. O'Connor celebrated his release in Helsingor, in northern Denmark, a couple of nights later in the company of Mick Dunne, who had made the journey over from Britain. The evening descended into another brawl as a group of twenty nazis battled with about ten locals in a bar.

O'Connor was one of several arrested but again was released the following morning as the police had insufficient evidence to charge him.

Browning, however, was increasingly annoyed at O'Connor's sojourn in Scandinavia and demanded he return to Britain to take charge of C18 affairs during his impending incarceration for *Combat 18*. He needed a reliable henchman to handle the growing dissent within the music scene and demoralisation within C18 ranks, and was fed up with O'Connor's romantic gallivanting overseas. When O'Connor's relationship with the Norwegian girl had ended, he agreed to return to England for good; but with his personal effects still in Gothenburg, needed one more trip to collect them. He had been in Sweden for only a couple of nights when he was again in trouble, this time for fighting with anti-nazis in the town square in Helsingborg. The authorities were not prepared to risk any further witness intimidation and kept him in solitary confinement for the four months he spent on remand. When the case came to court, he was found guilty and sentenced to three months imprisonment, but as he had already been on remand for longer, he was instantly released. He was also banned from re-entering Sweden for five years. During the trial, O'Connor had been made to read out a section of his Interpol file which stated, "O'Connor is extremely violent and is known to use a weapon."

The profile of C18 in Scandinavia was substantially enhanced by O'Connor's extraordinary few months in the region. His unrelenting aggression proved an inspiration to many Swedish nazis in the same way that Nakaba had been impressed by Browning going berserk at the Roskilde march in 1995. Evidence of this was clearly shown in *Kriegsberichter*, a nazi video magazine produced by a Finnish nazi who lived with Schilf. It was littered with pro-C18 references, interviews and clips. O'Connor appeared on the video sporting a balaclava and brandishing a handgun. The respect for C18, and O'Connor in particular, was evidenced by those attending his court case. Alongside Marcel Schilf and Erik Blücher were leading members of Scandinavian Blood and Honour, the National Socialist Front (then Sweden's leading nazi group) and the Aryan Brotherhood.

Despite the imprisonment of O'Connor and Lofdahl, their allies Blücher and Schilf emerged victorious in the battle with Nordland. They had a movement of activists, organised around the Blood and Honour network and the National Socialist Front (NSF), while Nordland had little organised support outside its publication and merchandising operation. They also benefited from small but regular gigs, as opposed to Nordland's infrequent, but large, events. Even in those areas where Nordland had been strong, principally the Stockholm and Gothenburg skinhead scenes, support was on the wane, as a combination of personal disputes and political splits broke up its network. Nordland's reputation was further hit by the arrest of 314 skinheads at one of its concerts in January 1998, headlined by the U.S. band Max Resist. This was followed by the disruption of two further gigs in February and March, leading many of its supporters to look elsewhere for concerts. These were found in the Scandinavian Blood and Honour scene, which was growing and increasing in militancy. Although many of its concerts were considerably smaller than those hosted by Nordland at its peak in the mid-1990s, they combined music and politics in a way that was absent from Nordland events.

Free from the debilitating feud with Nordland, Schilf and Blücher set about building their musical and political operations. In early 1997, their NSF accepted an invitation to visit the headquarters of the Danish National Socialist Movement (DNSB), led by Jonni Hansen. A short time after, NSF "propaganda minister" Bjorn Bjorkqvist attended a DNSB summer solstice party along with Norwegian and German nazis. The NSF also opened a dialogue with Erik Rune Hansen, the leader of the Norwegian National Socialist Movement (NNSB). The culmination of these links was a dinner hosted by the DNSB in late 1997, when an agreement on future cooperation was reached between the Danish, Swedish and Norwegian national socialist parties and the Scandinavian Blood and Honour network. This unholy alliance finally saw Blücher emerge from the shadows as a public figure, though not without a cost: an internal NSF video, obtained by the Swedish anti-fascist magazine *Expo*, showed him giving a pro-nazi speech followed by a stiff-arm salute. This destroyed any respectability he had left, especially in Norway, where the video was aired on national television. It also forced Blücher to be far more open about his nazism.

Not content with this historic Scandinavian pact, Blücher and Schilf were expanding Blood and Honour into Eastern Europe. Units aligned to them appeared in Poland, the Ukraine, Slovakia, Hungary and Serbia, with news, gig reports and interviews from these countries appearing in the numerous publications the two men put out. Blücher also took C18 into these countries. In spring 1999, a Slovakian C18 unit was formed, and produced a magazine similar in name and design to Browning's *Strikeforce*.

Blücher called more and more for direct action. In the *B&H Scandinavian Newsletter*, he outlined how the police had tried to suppress nazi activity and so had become legitimate targets:

> One fine day we will deal with the cowards and weaklings who let ZOG destroy our land without raising a fat finger. In the meantime we should mentally prepare ourselves for the coming onslaught of ZOG's zombies in blue. If they think it will be an easy match, they are dangerously mistaken. If we are not given the opportunity of sharing the democratic rights of the ZOG-sanctioned political parties; if we are driven underground, ZOG will experience a tide of resistance, causing havoc, civil unrest, violence and counter-terror. Zombies are by nature mindless and their shady string-pullers cowards. When the strings that control these ugly creatures are cut off, and their masters are confronted with the awesome power of Aryan wealth, they'll collapse like the dead-mind tools they really are."

A few months later, he issued a "last warning" to the "ZOG Government" to lay off the right-wing; an ominous portent of what was to come.

It was impossible to divorce Blücher and Schilf's venom at the Swedish Government from their own personal situation. Blücher was kept busy in the courts for his involvement in Ragnarock Records, while Schilf was ordered out of his apartment by the landlord after exposure by anti-fascists. He was also to lose Club Valhalla, which he shared with Blücher, after pressure grew on the Conservative politician who owned the building to kick them out. In 1999, Schilf moved several kilometres outside Helsingborg to Klippan, where he rented a large house, a barn and some adjoining land. The area was also home to a small but violent nazi scene. He dreamed of converting the estate into a nazi headquarters and music venue. The authorities again had other ideas, and a year later he was forced out after the Government bought the property from the landlord at a hugely inflated price in order to evict Schilf. All the time, Schilf's health was deteriorating. He had cystic fibrosis and was in and out of hospital in Denmark for much of the late 1990s. He continued to run his music business but it, too, was declining.

In the late spring of 1999, the long-promised battle with "ZOG" began. Three heavily-armed men raided a bank in Kisa, about 250km south-east of Stockholm, on May 29. The police arrived as the trio made their escape and gave chase but were met by a hail of bullets. Two kilometres out of town, the local police chief, who was in the chasing car, slowed down as he approached a sharp bend. His vehicle was sprayed with automatic gunfire from the three nazis. He escaped unhurt and took refuge in a nearby marsh. His attackers followed after him, lobbing three grenades and firing off several more rounds in his general direction. Thinking the officer was dead, the nazis continued their getaway, switching cars ten kilometres down the road. Their actions aroused the suspicion of two other police officers who had just come off duty and, deciding to investigate, they followed the men for some time. Fearing that they had been rumbled, the nazis screamed to a halt around a sharp bend and took up firing positions outside their car on the edge of the village of Malexander. The chasing police officers were caught by surprise as they came under fire, though at least one managed to shoot back, injuring one of the nazis. Both police officers were then killed in what appeared to be an execution: the officers were shot in the back of their heads by one of their own guns after they had surrendered their weapons.

The brutal murder of two policemen shocked the whole of Sweden. The injured nazi was later identified as Andreas Axelsson, former editor of *Storm Press*, the paper of a small nazi group in southern Sweden. Axelsson was a close political associate of the NSF leader Anders Hogstrom and one of the group's computer experts. Another man sought for the robbery was Jackie Arklöv, a man of mixed-race parentage whose mother came from Liberia but who was adopted at an early age and brought up in northern Sweden. At eighteen, he joined the army, where he received elite Ranger training and became a keen gun enthusiast. Arklöv idolised the Waffen-SS, discovered his hatred of race-mixing and became an ardent anti-semite. In 1994, he went to Bosnia and was recruited as a mercenary in the Croatian Ludovic Pavolic "anti-terrorist group". He commited several atrocities against Bosnian Muslims and served at a prison camp in Capljina. The following year he was to be sentenced to thirteen years imprisonment as a war criminal after witnesses testified how he tortured and abused Muslim prisoners, including a pregnant woman who he battered with a water hose, forced to suck a gun barrel and threatened with having the foetus cut out of her belly. However, he was exchanged for Bosnian Croat prisoners, returned to Sweden and joined the NSF.

Arklöv's involvement was supported by *Info-14!*. "Was it right of the two White comrades to bring along a coloured on their mission?" asked its statement, reproduced on Blücher's Blood and Honour website. "Many say 'No' but close their eyes to reality. This was an act motivated by the need to liberate the people's capital. It is the result that counts. A bank robbery can not be classified as a political action, even though it is politically motivated. Our position is clear. We find it correct to use Arklöv as a 'working partner'. And considering what sort of work they were engaged in, other candidates might be hard to find. As long as a person is not prepared to take Arklöf's place, this person should not criticise the decision to bring him along."

The third man arrested was Tony Olsson, a member of the defunct Reich Front who was already serving six years for accepting a contract to carry out a murder. He was believed to have joined the Aryan Brotherhood while in prison. The day before the robbery, Olsson was performing in a controversial rehabilitation programme established by the National Theatre, in which he testified on stage to his nazi faith and anti-semitic ideology. It later emerged that Axelsson was employed by the National Theatre as a driver and had taken Olsson to and from prison for performances. Olsson disappeared after the show in Stockholm the day before the bank robbery. He was later arrested in Costa Rica after his mother and a journalist were followed by Swedish police. Although Sweden had no formal extradition agreement with Costa Rica, the local authorities agreed to a diplomatic request and raided their hideout. They recovered over £75,000 of the stolen money.

While the murders were the result of a botched armed robbery – believed to be one of several carried out by this group – they acted as a signal to others. "It was the sounding alarm for racial war," says Stieg Larsson. The nazis said policemen were legitimate targets. "The shootout between 'National Socialist bank fund liberators' and ZOG's troopers is seen by many radicals in Sweden as just revenge and rough justice for the police murder of the patriot Martin Krussall, who was liquidated by a 'copper' in Malmo on the 29 November 1991," wrote Blücher, using the pseudonym Max Hammer. It was, he announced, the beginning of the "radical backlash taking place in the otherwise so oppressed and depressing Swedish ZOG society."

Info-14! sought to make a connection between the death of the policemen and their state function. "These men did not die as fathers, they are nobody's children, they were not innocent. They made their choice, just as the men who entered the bank in Kisa. They wore the State's uniform to uphold its criminal laws. They took order from the Jewish chief of Police and the Soviet minister of justice, and they worked to arrest Swedish youth who dare to have their own opinions. Their goal was to put Swedish youth in jail just because they wanted to use their own traditional symbols. People who engage in this type of terror, deserve no mercy. No innocents died – policemen died." Blücher reproduced this blood-curdling message on the Scandinavian Blood and Honour Internet site.

A month later, a sophisticated bomb was placed under the car of two well-known Swedish journalists who had been at the forefront of exposing Blücher's music operation. Peter Karlsson and his eight-year-old son only escaped death because they had reinforced seats for traffic safety. Both were badly injured. Only weeks before, Karlsson and his wife Katarina Larsson had written a story in a national newspaper exposing nazi infiltration of the armed forces. They had previously been responsible for halting production of Blücher's CDs at the Ritek Corporation factory in Taiwan and had got a CD plant in Italy to cut ties with Ragnarock Records. Long the targets of nazi abuse, the pair had applied for, and obtained, a security block on personal information, barring the release of their address and car registration, which is openly available under Swedish law. Peter Karlsson, in particular, was also blamed for a beating Schilf received from anti-fascists.

The nazis revelled in the attack. Blücher, writing on the Internet as Max Hammer, said, "As for the bombing of the Antifa journalist Anders Carlqvist (Peter Karlsson), this was an act of not only justified self-defence but also a natural conse-quence of his lying and criminal activity." *Info-14!* gloated, "The hand of fate still caught up with them one summer day. They were exposed with a bang! *Info-14!* regrets the fact that a child was wounded in this war which initially was declared by the State against Swedish patriots. Apart from this, no regrets!"

Forty-eight hours later, at about midnight on June 30, police answered an anonymous call alerting them to a car break-in the harbour area of the city of Malmo. As an officer opened the driver's door of the vehicle, he triggered a bomb so powerful that its detonation was heard across the city. He took the full force of the blast, receiving massive injuries to his face and upper body, and would have died if a colleague had not been able to administer first aid and stop the flow of blood from his wounds. At the time of writing, the case remains unsolved. That it came so shortly after the Stockholm bomb has made some people think there is a connection. While the police have concentrated their inquiries on a local Hells Angels gang with access to serious weaponry, it must be remembered that the Swedish nazis have ties with not only the Hells Angels but also the rival Bandidos. *Info-14!* supporters are closely linked to individuals in the Brotherhood bike gang. Malmo was also the city where police had shot dead a nazi in 1991, something that the Swedish nazis had not forgotten.

Three months later, the anti-fascist trade unionist Björn Söderberg was shot dead on his doorstep. A skilled negotiator for the syndicalist union, he had provoked the nazis when he discovered that Robert Vesterlund, the editor of *Info 14!*, worked in his workplace and was not only an active trade unionist but was about to be elected onto the local union executive. The day the revelation hit the press, a request to the police registry for Söderberg's passport photograph was made from a Post Office box belonging to Hampus Hellekant, aged twenty-three. Two days after the execution, Hellekant, Jimmy Niklasson, twenty-one, and Björn Lindberg-Hernlund, twenty-three, were arrested for murder. It later emerged that an alias previously used by Hellekant was the name behind the application to obtain Peter Karlsson's photograph. He had been behind the writing of several bogus letters sent out in Karlsson's name in 1999 and he had also attempted to gather information on the press and photography agency Embla Photo, which supplied material to *Expo*. The police found lists of names and addresses, including details of Andreas Rosenlund, a former editor of *Expo*. Alongside was written, "Check Andreas Rosenlund, social number, car and address. Children. Order passport photo."

The three men were later convicted and sent to prison for between six and eleven years. They were caught because the Swedish Security Police already had them under surveillance as possible suspects for the car bombing of Peter Karlsson. What was not reported was that two of the three men were wearing C18 tee-shirts at the time of their arrests and had considerable

C18 propaganda in their possession. There was no evidence implicating Vesterlund in the killing but he was subsequently convicted for being in possession of a handgun when he was arrested.

These were just the most serious of many incidents in Sweden in 1999. There were others. Someone fired a bullet through the window of Kurdo Batsi, editor of *BlackWhite&Expo*. A trade union office in northern Sweden was bombed. Dozens of local politicians and anti-racists received threats and small-scale attacks. While the number of incidents was not greatly different from previous years – indeed three deaths was fewer than the nine people murdered in 1995 – the targets were different. "The State" had become the main enemy. This process began with the growing popularity of *The Turner Diaries* from 1990, including its translation into Swedish, and was developed by the growth of C18 in Scandinavia. Though there is nothing linking Schilf or Blücher to any of the acts of terrorism, they both distributed in huge quantities material that openly advocated terrorism and concepts such as race war and leaderless resistance.

C18 in England was asked to release a statement claiming responsibility for the car bomb attack. The request was withdrawn due to the already intense police interest in C18 internationally. While the bomber remains at large, two people involved in passing money to him were both involved in the C18 network in Sweden. And only days after the murder of union official Björn Söderberg, Will Browning and Darren Wells travelled to Norway to meet C18 representatives from Sweden, Norway and Germany. Among the requests made was that a Swedish nazi, who had been involved in one of the terrorist incidents, be safe-housed in London until the police operation was scaled down. This request was granted and the Swede flew into London to lie low.

Things quietened down after 1999. More determined opposition from the Swedish people and the press forced the nazis on the defensive. On the day of Vesterlund's arrest on suspicion of involvement in the Söderberg murder, four of the main national newspapers reproduced the photographs of sixty-two key nazis in the country. Coming from a country like Sweden, which prides itself on its liberalism and tolerance, it reflected the danger to democracy that the nazis posed. And it seemed to work. "The nazis physically exhausted themselves," says journalist Stieg Larsson. "However, the political movement and philosophy behind it remains. They will be back."

CHAPTER SEVENTEEN

Wilting at Home

BOTH SIDES LEFT the Chris Castle murder trial issuing threats against the other. David Myatt had failed to challenge Will Browning to a duel in the courtroom, so did it in writing immediately afterwards. "Browning himself is welcome at any time to challenge me to a duel for saying and writing these things. And I will accept such a challenge – but I insist such a duel by fought in an Aryan and thus honourable way, according to our ancient Aryan customs. In part, this means fought with deadly weapons, with there being a high degree of probability that one of us is killed ... No one is to blame for this tragedy which has befallen our cause but Browning, for instead of choosing the honourable way, the Aryan way, he choose to cooperate with the System we are all pledged to fight and destroy."

Myatt's fantasies of pistols at dawn were temporarily shelved when police raided his home in connection with racist material on the Internet. Steve Sargent and Herve Gutoso suffered similar raids. Though all three men were later released without charge, the arrests had a debilitating effect on their National Socialist Movement, coming so shortly after the trial verdict that already isolated the group.

In mid-March, 1998, Myatt met this author in a pub in the Shropshire farming town of Craven Arms to deny allegations that he was a Satanist. Arriving in his customary Barbour jacket, flat cap and corduroys, the ginger-bearded nazi claimed to have only briefly flirted with "the occult" some twenty-five years before. He denied any connection to the Order of Nine Angles (ONA) but was forced to admit that he had opened four P.O.

boxes from which the cult had operated between 1983 and 1994. "I only opened them as a favour for a friend," he lamely commented. When pressed with evidence that his own political writings had been distributed from these addresses, he said that the box was shared by a friend whose identity he had promised to keep secret. Myatt was also forced to concede that NSM supporter Richard Moult was "Christos Beest", the new leader of the ONA, and that he was actually living with Moult and his partner.

Unable to convince me that he was not a devil worshipper, Myatt challenged me a duel. He handed me a three-page document entitled *Why Duelling is Right*, which included the *Etiquette of Duelling*, the rules by which he fought his battles. It was impossible not to laugh but he was serious. "If a person is innocent of some charge or accusation, they are innocent, regardless of how much abstract evidence is produced which seems to condemn them," his document read. I told him that, from his bizarre logic, a child molester is not a child-molester if he fights and wins a duel.

According to Myatt's rules, a duel is to be fought with either single-shot pistols, swords or with knives with blades at least nine inches long. "The duel is a private affair between the two individuals concerned. As such, only the nominated seconds, and a referee – acceptable by both sides – must be present. It is against the etiquette of duelling for any other people to be present." Once both parties accept, the two combatants arrive at the set place at a set time, preferably at dawn. "The duellists stand back to back. At a sign or word from the referee they then walk a set number of paces agreed beforehand (ten being usual) before turning to face each other. The referee then says, 'Take aim!' at which they take aim. The referee then says, 'Fire!' at which they discharge the weapon. It is considered dishonourable conduct to aim and/or fire before the referee gives the signal to so do. Should one person fire and miss, or hit and injure, the other duellist before that duellist has also fired, then the person who has fired must wait, without moving, until his fellow duellist has also fired, if he is capable of so firing. Honour is satisfied if the duel is undertaken in the above manner."

Staring me in the eyes, Myatt said his threat was serious. I said I would ignore it. Myatt said this proved I was a "dishonourable coward" and that he was innocent of the Satanist charge. This surreal incident, in a busy lunchtime pub, ended when Myatt ordered me to turn off my tape recorder and then boasted of having successfully fought two previous challenges. "I killed one and wounded another," he claimed.

Yet for all his bravado, Myatt was losing the will to fight. He quit the leadership of the NSM – to be replaced by Tony Williams – and the group slid into obscurity for the next twelve months. Steve Sargent continued to bring out *White Dragon* but his political activism was also decreasing as he became disillusioned with the movement. He attacked the *World In Action* programme about his brother's MI5 links as "a disgusting stitch up of one man" but his own support for Charlie was waning. Martin Cross was also re-evaluating his friendship with Charlie Sargent, believing that the C18 leader knew that Castle was coming round that day but had kept quiet hoping there would be a fight.

The police, meanwhile, had not given up the chance of nailing Browning for the Danish bombs. In March, officers from the Tactical Firearms Unit smashed their way into his house. A startled Browning, who had been alerted to activity outside his home by his two German shepherd dogs, was met on the stairs by several gun barrels pointing at his head. He was then led outside, naked, to a waiting van. His partner was instructed to shut herself in the bathroom with the dogs while officers conducted a thorough search of the house with machines that would pick up any traces of explosives. Leading the raid and the subsequent interrogation was the Organised Crime Squad officer who had headed the British end of the Danish operation. Browning refused to answer questions and was released on police bail pending examination of items taken from his house. Nothing incriminating was found.

★   ★   ★   ★

WILL BROWNING WAS deeply affected by the death of his Chris Castle and his own imprisonment for the production and distribution of *Combat 18*. The guilt of watching his friend die in his arms vied with his obsessive hatred of "the State". Many of his long-held views were changing. He had re-evaluated his politics while in Brixton Prison, engaging with black inmates about the advantages of black nationalism and racial separation, and blamed the Government for his friend's death. He chose to articulate his changing outlook in *Strikeforce*, a new C18 magazine. Gone were the threats to murder all blacks, Asians and Jews, to be replaced by something completely unusual:

> We are left-wingers. We are revolutionaries! When people talk of 'left-wing' today they are referring to Communists, Marxists, anarchists etc, and when they speak of the 'right-wing' they are talking about US. How can this be? We are anti-Government, we want to be given our own land where we can govern ourselves. The root of our problems is the Government and not the blacks or muggy reds. Strike against the Government and its lackeys both inside and outside our movement. It is the Government who try to destroy us, imprison us, murder us. It is the Government that floods our nations with non-whites. It is the Government who controls the media. It is the Government we must target!

The article caused derision among British nazis. "I don't know what he was on about," said one C18 supporter. "To say that we had more in common with the Left was just offensive. I'm no Communist." But Browning cared little. He was happy to write off much of the far-right. "We might be forty but it's a good forty," he was repeatedly heard to say about his hardcore support. He was happier with a few dozen loyal soldiers than constantly having to watch his back in a movement of several hundred. It was a stance that only added to his isolation.

Browning's conversion was not as ridiculous as it first appeared. He might have gone over the top in declaring himself a left-winger but he was only the latest of a growing number of nazis who viewed the state as their main opponents and replaced their opposition to communism with a similar hatred of capitalism. The roots of this conversion were to be found in the early Nineties. The collapse of state socialism in Eastern Europe and the break-up of the Soviet Union left the United States as the world's only superpower. When President George Bush announced during the 1991 Gulf War that he desired to see a "New World Order", the nazis had found a new international foe. This drive for a homogenous world – based on American capitalism – continued under President Clinton, with his vision of a single global economy.

The concept of an evil, one-world government is not new. Christian fundamentalists claim it is foretold in the *Book of Genesis* and is a precursor for the clash between Christ and the anti-Christ and the battle of Armageddon. Earlier this century, Soviet communism was viewed as its likely vehicle. Since 1991, American capitalism has replaced it, say the extreme-right. In this worldview, Jews are – as usual – seen as the driving force behind the plot for global domination; hence their perceived influence on the U.S. banking system and the country's strong support for Israel. Browning's rejection of capitalism and his adoption of an anti-state position was a crude and simplistic version of what others were articulating around the globe.

Browning was even more outspoken in the second issue of *Strikeforce*. In an article entitled *They ain't alright just because they are white*, he laid into just about everybody on the Right. "I've been involved in the so-called 'right wing' for a number of years now, but when I step back and look at the so-called movement, especially more recently, I can't help saying to myself 'Why am I surrounded by such 'misfits'?" While accepting that many joined the right wing out of genuine idealism, the majority were made up of "cowards", "inadequates and losers", "faggots", "drunken bums" and the "sickos and weirdos". The problem now, he concluded, "is that since the war the pro-white groups have been desperate for the numbers and will accept absolutely anyone just because they're White and call themselves racists. It doesn't matter what sort of lowlife they are as long as they see 'our way'."

Browning, in his own limited way, was undergoing a political transformation. He argued privately that class rather than race was the defining relationship in society, although he continued to argue for racial separation. He even read a biography of Che Guevara, the Marxist guerrilla leader who tried to transform Third World liberation campaigns into revolutionary upheavals, and enjoyed watching the film *Michael Collins* for its anti-British sentiments. But in the end, the Beast did not have strength of his convictions to make a clean break. Despite trying to claim that a streamlined C18 was clear of "misfits", he must have known deep down that the reality was different.

Gathering together thirty of his closest supporters in east London, he set out a five-year plan of action. "You are C18 proper," he told those present. "We estimate that to accomplish anything worthwhile we will need about five years of building. Some may think that this sounds a long time but believe me it goes quick as fuck. It is already five years since C18 first started and here we are almost starting from scratch." Browning explained the financial position of the group, the £50,000-worth of stock, which he said was "money in the bank", and the £25,000 owed, all of which he claimed was not bad considering the difficulties of the past eighteen months. He said that with ISD Records hoping to raise as much as £15,000 a year through the production of five or six CDs and with the group beginning illicit booze runs from France, C18 would be financially self-sufficient very quickly. He also hoped to found boxing gyms in the north of England and east London. "After five years of this sort of training we should have a tight little firm," he concluded.

He also dealt with rumours that Steve Sargent was going to attend a forthcoming concert. "Everyone has to turn up on the twenty-seventh of this month for the NF gig in Coventry," he said. "Hopefully Sargent might think we ain't gonna be there and turn up, then we can bury the cunt once and for all." On the day, C18 supporters arrived with an assortment of weapons.

Browning carried a machete under his jacket. Much to his disappointment, Sargent was nowhere to be seen.

Browning's fixation with the Sargents irked many in his orbit; some in Blood and Honour were sick of him turning up at gigs armed for battle and interrogating those he believed to be in contact with the NSM or who had not condemned the Sargents sufficiently. A less political leadership now ran Blood and Honour and, while many of them had previously been aligned with C18, they were taking a more independent line. No longer absolute was their slavish obedience to C18, as an editorial in *Blood and Honour* made clear. "Firstly B&H will be written independently and NOT jump on any bandwagon and create lies and gossip about people we should be classing as allies. There is too much negativeness within our movement. So it's time to end it."

The editorial of *Strength and Will* – published by Avalon lead singer Graham Thompson, who once wrote a song entitled "C18 Are Calling" – made a similar appeal. "We would more than welcome folk from Blood and Honour, British Movement, Hammerskins, BNP, NF, Third Position and any other like-minded individuals who can see our way forward TOGETHER." In neither publication did C18 get a mention.

However, talks aimed at unifying the two wings of the nazi music scene – Blood and Honour and Rock Against Communism – foundered. Browning was adamant that Brad Hollanby could never be allowed to return to Blood and Honour, while several of the Rock Against Communism group refused to countenance an alliance with Browning. As the organisers sought a resolution, it became clear that their allegiances were shifting away from C18. In June 1997, a gig in rural Northamptonshire was initially billed as a C18 event, but they were conspicuous by their absence. It had been organised by a local nazi and former Hells Angel who was one of the most persistent in calling for a shift away from C18. It was clear that Browning would find a very different Blood and Honour to the one he left when he was imprisoned. "C18 will have to toe the line," said one organiser.

Even so, no-one was willing to confront Browning head-on. The Beast still terrified people. The chasm crystallised into a dispute between traditional boneheads and the football casuals. A Blood and Honour gig in south London descended into chaos when Headhunter Andy Frain, the Nightmare, began randomly attacking skinheads, starting a brawl in which Darren Wells hit Avalon lead singer Graham Thompson. Mark Aktinson's partner Liz also had a dispute at the gig with several women she had been badmouthing, including Gail, the wife of Blood and Honour organiser Simon Dutton. Liz was forced to take refuge in a friend's car and, with Atkinson in prison, was quietly ostracised by most in C18 until his release.

In the summer of 1998, the non-C18 section of Blood and Honour made its move and began to stage events without telling C18. An angry Browning saw this in typically black-and-white terms: they were shying away from political confrontation in favour of a social scene for weekend rebels. He wrote:

> We've seen through the 'self-preservation' society who manoeuvred themselves into positions of trust with the Blood and Honour movement. Their self-elected little clique who slithered in with smiles then sneaked around amongst us, the treacherous vermin who saw the death of a comrade as an opportunity to capitalise on whilst our backs were turned have been uncovered as the traitors who always come to our gigs with smiles, appearing friendly to our faces but always plotting behind our backs. They constantly attempted to subvert our movement with their poison and lies ... So good riddance to the little clique who failed in their attempts to turn B&H into some sort of pop-scene, those cowardly weaklings who tried to turn the movement of Ian Stuart into a worthless pressure valve for the system with meaningless gigs and pointless fanzines, going nowhere just as ZOG wants it to go.

Yet the Beast seemed to have mellowed. Whereas once he would have been itching to beat his former associates to a pulp, now he seemed content to let them off. Less charitable was his henchman Del O'Connor, who took the fallout personally. He was organising the Ian Stuart Donaldson memorial gig in Wigan when he learnt that Stephen "Stigger" Calladine was secretly planning his own rival event in conjunction with the British Movement. In a fit of rage, O'Connor planned to "stab Stigger up" next time he saw him. In the event, the two gigs passed off without trouble and, while Stigger's concert was the larger, attracting 180 people, there was a decent turnout of 120 at the C18 event. Leaner and fitter was how Browning saw the post-split C18 wing of the music scene, believing that while numbers might be down, gigs would be without the backstabbing that had bedevilled the movement – even though he had been responsible for much of it.

Browning's five-year plan entailed him keeping out of the limelight but he was unable to ignore his enemies for long. He hated them too much. The Beast began plotting another bombing blitz. Shortly after the memorial gig in Wigan, he and O'Connor travelled to Germany to discuss the plot with his close friend Thorsten Heise. Browning proposed sending a C18 supporter from Britain to make the bombs, again to be sent in videos, if the Gemans could obtain the necessary materials. Both O'Connor and Heise were unhappy, believing that C18 had attracted too much attention for them to get away with it. Much better, they argued, to lie low for now. Though unconvinced, Browning was forced to accept.

O'Connor's lack of support annoyed Browning. He later complained to friends that O'Connor seemed more interested in arranging tee-shirt deals than building a serious terrorist organisation. O'Connor, meanwhile, saw the German escapade as the latest example of C18's futility. The Wigan-based enforcer was also beginning to resent Browning, feeling that he was doing the group's donkey work funded only by his income support, while the C18 leader was working and collecting monthly payments from Marcel Schilf. On a two-week trip to the U.S., O'Connor contemplated a life away from C18. When he was left stranded without transport at a Christmas gig in Coventry a few week later, to the amusement of an unsympathetic Browning, his mind was made up. In late January 1999, O'Connor packed his belongings and moved to Dallas, Texas.

Oblivious to O'Connor's disappearance, Browning mobilised his supporters for the annual Bloody Sunday demonstration on January 30. He hoped to attack the march and catch a few NSM supporters in the process. It was to be the largest C18 outing for several years, with its ranks being swelled by the presence of three dozen Chelsea, Reading and Oxford hooligans. A mob of over eighty arranged to meet at Waterloo Station at 11am but, with the police swamping the area and photographing faces, they dispersed to pubs around the Embankment and Covent Garden. Eventually the police turned their attention to the march itself and an organised National Front protest along Whitehall, allowing C18 to slip their surveillance and mob up again in the Tom Cribb pub in the Haymarket, just off Leicester Square. As the demonstrators approached Trafalgar Square, the C18 mob left the pub and ran at them. A few punches were traded before police reinforcements arrived and pinned the nazis on the sidewalk, where they were held for thirty minutes before having their mugshots taken.

C18 hailed the Bloody Sunday event as a huge success. They had embarrassed the police and shown their internal rivals that they were very much alive. The day ended on a high when Atkinson bumped into Steve Sargent's friend Rob Hilton at Euston Station and put him on his backside.

The glee was to be shortlived. Unbeknown to the mob out that day, they had been infiltrated by BBC television journalists from the *MacIntyre Undercover* series, which was investigating the Chelsea Headhunters. Donal MacIntyre and his team had won the confidence of Jason Marriner, a leading Headhunter and close friend of Darren Wells. C18 was not a target for the journalists, but when Marriner boasted of his role in mobilising hooligans for the Bloody Sunday event, it was too good an opportunity to miss; they joined the mob and filmed them in action. Also implicated in the eventual programme was Andy Frain. In a car driving to a planned clash with Leicester hooligans – an incident that would see both Frain and Marriner sent to prison – the Reading Nightmare boasted of apparently slashing an off-duty policeman across the face. In another incident, Marriner recounted the tale of Frain upsetting Jewish Holocaust survivors when he climbed into an oven at a former concentration camp before re-emerging and giving the nazi salute.

Browning and his gang were under attack from all sides. In mid-February, British Intelligence followed a minibus of C18 supporters to a concert in East Germany. The spooks had learned about Browning's latest bombing plans and decided to monitor his movements closely, especially as there was a chance of a meeting with Thorsten Heise. However, they were never to know whether the two men met, as Browning slipped away from the concert for two hours, losing his tail in the process.

C18 hit the national headlines in early March after *Searchlight* exposed a dozen nazis in the British Army, including three who had been present on the Bloody Sunday counter-demo. Darren Theron was a serving member of the Parachute Regiment, while Karl Wilson and Mark Taylor belonged to the Lancashire-based Kings Regiment. Theron had once been pictured on the front cover of *The Stormer* standing over the dug-up remains of human bodies while on duty in the former Yugoslavia. A week later – and unconnected to the *Searchlight* article – the homes of fourteen C18 supporters were raided by police, including those of Theron and Wilson. While the authorities publicly claimed that these raids were the result of an eighteen-month army and police investigation, they had in fact been co-ordinated by MI5, which had taken over responsibility for monitoring C18 during 1998. The army had looked into nazi influence in the Parachute Regiment but no action was taken by the Military Police.

Browning was deliberately ignored in the raids. The police seemed happy to give the impression that this signified some greater intrigue. This point was made verbally to at least one of those raided, with an officer insinuating that Browning was an informer and highlighting the injustice of others being targeted because of his activities. Browning was acutely aware of how others would perceive the fact that he had not been raided, moaning to anyone who would listen that it was a police stitch-up. The raids were also an intelligence-gathering exercise, giving police the opportunity to copy phone books and photographs and to approach C18 supporters for information. A rumour swept C18 that one of those raided was offered £1,500 a month to turn informer.

Two weeks after the police raids, Browning, Wells and Darren Theron flew to Vienna, where they were to be picked up and taken over the border into Slovakia. Under the cover of a concert, Browning was due to hold discussions with Erik Blücher, Thorsten Heise and representatives of Serbian and Slovakian C18. His gloom at the state of the movement in Britain had been lifted by its growth in Eastern Europe, particularly the Czech and Slovak republics and Serbia. In Slovakia, a pro-C18 magazine appeared, while ISD Records produced a Serbian compilation CD entitled *Anthems of Ethnic Cleansing*. Direct contact with the Serb nazis, many of whom were active followers of the paramilitary White Eagles, was undertaken primarily by Kevin Watmough, who had taken over responsibility for propaganda.

Browning was never to reach Slovakia. As soon as they landed in the Austrian capital, the trio were picked up by immigration officers and handed over to the MI5 operatives who had followed them on the flight, even though they were outside their legal jurisdiction. Browning was told bluntly that the authorities were aware of his plans to send more bombs and that if anything of an explosive nature arrived in Britain they would not let him escape justice again. The MI5 policy of harassment continued on his return. He received a large bouquet of flowers sent by "Ian" from a florist in Manchester. The accompanying card carried a witticism about his failed trip. On another occasion, Browning was stopped on the street; his mobile phone was taken from him, dropped on the ground and stamped on. These two incidents, though unsubtle, did succeed in rattling the C18 leader. But something outside his control was about to draw M15's attention in a different direction.

* * * *

ON APRIL 17, a twenty-two-year-old engineer called David

Copeland left his Hampshire home and travelled to south London. There he planted a crude but deadly nail bomb in a busy Brixton street. It exploded some time later, injuring dozens, some seriously. A week later, he put another bomb in Brick Lane, the symbolic heart of the Bengali community in east London. He thought it would explode on market day, but fortunately had got his dates wrong; few people were around when the bomb ripped through a car. Six days on, and with the capital in a state of some alarm, Copeland left a third bomb in a crowded gay pub in Old Compton Street, Soho, as workers unwound ahead of a Bank Holiday weekend. Three people died and many others were seriously injured, with several needing amputations.

The carnage was a remarkably wicked act carried out by a quite unremarkable person. With no military or explosives experience, Copeland downloaded bombmaking instructions from the Internet and bought the necessary equipment from local hardware and fireworks shops. Though a cable fitter on the Jubilee Line extension in east London, he had little electrical knowledge and had even proved unable to turn on power from the mains in one bedsit he lived in. Yet he was able to build several working bombs without a problem.

Copeland was little different from many others who join nazi groups. He suffered from low self-esteem and insecurity over his lack of height, and joined the BNP as a means of personal empowerment and to achieve a sense of superiority over others. The party's homophobia and machismo banished some of the insecurities he felt over his sexuality, having long believed that his family and friends thought of him as being gay due to his lack of a girlfriend. Through the BNP, he came into contact with more extreme groups and it was not long before he began to believe in the destiny of the white race to triumph over others. Mixed with Christian Identity, a theological justification for blatant racism and anti-Semitism which depicts the white race of Northern Europe and North America as the Lost Tribe of Israel – God's chosen people – it became a poisonous cocktail which eventually led him to his terrible acts.

The police had few leads to go on. While Copeland had been involved in nazi groups for over two years, he had carried out the bombings alone, due mainly to his mistrust of others. Many theories about the perpetrators were aired, with C18 featuring heavily in the media speculation. Officers who had been monitoring the group closely over the previous six months quickly concluded that this was not a Browning operation, but did not discount the possibility that it was a renegade faction or rogue former member. The media, meanwhile, went for C18.

Between the Brick Lane and Soho bombs, Del O'Connor became the journalists' leading suspect. O'Connor had launched White Wolves C18, and a phone call and several letters claiming to be from the White Wolves took responsibility for the bombs. At the same time, O'Connor disappeared. News of the police search for him reached the *Daily Mirror*, quickly followed by the rest of the press. O'Connor was in Texas, unaware of the commotion at home. Browning, meanwhile, was feeling the pressure. With the press on his back and even his mother being interviewed by one newspaper, his persecution complex went into overdrive. He viewed the intrusions as unwarranted, despite leading a group that openly advocated terrorism. He became utterly paranoid and convinced that the Brixton bomb was a plot by the state to fit him up. "They've definitely trying to set me up," he told friends, on hearing that the second bomb exploded in a red car; at the time he drove a maroon Ford. Others in C18 were more directly embroiled in the investigation. Darren Theron, who had only recently been booted out of the army, was raided only hours before Copeland was caught.

When Copeland was finally arrested, it emerged that he was the NSM's Hampshire and Surrey organiser. Tony Williams promptly closed down the NSM, fearing that he might be implicated in the bombings because of Copeland's membership. Steve Sargent was furious with this decision, which proved to be the death knell for the NSM.

★　★.　★　★

WITH FEW FRIENDS left at home, Browning cast further afield for the support. In the summer of 1999, he led a twenty-strong C18 group over to Northern Ireland to a Loyalist/C18 gig in Portadown to celebrate the Twelfth of July, the most important date in the Loyalist calendar. It had been organised by Ian Thompson, a leading member of the Loyalist Volunteer Force and close friend of Browning. The C18 group laid a wreath at a ceremony to commemorate Billy Wright, the assassinated LVF leader known as King Rat, and included several masked men fired shots into the air. Then the men joined around forty right-wing Loyalists the gig, the music being provided by No Remorse, Warhammer, Razor's Edge and a local flute band. The following morning Browning, who had stayed at the organiser's house, was picked up and taken to meet the acting leader of the LVF. For once nervous, Browning offered to raise money for the paramilitaries through the production of sectarian CDs, while privately he coveted the Loyalist's bomb-making capabilities. However, no deal was done. The Loyalist leader – who went on to be arrested in the United States – appeared less than impressed by Browning.

Six months after the Portadown gig, Ian Thompson was charged with possession of a sub-machine gun and bomb-making components. In 2001, he was jailed for nine years.

With the loss of the LVF link, C18 limped along. Its gigs continued but were sporadic and poorly attended. Even Browning was politically jaded and planned to move. His property had increased in value substantially due to the house price boom and the extension of the Jubilee Line into south-east London. He could now afford to sell up and buy a larger place on the south coast, with Dover his preferred choice. He remained in contact with his supporters at home and abroad but rarely travelled outside the capital.

In the summer of 1999, Del O'Connor was deported from the U.S. for overstaying his three-month visa and was duly arrested at Gatwick as part of the wider police operation initiated against C18 some months before. He was bailed pending further investigation after several C18 activists told police that racist material found in their houses belonged to O'Connor. Browning believed O'Connor was now an informant, and word spread of a possible clash, particularly after the Beast learned that his former henchman had spent time in Scandinavia with Marcel Schilf and the Blood and Honour network.

Browning's enthusiasm was reinvigorated by the bloody events in Sweden – the deadly attacks on policemen, trade unionists and journalists. However, he backed down when asked to make a statement of responsibility in London, fearing yet more police attention. His reluctance was justified when four people close to Thorsten Heise were arrested in the autumn of 1999 and bomb-making equipment and weapons were found. German police had picked up intelligence that this group planned to hit back at anti-fascist targets in response to an earlier attack on Heise's own home. Heise, meanwhile, was imprisoned for attacking a policeman, and his Aryan Brotherhood was ostracised from much of the scene after a violent clash with German Blood and Honour supporters.

As if Browning did not have enough enemies, the Bloody Sunday march in January 2000 saw a potentially more serious threat emerge in the shape of the London UDA chief, Frank Portinari, who was now out of jail. They had once been close friends but fell out after the imprisonment of Charlie Sargent. The UDA leader was not convinced of Sargent's guilt, having known him since the late Eighties. He was reluctant to become embroiled in C18 affairs, but Mark Atkinson's attack on his sidekick, Rob Hilton, forced him off the fence in favour of Sargent. Yet the balance of forces, at least numerically, seemed to favour C18, and Portinari turned up at Browning's house asking for a guarantee that the Derry Apprentice Boys march, held in London every spring, would be ignored by C18. Browning consented and told him that he had no problem with the UDA but simply Hilton. Even so, Portinari was heard publicly voicing his contempt for the C18 leader during a visit to Belfast that Easter, and at least one Sargent supporter reckoned Browning was a "dead man".

Portinari began to gather a large enough group to challenge

Browning's authority with the launch of a UDA front, the British
Ulster Alliance (BUA), in early October. As the Bloody Sunday
demo approached, rumours began to circulate – eagerly spread
by Browning's enemies – that C18 was going to be attacked by a
united force of the BUA and hooligan Warren Glass's west
London firm. Browning also heard these reports and mobilised
his firm under the guise of attacking the Republican march. On
the day, Portinari's dozen or so supporters were swelled by a
similar number of Chelsea and Reading hooligans, led by Andy
Frain and Warren Glass, and some NF supporters who made
their way up from their official protest in Whitehall. They met
up at the Globe pub opposite Baker Street tube station, a venue
regularly used by soccer hooligans on England match days.
Portinari's followers tried to attack the marchers as they reached
Euston but were held back by police. Meanwhile, Browning and
fifty supporters were held in a pub near Russell Square station
by police for several hours. The expected intra-Right clash never
materialised, as the two groups largely ignored each other. Frain
and his hooligans even linked up with C18 later in the day.

Six months later, two of the early C18 activists confronted
Mark Atkinson in a pub in Egham, Surrey. They demanded that
he explain his allegiance to Browning and informed him that he
and the C18 leader were going to get "whacked" by the UDA. It
was not a good few weeks for Atkinson, who was on the receiving
end of two beatings at the hands of fellow west London nazis.
The first was when a drunken Atkinson turned up on Simon
Dutton's doorstep spoiling for a fight. Dutton initially refused to
answer the door, waiting until the C18 man had turned to leave
before coming out and kicking him down the stairs. Dutton also
told Warren Glass that Atkinson had been issuing threats against
him. A few days later, Glass caught up with Atkinson at work
and gave him a hiding.

The temperature between C18 and the London UDA rose to
fever pitch during the summer of 2000. Browning and Atkinson
were restrained from attacking Portinari and Hilton by their fear
of the UDA in Northern Ireland but this did not prevent both
sides continuing the rhetorical war. At a BUA meeting, held in a

Euston hotel in the company of several close supporters of Belfast UFF leader John Adair, Portinari accused Browning of being a *Searchlight* informer. A few weeks later, Browning and a twenty-five-strong mob turned up at a pub where the NF were drinking following their Remembrance Sunday march to the cenotaph. He belligerently quizzed NF members about their support for Portinari and had to be placated. That day also witnessed Browning's first face-to-face contact with the Loyalist killer Steve Irwin, who had travelled to London in the company of the West Midlands NF, some of whom were strong C18 supporters. Irwin had been released from prison only a few months before as part of the Good Friday Agreement, after serving only seven years of a life sentence for one of the most notorious slaughters of the entire Troubles: the multiple murder of Catholics at the Rising Sun pub in Greysteel on Hallowe'en night. He had long been a staunch nazi but this was his first contact with the C18 leadership in London. He gave Browning his full support.

Irwin was acting on his own initiative and UDA chiefs reacted with fury when they learned of his backing for C18 in the dispute with Portinari. Irwin was visited one morning and asked to explain himself. Since coming out of prison, he had been distancing himself from the UDA, preferring closer links with the LVF. He had remained in contact with several other UDA activists from the Londonderry area, many of whom had also begun to side with the LVF. "He is considered a hothead and unpredictable by the UDA," says one RUC officer. "Irwin has started to form his own grouping away from the UDA with some of those in the Londonderry and Coleraine areas." According to one supporter of this group, who spoke to a Sunday newspaper in Northern Ireland, the group has access to guns and explosives. His LVF links include the Lisburn unit, one of whose leading figures appeared at a C18 gig in March 2001 with several other LVF supporters and read out a statement of support from the stage. Leading the group was Alfie Phillips, a close friend of the late Billy Wright and one of the original LVF "Rat Pack". He also had been released from prison – where he had been serving

a sentence for murder – under the Good Friday Agreement. He
is now a senior member of the LVF command. The gig also saw
representatives from C18 units in Sweden, Norway, Denmark
and Germany present. It was its biggest event for several years.

The re-emergence of a Loyalist connection was a boost to
Browning at a bad time. He had been arrested again and charged
– almost two years after the event – with affray over the 1999
attack on the Bloody Sunday march in Trafalgar Square that was
filmed by *MacIntyre Undercover*. The state was never going to
leave him alone, he decided. His morale plunged further in
January 2001 with the death of Marcel Schilf, who lost his long
battle against cystic fibrosis. The relationship between the two
men had not been close for a few years but Browning was greatly
affected by his death. He believed that Schilf was a man of action
and had died loyal to his cause. He even thought that the Dane
was a greater figure than Ian Stuart Donaldson.

The Beast now knows that he will never attain his ultimate
goals. The police and Security Services now monitor his group
so closely that little escapes their attention. When Steve Irwin
came to London in November 2000, he was picked up and
questioned by Special Branch. The same fate awaited Mark
Atkinson when he tried to board a plane to Belfast six months
later. Two other C18 supporters were stopped by police at
Stansted Airport on their return from Schilf's funeral in Sweden.
When London C18 met up to travel up to the concert in March
that LVF supporters attended, police had the location under
surveillance. Browning had slipped through their net once before;
they were not prepared to allow it to happen again. For them
too, this was now personal.

CHAPTER EIGHTEEN

Kids in a Candy Store

COMBAT 18 BEGAN as a London street force out for a fight. Its origins and many of its activities were firmly British. The gang mentality, the enjoyment of fighting and the culture of drinking had been major elements of British youth culture since at least the 1950s. The pent-up frustration, marginalisation and resentment of those involved led them to lash out at those they despised. While supporters were united and motivated by political ideology rather than simply fashion or music, their actions and mentality differed little from other manifestations of youth subculture, particularly football hooliganism, from which many of them came. They talked of "protecting your manor", "taking liberties" and "respect".

Over time, C18 adopted an ideology. It would describe itself as a revolutionary, national socialist, terrorist organisation. Its enemies were no longer individual blacks or Asians but the political, cultural and economic system which, it claimed, discriminated against white people. It borrowed a considerable amount of its terminology from the United States – concepts like ZOG, leaderless resistance and race war – where, over the past twenty years, an increasing number of whites have given up the electoral process and turned to terrorism. By 1995, C18 was advocating a race war in Britain. Charlie Sargent was addressing meetings around the country calling for his followers to begin killing and burning out their political and racial opponents; David Myatt was instructing readers to begin a covert and overt war to undermine and destabilise "the System"; and Will Browning, through the pages of *Combat 18*, was reproducing bomb manuals and lists of potential targets, and exhorting,

"Now you have the technology, bomb the bastards."

Yet when it came to it, only a dozen people were prepared to carry out what they had preached. Only the eight who had some prior knowledge of, or role in, the Danish bomb plot, and a few others involved in the attempted armed attacks and firebombings on their opponents in the music scene, took up the call to arms. When violence did occur, it often revolved around the motivation and planning of one man: Will Browning. In its stated aim to spark a race war in Britain, C18 failed. Indeed it would never pose any serious threat towards the state, either politically or militarily; what aggression it did unleash was often directed at fellow racists. C18 was also largely ignored by most anti-racist and anti-fascist groups, for whom the nazis posed a physical rather than a political threat.

Browning was fond of telling people that C18 was the target of the largest police and security operation to have befallen any neo-fascist group in Britain. It is true that the authorities now keep a watchful eye on the group, to the point where no leading C18 activist can travel abroad without being pulled in for questioning by Special Branch. Yet this was a cause of the decline of the group rather than a sign of its success. It was also riven by its internal feuding, the weaknesses of those it attracted and its unattainable political goals.

Writing on the C18 website, Kevin Watmough explained the ideals of their nazism. "The concept of honour is central to National Socialism and all National Socialists are obliged by their honour to act in certain ways: with nobility of character ... In this way National Socialists embody all that is best in our race and in the civilizations that our race has created over millennia." Like David Myatt, he sought to place C18 in a direct lineage with the original Nazi Party.

> Many who call or have called themselves National Socialists since the immolation of Adolf Hitler have either not understood the concept of honour or ignored it. It needs to be stated and repeated as often as possible that unless a person is prepared to strive to be honourable – and to take

a real oath on their honour to the Cause and the Leader –
then they have no right at all to call or describe themselves
as National Socialists. An oath on honour means what it
says – to break that oath is dishonourable, a cowardly act,
and as such deserves death or everlasting ignominy.

What this means on a practical level is that each National
Socialist will set themselves standards – of behaviour, dress,
conduct and so on – and then strive to attain and maintain
those standards. This means that each National Socialist
will also not compromise on those standards: we will not
accommodate ourselves to the many and varied forms of
decadence and degeneracy that exist today. Most
importantly, our honour means that we will not undertake
– to further the cause or otherwise – any acts or actions
which are dishonourable.

Few in C18 ever approached these "ideals", or even really
understood nazism. "They're all hypocrites," Chelsea hooligan
Andy Frain told me back in 1995 in relation to his friends in
C18. "They all talk about Adolf Hitler and national socialism yet
few of them understand what it means. Most of them have black
mates anyway." A year before, Frain had attended a local election
count in the company of the BNP candidate and other racists.
Also present were a few black men who had turned up at the
request of a Labour Party councillor in case of trouble from the
BNP. During the evening, an embarrassed Frain came up to the
group, which included several people he knew well, and apolo-
gised for being with the BNP. He told them it was nothing
personal.

Far from being "honourable" Aryan superheroes, the few
who most studied the ideology were weirdoes and misfits –
uniform fetishists, fantasists, Satanists – whose personal
behaviour bore little relation to the standards they placed on
others: men like David Myatt. No-one who has met Myatt can
describe him as ordinary. His obvious intelligence contrasts
sharply with his bizarre political views, his devil rituals and
fantasist role-playing enacted through the Order of Nine Angles,

and the unrealistic standards he sets for human behaviour. He is out of touch with the real world, apart even from those around him in C18. Anyone who views the skinhead thugs and drug-dealers of Romford C18 as "Aryan warriors" is bound to feel continually let down.

In common with many who judge others by the twisted ideals of nazism, Myatt's own life is a sham. He altered his story several times when confronted with evidence of his Satanism, then tried to flatter me by saying how we were much alike and how people with strong ideals should be on the same side. When that failed, he challenged me to a duel to "determine who was telling the truth". While Myatt is one of Britain's foremost post-war national socialist thinkers – the competition is not very stiff – he fails to live by what he preaches. He talks of facing a "Holy War" in which people must be prepared to take casualties, yet on each occasion when he has felt any sort of political pressure or media exposure, he has run away. Following his imprisonment for racial violence in 1974, he became a Benedictine monk for eighteen months; in 1984, after being exposed for trying to establish a nazi-Satanic commune in Shropshire, he announced he was turning his back on his political activities for Taoism; in 1998, when confronted with his links to the ONA, he dropped out of the National Socialist Movement and converted to Islam; and when, in the summer of 2000, his involvement in the National Socialist Movement was reported on a BBC documentary, he wrote to *Searchlight* offering to pen an article retracting his past racism and explaining his conversion to Islam. *Searchlight* refused his request but offered to conduct an interview with Myatt. First he wanted it to be done by mail, then in his home and finally in his local mosque, before eventually declining. Five months later, and obviously thinking the press attention had waned, Myatt reappeared within the nazi scene, this time advocating Steve Sargent's new group the Albion Fynd. He now claims that nazism is compatible with Islam.

Tony Williams is another who seems to play at nazism. Benefiting from a healthy trust fund left by his father, he has time to write and pose for photographs in a variety of nazi

uniforms. However, when his commitment was put to the test –
following David Copeland's arrest for the London nail bombings
and the discovery that he was an NSM organiser – Williams
closed down the NSM and hid from the world. When confronted
by two Essex NSM supporters days later, demanding computer
equipment and membership lists, the brave nazi warrior broke
down.

While plainly racist, few of the foot soldiers understand nazism
beyond thoughtless statements about the superiority of "Aryans"
and Jewish conspiracies, and even much of this is show. Few
C18 supporters, for example, truly did not believe that the
Holocaust happened. Yet they were preoccupied with it, and
with the so-called ZOG plot. Why? For those who understood
the politics, refuting the Holocaust was a necessary requirement
for the rehabilitation of national socialism as a political force.
The vast majority, however, saw Holocaust denial as simply a
means to shock and offend. The authors of *Combat 18* knew full
well that reproducing pictures of C18 supporters lying on the
slabs in concentration camps would horrify most decent people,
especially Jews, many of whom had lost relatives in the gas
chambers. When the media reported these abuses, the sense of
personal importance felt by the culprits increased.

It is also true that many involved saw their activities as a way
to stick two fingers up at a society they despised. They were
angry young white men who felt alienated from an increasingly
multiracial land and one where women are more self-confident
and empowered. Many were unemployed or in short-term
manual work with little job security and long-term prospects. It
was far easier to blame the arrival of black people in Britain than
a modern economic system that leads to cycles of unemployment
and to low-paid jobs. Through C18 and its offensive propaganda,
they were able to strike out at those they resented. The more they
offended, the better. Their incoherent rage and striving for
power through fear and violence only highlighted the impotence
of their own lives.

This sense of power and self-importance was a motivating
factor for Charlie Sargent. A one-time drug dealer and petty

thug, Sargent was going nowhere. He had no job, no money and no prospects. In leading C18, he became somebody. He relished the role – as was evident from the newspaper interview in which he shamelessly claimed credit for the Dublin football rampage. He was also able to supplement his meagre income by producing magazines, tee-shirts, organising music concerts and selling CDs. Standing in the dock during his murder trial, stripped of his political cloak, Charlie reverted to the real Paul David Sargent: small, unimposing, dishonest and lacking in confidence.

Will Browning had different motivations. From an early age he had rebelled, often violently. Much of his teenhood was spent under some kind of supervision, separated from family and friends. Soon after arriving in London, he was again behind bars. Browning was full of hatred and cast it onto society and the apparatus that enforces its control. He seemed unable to form close relationships and had little contact with his family, even disowning his mother after she handed over a photo of Browning to a tabloid journalist who turned up at her Jersey home. "She's collaborated with the system," he said in anger. "I'll never forgive her." He could not answer any argument without resorting to violence and was preoccupied with how others viewed him. C18 was his outlet. He complemented Sargent's big mouth perfectly. Even after his commitment waned in the wake of Chris Castle's death, he remained in C18 because it still gave him his best opportunity to orchestrate violence.

While Sargent and Browning received most media attention, others in C18 basked in the public notoriety. They too became important for a day: noticed by some, feared by others. The press gave C18 considerable local and national exposure and as a result undoubtedly boosted the egos of many of those involved. However, the coverage cannot be said to have helped the group; very few people joined C18 during the second half of the Nineties as a result of TV or newspaper coverage. This was largely because there was no publicly-available contact point; even if there had been, anyone who appeared out of the blue would have been treated with mistrust and suspicion. The media, if anything, contributed to the demise of the group by forcing the police to take a firmer line. For example, the discovery that Nimbus (UK) had produced *Barbecue in Rostock* eventually forced ISD Records to relocate to Scandinavia, greatly reducing the money-making potential of C18. The revelation that Charlie Sargent was a police informer helped to destabilise and split the movement, and the *MacIntyre Undercover* expose of the Chelsea Headhunters helped imprison the dangerous Andy Frain. The press also identified those involved in C18, making anonymous attacks all the harder, a point admitted by Steve Sargent.

Most of those involved in C18 were in it for the fighting; for many, it was a way of life. C18 supporters were into football hooliganism, street and bar brawls and blood sports. The politics gave a semblance of justification for causing trouble. Most of what they called political action owed more to drunken, yobbish behaviour than coordinated terrorist strategy. They shared with BNPs supporters the same resentment and scapegoating, but this came second to their lust for fighting. Violence, and the resulting "power" and "respect" gained from it, dominates C18. This explains the lack of women and people over forty in the group.

It is laughable when Myatt, Watmough and Browning talk of Aryan superiority and the "creation of a new man". A cursory glance of C18 supporters around the country highlights the low-lifes involved. Browning's main contact in Newcastle has several convictions for burglary, including the homes of elderly women. In Gateshead, the lead singer of a C18-aligned band is a bare-knuckle fighter. In County Durham, a group of nazis who staged a C18 gig in 1998 are involved in badger baiting. In Yorkshire, one of the main instigators of the violence of the mid-Nineties also sold hardcore porn and snuff movies. In Oldham, some of the football hooligans involved in C18 are drug dealers and organise booze runs from France. In South Wales, one of the main C18 activists during the Nineties organises dog fights and deals drugs, as does another leading member of Blood and Honour in the same area. In east London, the C18 unit that killed and threw a dog through the window of a family home is also involved in drug dealing. One of the group has a conviction for "rolling" gay men and another is a nazi despite having two children with a black woman. In west London there are the Deviants, who talk about racial superiority while sampling the sex trade in every corner of the earth.

The Americans would use the description "trailer trash" to describe many of the people attracted to C18. In 1993, a leader of the Ku Klux Klan was less than impressed when he met up with C18 while on holiday in England. He was taken to a pub in east London one Sunday lunchtime and was entertained by strippers. He looked on, horrified, as the C18 mob howled in delight at the women on stage, several of whom were black. He was not the only foreign nazi to find their behaviour immature. Only someone with such a warped mind as David Myatt could possibly consider these people to be Aryan warriors and the vanguard of the master race.

★   ★   ★   ★

GLANCING AROUND THE front room of the Chelmsford flat Steve Sargent shared with Herve Gutoso, I began to get a picture of a C18 activist. The place was littered with clothes, newspapers and cigarette butts. The floor had not been vacuumed for weeks. In the kitchen, a week's worth of washing up lay stacked up in the sink and across the work surfaces. One cupboard contained almost twenty tins of macaroni cheese and a similar number of Ambrosia custard, but little else.

Despite being aware of who I was, Sargent spoke freely about his involvement in C18. He knew I would never portray him in a positive light but seemed content enough with the notoriety attention gave him. He spoke frankly and honestly about the prospects for the Right, which were few, he conceded. He did, however, have a sense of humour, which I had already witnessed in his writings.

Yet, sitting on the floor, going through a scrapbook of newspaper cuttings about C18, he was like a teenager who couldn't grow up. Nothing excited him more than recounting stories of the good old days, the adrenalin rush moments before a fight and the camaraderie of the Sunday drink-up. He was at his happiest when talking about his sexual conquests, which he was the first to admit were few and far between. One story I heard was of a blossoming relationship with a Slovakian skingirl who ran a nazi mail order business. Head over heels in love, Sargent travelled across Europe on a coach (he was scared of flying) only to find that her ex-boyfriend had moved back into her flat. Rather than return home early or find any place to stay, the disappointed Sargent kipped down on the spare bed a few feet away from the couple. He even boasted to me about buying second-hand porn mags from the local market at 40p each, and how his flatmate would shit in padded envelopes and send them to people he did not like. Sargent was then thirty-two, but I left with the impression that he was half that age.

Will Browning was different. I met him on a few occasions during the the Sargent and Cross murder trail, which I was covering for *World In Action*. He had a strong character and dominated the people around him, a point recognised by Det Supt Steve Reynolds, the officer who headed the murder case. It was easy to see, by his presence and the way he carried himself, how he had emerged as the street leader of C18. His puritanical views also marked him out: he was disgusted by the sexual exploits of the West London Deviants, and for that matter most of the C18 activists during their trips to the red-light centres of Continental cities. He too was not "normal", but for different reasons than Steve Sargent. He was a deeply paranoid person who continually thought people were out to get him. "You'd better not be stitching me up," he said to me, menacingly, during a break in the trial. He would refer to me as "Slippery" or "Slips" in our brief conversations. He also once produced a pair of pliers from his coat pocket and told me of a tree in Epping Forest he had earmarked for me if I crossed him.

Yet there was a certain quality about Browning that stood him apart from most of the others in C18. He was a man of his word, and fiercely loyal to his friends. Sometimes he was too loyal for his own good, and the trust he placed in his friends was often not repaid. Time and again they coughed to the police to escape punishment. Few people in C18 would have remained silent for ten days under intense questioning, despite facing possible imprisonment and after seeing a close friend die in their arms. Browning did. Charlie Sargent was a good example of those who had no hesitation in saving their own skin in the face of adversity.

The seeds for C18's destruction lay in the very people it attracted – the misfits, the weirdoes, the low-life, the drug pushers, the deviants. Given the violent tendencies of those involved, the egos, the paranoia that consumes nazi groups generally, and the large sums of cash generated by the music scene, rivalries and confrontations were inevitable. In addition, the lack of a coherent and generally understood ideology and an effective leadership meant that there was little cementing these people together. Even the leaders wanted different things: Charlie Sargent was in it for himself, seeking to extract as much personal gain as he could; Will Browning wanted to enact his violent fantasies; Steve Sargent just wanted a simple life where he could live and drink amongst like-minded friends, however few they were.

"Britain is finished," Browning told *World in Action* journalist Andrew Bell and myself during one meeting. In a brief but illuminating discussion, he tried to explain his dream. "Let us have a small island somewhere off Scotland or Scandinavia where we can be alone and away from society, that's all we want." He railed against the capitalist system. While he conceded that this system wasn't totally run by Jews, he did claim that "about two hundred of the three hundred families which run the world are Jewish."

He was less articulate when asked to explain his alternative society, how it would be run and what democratic structures would be used. "We'd run it wouldn't we," bemused at the perceived stupidity of the question.

"Yes, but would you have a popular democracy or would you run it as a dictatorship?" enquired Bell. "If it was run as a dictatorship, how would the leader be appointed?"

Browning was flummoxed, seemingly unsure of what we were getting at. There followed an embarrassing silence as he sought an answer, before the talk turned to another topic. In a thirty-minute discussion, Browning unwittingly gave an insight into his mindset and motivation, which we concluded at the time was simply revenge and defiance. "We just can't let them win," he said. "They" were not clearly identified: at times it meant Steve Sargent and the NSM, while at other times it meant the state and its apparatus. Occasionally, it meant the 300 families who apparently controlled the world.

Another feature of those attracted to C18 is a self-destructiveness that drives many towards drink or alcohol abuse, prison or self-harm. In 1995, I had three meetings with Neil Parish, the former leader of Blood and Honour, as he tried to rebuild his life outside the nazi scene. Three years earlier, he had been raking in over £1,000 a week in orders, as well as cash money from sales at gigs and meetings, and his wife had just had a second child. Life seemed to be going well. An arrest for possession of a CS gas canister following an attack on a gay pub in Kings Cross in August 1992 changed all that. With forty previous convictions, he knew he was going to prison and his life quickly fell apart. When I met him, he was desperately trying to start afresh, but finding it hard. He had been shunned by most of his former comrades – who accepted Charlie Sargent's accusations that he was a thief – and led a lonely existence picking sprouts for a pittance to support a wife and three children. Parish had just decided to sell his story to the *News of the World*. The paper was eager to listen but had no intention of paying him. They even had a photographer hidden in a van down the road, poised to take an illicit snap if he refused to have his picture taken. Parish badly needed the money but admitted to me that he also needed to make a public confession about his past to convince himself, his newly-found friends and, most importantly, his family, that he was truly out of it.

In the summer of 2000, Parish appeared on an TV programme produced by Leo Regan, who, seven years before, had brought out a book depicting the lives of Parish and other Blood and Honour activists. Parish's marriage had long since ended and he was now settled with a new wife and child somewhere in Lancashire. He still held many of his racist views and admired the murderer David Copeland but remained out of the nazi scene. During the course of the programme, Parish's new wife walked out on him following a violent row and he was sent for anger management therapy.

The programme reminded me of the many people I have met who contributed to this book. Several had lives not dissimilar to Parish. Many carried the baggage of a troubled and violent world. For Parish, it was a childhood in a children's home, long days and nights hanging around shopping centres and street corners as a teenage skinhead, crime and substance abuse. Rejection and bullying are just two of the themes that reappeared in many of the people I met. Understanding that does not mean you ignore or excuse what they are doing now. It does indicate that solely criminalizing these people will not help prevent them from continuing their activities or stop the next generation of violent nazis emerging in the future: quite the reverse.

Steve Sargent later mocked Parish for appearing in the programme, claiming that he was a misfit who brought shame on the Right. "The programme set out to ridicule the right-wing and with the help of the human garbage, Nick, Neil and Colin [all former skinheads in the programme], they pretty much succeeded. It was inevitable that the worst possible people would be attracted to take part in the book in the first place. With a TV camera to perform in front of, the scum will always rush to the fore."

Browning, meanwhile, dismissed David Copeland as a "nutter" and "mad", claiming that his indiscriminate carnage was a result of mental illness rather than political ideology.

For both Sargent and Browning, such criticism shows a lack of self-awareness. There are too many similarities between Parish's life and that of Sargent; likewise between Copeland and Browning. Copeland – who was convicted in June 1999 of the murders of three people and received six life sentences – saw nazism as justification for his violent fantasies. While Browning never inflicted such destruction, his own thirst for violence also began well before he became active in C18 and his victims included many innocent and non-political people. In the early days of C18, he had many of the same thoughts of igniting a race war that consumed Copeland; it was only later that he began to refine his targets. The level and nature of the bloodshed might have been different but the mentality was the same.

The future of C18 depends on Will Browning and his stomach for more trouble. He is the only person in Britain who can take C18 beyond the street gang that most of its supporters are content with. Internationally he is still revered. But even if Browning wants to carry on, he is faced with a police force unwilling to allow him to slip through the net again. Few others will stand by him as arrests pile up and harassment grows. He also, like Parish, has to choose between his family and a life in prison. Mark Atkinson is emerging as the driving force behind a resurrection of C18, helped by his Loyalist links, but has neither the intelligence or inclination to make the group anything other than a thuggish gang.

The future for the Sargents appears bleaker. Charlie languishes in prison and will not be released until at least 2015. He has been ostracised by most of the Right and lost most of his friends. Steve Sargent remains nominally active with his new grouping, the Albion Fyrd, which combines nazism with English mythology. This, however, is no more than a paper organisation, a symbol of his own isolation and defeatism. Darren Wells seems more interested in starting a new life abroad than building C18 in Britain. Mick Dunne and Eric Wallis, to name but two, bottled it as soon as the going got tough.

C18 will continue in some form but will never again challenge the BNP for political hegemony of the Right. It may simply remain a vehicle for intimidation and street violence. The danger, however, is that it will inspire violence in others. David Copeland was motivated by the sort of ideology that C18 brought over from the U.S. He had little time for C18 itself but did become regional organiser of its splinter group, the NSM. He wasn't alone. Two weeks before Copeland planted his first bomb, nineteen-year-old Stuart Kerr left his dingy bedsit just outside Chichester, Sussex, at one o'clock in the morning and walked a mile to an Asian shop he and two friends had been targeting in the preceding few weeks. He hurled two petrol bombs at the shop window. He later set alight a police car inside a police compound and cut his own arms. Like Copeland, Kerr was fascinated with Third Reich ideology and covered his bedroom walls with nazi posters and newspaper cuttings. His bookshelves contained biographies of Hitler and his tape collection included Will Browning's No Remorse. Kerr was also in contact with C18.

For a short period in the Nineties, Combat 18 believed its own propaganda. "We were like kids in a candy store," one former activist told me. "You should have seen what we had at our disposal. There was no problem with money, guns or even explosives. We had them all. Friends of ours were simply climbing over fences of the unguarded weapon dumps and walking away with stuff. We really thought we were going to do something which hadn't been done before. The mood of those around Browning was electric. People were reading the stories of Robert Matthews and The Order and saying, 'Yeah we want to do the same.' Some were learning about the concept of leaderless resistance and thought it was the correct thing to do. People were fed up with political parties. Looking back it was all unrealistic but we were well up for it. Perhaps we just got carried away with events."

Epilogue

THIS BOOK WAS to have ended with Combat 18 in decline; indeed, its original sub-heading was to be *The Rise and Fall of Combat 18*. Charlie Sargent was serving a life sentence, while Will Browning was facing trial over an attack on Bloody Sunday demonstrators and seemed to have stepped back from politics. Without its two leaders – and with constant police and media scrutiny – it seemed C18 had nowhere to go. That was before the extraordinary events of the summer of 2001.

Socially, economically and racially, Oldham is little different from the swathe of former textile towns along the "M62 corridor" linking Lancashire and Yorkshire. A blue-collar town in the foothills of the Pennies, seven miles north-east of Manchester, it is still emerging from the collapse of British manufacturing, with some success – it boasts an unemployment rate lower than the national average. Most of the cotton mills have gone, to be replaced by other employers like Ferranti, but the redbrick housing of the stereotypical northern town is ubiquitous. Like the other M62 towns, it also has a substantial ethnic minority community: about twelve per cent of the 219,000 population is of Asian origin.

Where Oldham differs from other towns is in the volatility of its ethnic mix. Tension between whites and Asians, and between the different Asian communities themselves, has been building in the town for several years, though rarely has it made national headlines. That changed when, in April, a BBC radio journalist reported that young Asian men were establishing "no-go" areas for white people in one part of the town. A few days later, the report seemed to be vindicated when seventy-six-year-old Walter

Chamberlin was attacked and badly beaten by four young
Asians as he returned home from a rugby match. Though Mr
Chamberlin and his family viewed the assault as thuggery rather
than racism – and though he was not walking through an Asian
area at the time, as some reports suggested – the media went into
a frenzy and Oldham was catapulted into the spotlight. It was a
godsend to the racist gangs.

Oldham provided C18 with a unique opportunity to play a
role in major racial disturbances. By that summer, the town
was one of the few places left where it could claim any sort of
local unit: up to fifteen Oldham hooligans had attended a C18
gig in Coventry just six weeks before the attack on Walter
Chamberlin. Local activists were also involved in the Fine
Young Casuals (FYC) football mob and had long associations
with racist gangs such as the "Oldham Irregulars" and the
"Fitton Hill Whites". They were perfectly placed to orchestrate
a backlash.

They also had powerful allies from out of town. On April 28,
a week after the attack on Walter Chamberlin, 450 hooligan
followers of Stoke City went on a rampage through the largely
Asian area of Westwood on their way to Oldham's football
ground. Stoke's "Naughty Forty" is one of the largest and most
active soccer gangs in the country and, with a big turnout for
what was their last game of the season, had decided to exact
revenge for the assault on the pensioner. Initially, the Fine
Young Casuals were oblivious to their rivals' intentions and
turned out in the town centre to confront them. A couple of
Oldham hooligans even fired flares into the Stoke mob but were
soon forced to concede that their paltry mob of forty could have
little impact on the hordes of Stoke. A brief discussion between
leading figures from both gangs saw the mobs unite and march
together through Westwood. Cars and houses were attacked as
the hooligans, with no police escort, went through the area like a
marauding army. After the game, which was marred by racial
chanting, the hooligans regrouped for their return walk into
town. This time young Asian men, who were not prepared to see
their areas invaded again, had linked arms and made a defensive

line across the street. Community activists pleaded with police to redirect the racist hooligans away from the estate but to no avail. A police van drove through the Asian lines to clear a path.

Inspired by the Stoke firm, Oldham's racists mobilised other hooligans a week later. The National Front had applied for permission to march through the town and, despite a Home Office ban on all political marches in the town, were determined to show. The NF were, however, a sideshow for the hooligan mobilisation. Various mobs had phoned the FYC pledging support, including even the Burnley "Suicide Squad", who normally counted among Oldham's local rivals. As many as fifteen Stoke returned and were joined on Saturday, May 5, by over twenty from Stockport, ten from Huddersfield and a few from Manchester City and Burnley. Linking up with them were C18 supporters from London and Liverpool. David Tickle from Wigan came with two leading Loyalist Volunteer Force supporters, including one who was on the run from the authorities in Portadown. The numbers out that day would have been even greater had not several Oldham hooligans been on a stag weekend in Shrewsbury.

Over 100 hooligans and nazis began to gather in several Oldham pubs. The police stopped an impromptu march into the main shopping street and held forty racists outside Barclays Bank for several hours but the rest, now numbering about seventy, regrouped in a pub called the Ashton Arms. Though at one point surrounded by police, they were later able slip away and head for another pub on the edge of an Asian area. They were soon spotted by local Asian youths. In the ensuing fight, one Stockport hooligan was stabbed. There was considerable anger in the Asian communities that the police had not contained the thugs earlier in the day.

For the next three weeks, C18 activists in the Fine Young Casuals toured neighbouring towns to drum up support for another mobilisation on May 26. Eight of the FYC travelled to Stoke to meet their hooligans before a play-off match with Wigan. On May 19, one of the FYC went over to Liverpool and linked up with Karl Wilson, an Everton hooligan who had been thrown out of the army for his political activities. Wilson had been present in Oldham on May 5 but this time was urged to bring people with him. On the same day, other C18 hooligans from Oldham were in contact with the Chelsea Headhunters, who were in Manchester for their team's match at Man City. Several Headhunters, who also have a close link with Stockport, had intended to travel through to Oldham after the game but this plan was abandoned because of serious fighting during and after the City game. Another Oldham C18 activist made contact with some Blackpool hooligans. The FYC friendship with thugs from Shrewsbury, Newcastle and Stockport was also utilised. This would be the big one, they were promised.

Saturday, May 26, saw the C18-inspired chain of events that would end in a mass disturbance and put race riots back in the headlines for the first time in years (see Prologue): the gathering of a white mob on the outskirts of Oldham from early morning; the plan to march provocatively through an Asian estate; the repeated attempts to escape the police; and, finally, the incident on the edge of the Glodwick estate that may have sparked the Asian riot.

That day also saw a clash between BNP leader Nick Griffin and two of Will Browning's lieutenants. Griffin was brought to the Britannia pub, where the white mob was gathered, by his Oldham party organiser Mike Treacy. As the two BNP men began to glad-hand some of the local hooligans, Mark Atkinson and Darren Wells wanted a quiet word.

"Daz, shall I do him?" Atkinson asked Wells as they approached the BNP leader.

"No. Let's talk to him first."

The conversation was short and to the point.

"Why do you keep slagging C18 off?" asked Wells.

"I don't," replied Griffin, defensively.

"When you were on trial for *The Rune* magazine you told the judge that the police should be concentrating on C18 publications rather than yours."

"I meant Charlie Sargent and the fact that he was allowed to do what he did while being a police informer. I don't have a problem with Will Browning. When I said that, people had already been done for the Combat 18 magazine so they couldn't have been done again."

"Shall I do him Daz?" Atkinson repeated, much to Griffin's horror.

"Look, I don't have a problem with C18. We shouldn't fall out over petty things, after all, we're all on the same side. We should all pull together."

Griffin's attention was diverted by Treacy, who wanted to introduce him to a hooligan from the nearby Limeside estate. On hearing about the strength of racist sentiments on Limeside, Griffin decided that they should put in an appearance there immediately. Anything to get away from the C18 boys.

The violence of that night was repeated the following evening, when over 200 white youths gathered in an attempt to march on the Asian Glodwick estate. They were prevented by a heavy police presence, but there was again serious trouble. On the Fitton Hill estate, white youths called and then ambushed an Asian taxi driver. Asians again built burning barricades, bombarded the police and firebombed the offices of the *Oldham Evening Chronicle*. A speeding car was driven at police lines, forcing seven officers to dive for cover.

The C18-hooligan network immediately planned yet another attack for the following Saturday. Will Browning, however, was reluctant to get involved, as he was due in court in August and didn't want to make matters worse. This caused a sharp exchange between him and Mark Atkinson, who said the situation demanded sacrifices from everyone, even if it meant prison. London C18 eventually decided to skip the Saturday gathering in Oldham, where they knew the police presence would be huge, and concentrate instead on the England v Pakistan cricket Test match at Old Trafford the following day. With a national TV audience, this would be the perfect opportunity to make a splash. Martin Fielding, the C18 activist from Oldham, and Evertonian Karl Wilson bought bundles of tickets. Some Stockport hooligans also expressed an interest and two cars were arranged from London. Despite his initial reservations, even Browning expressed an interest in going.

The Saturday saw another hooligan turnout, largely orchestrated by Fielding. This time they decided to meet later in the afternoon, again outside the town centre. Over fifty BNP activists were also out leafleting in what was the last Saturday before the Election. It was almost three in the afternoon by the time that Fielding began meeting up with the firm. There was a strong showing from Manchester United, led by a notorious hooligan who, until the late Nineties, had been leader of the Fine Young Casuals. While many United fans were Catholics and generally less nationalist or racist, many of the younger hooligans did not fit this mould. The thirty United boys were matched by a similar number from Oldham plus a smattering from Stockport. The local Limeside Boys were also in the area but remained apart to avoid police detection. Fielding was also in contact with forty Stoke hooligans who were watching the cricket at Old Trafford and who intended to come into town after the end of play. By four in the afternoon, a firm of nearly eighty men was gathered in two pubs, ready to confront the Asians.

In the end their best efforts came to nothing. The police, who received a tip-off about their presence, arrived at the pubs in numbers. After the events of the previous weekend, they were now determined not to let the hooligans run amok again. Fielding and the others were hauled out and lined up against a wall. Photographs were taken, with some of the hooligans even being forced to remove their tops to reveal tee-shirts and tattoos. They were eventually released, but a combination of heavy rain and riot police prevented any major disorder. There was still the cricket the following day.

Browning decided to forego the cricket; he disliked the game even more than football. His non-appearance was further evidence that he was losing interest in nazi politics, though he would never admit this publicly. Two London cars did make the journey, however, bringing ten C18 men. One East Ender brought the C18 banner: the words "Combat 18" above a death's head logo with the motto "Whatever it Takes" written below. An

Oldham lad had promised to run onto the pitch during the match and plant the flag in the wicket; this would not only generate huge publicity but was thought likely to provoke the large and volatile Pakistani support into a riot. The same person had pulled a similar stunt when his football team had been relegated and he had run onto the pitch and stamped a team scarf into the centre circle. Such behaviour had earned him the nickname "the Main Attraction".

Everton hooligans, numbering up to thirty, were the first to arrive at Old Trafford that Sunday morning. Their leader hoped that by dressing up in an English cricket top and white hat, his presence would go unnoticed, but the police were obviously aware of the plans and were intent on stopping the C18 mob and hooligans from getting into the game. The Scousers were blocked from entering the ground and, after the usual photograph session, were told to leave the area. The Oldham and Stockport firms, totalling twenty-five, were also caught; a few who slipped in independently were soon rounded up and evicted. The London contingent heard of the police operation while coming up the motorway; while they knew their chances of getting in would be slim, they felt obliged to persevere. They were greeted by several riot vans and evidence-gathering teams.

Prevented from entering, the C18 group headed to a nearby pub where they waited for the Oldham and Stockport lads to arrive. Even here they were not safe from the police and within a few minutes they had company. Mark Atkinson was pulled out of the pub and made to open up the car for police inspection. He did so grudgingly, knowing that the C18 flag was neatly folded inside a bag. An officer picked it up but unfolded it back-to-front and required other officers to tell him to turn it round before he realised what it was. Atkinson was asked to stand by the flag so the police could take photographs but, unsurprisingly, he declined. The only bit of light relief for the C18 group was when a fellow Londoner, who was sitting in the pub alone, was mistaken for a nazi by the police and was rounded up with them.

It was a frustrating day for the racists. Yet overall, C18's contribution to provoking the Oldham riots had been one of its

most significant acts. Some even claimed it was the start of the
race war they had been propagating since C18's inception in
1992. Paradoxically, it had occurred at a time when C18 was
virtually defunct as a national organisation. Oldham was probably
the only town in the country where they could still boast a proper
unit. This unit was also closely tied up with the local football
hooligan gang – and that was vital. Highly politically-motivated
– something unusual for a soccer gang – the Oldham mob
travelled to meet other gangs to elicit their help and orchestrate
trouble. In turn, the C18 activists from around the country who
responded – though few in number – gave great encouragement
to the locals. Speaking to a BBC news crew a couple of days after
the riots, one Oldham youth said, "C18 came into town to help
us and we were happy to have their support."

★　★　★　★

ON THURSDAY, JUNE 7, 2001, the BNP enjoyed its most successful-
ever General Election. Party chairman Nick Griffin – who
appeared at the count with a gag over his mouth in protest at a
ban on post-result speeches from the rostrum – won 6,552 votes,
or 16.4 per cent of the poll, in the Oldham West and Royton
constituency. This was more than the LibDems and was the
highest-ever nationalist vote in a UK General Election, beating
even the National Front vote in West Bromwich in 1973. In
the other Oldham seat, Oldham East and Saddleworth, BNP
organiser Mick Treacy won 11.2 per cent of the vote, while in
nearby Burnley another BNP candidate gained a similar percent-
age. It became one of the big stories of the Election, with the
smarmy but articulate Griffin appearing on *Newsnight* and the
Today programme to defend his views, carefully tailored for
public consumption.

The racial disorder of that summer had much to do with it.
The events in Oldham were followed by an unexpected wave of
disorder. In Burnley, a weekend of violence climaxed in more
than 200 youths attacking shops homes and vehicles, with riot
police forced to head off fights between whites and Asians. In

July, 200 people were injured and thirty-six arrested in the Manningham district of Bradford after clashes between police and around 1,000 mainly Asian youths in a riot that suprassed even Oldham in its fury. A few days later, police arrested forty-nine whites and Asian after racial clashes in Stoke. Leeds also saw disturbances. These deplorable incidents, and the relative electoral success of the BNP, may suggest a worrying revival of the far-right in British politics; but it is not at all clear (at the time of writing) whether any of it will be sustained.

One man at least seems to have opted out. On Wednesday, August 29, 2001, Will Browning and two others, Matthew Osbury and David Haldane, pleaded guilty to threatening behaviour while protesting at the Bloody Sunday march in London in 1999. They had been charged initially with affray – which they denied – but the prosecution accepted a guilty plea on the lesser charge. The judge agreed that it was clear that Browning and the others had gone into central London that day with the clear desire to disrupt a peaceful protest. Sentencing was deferred for reports until October, when Browning and his co-accused were fined and each ordered to complete eighty hours community service.

It was a relatively minor conviction but one that debilitated C18 as an organisation and Browning personally. Since being charged a year before, the C18 leader had become a political recluse. He played no part in any of the forays north during the summer of 2001, nor had he been abroad on any political business. And he left the court a bitter and angry man. He felt that the prosecution was politically motivated, coming so long after the incident had occurred, and was a consequence of his defeat of Charlie Sargent in the internal C18 leadership feud. He was however, relieved not to be facing a lengthy sentence. To some degree, his trial became a suitable excuse for inaction.

Browning's hatred of Charlie Sargent burns as strong as ever. He still derides the rival Blood and Honour scene as weekend rebels and idiots, and relishes every misfortune or incident that afflicts it. He despises the Kosovans and Albanians – the folk devils of the latest media refugee panic – who he claims are taking "our jobs", and sporadically rails against Asian gang violence. However, he is uninterested in the issues concerning most domestic nazis. "Britain's finished," he is fond of telling people, rather grandly. When leading members of the NF approached him to help attack anti-fascists at a St George's Day march in Leicester, he told friends that he couldn't care less. His mind is focused on the state – its structures and agents. In that, he includes the Sargents. Browning knows that he is not going to achieve anything politically. He has given up hope of igniting racial conflict. But he is still fighting a private war: a war that goes beyond C18, back all the way to the childhood taken from him by authority.

On September 12, 2001, Will Browning contacted an acquaintance on his mobile phone, in a state of high excitement. "Have you seen it? Have you seen the news?" he gabbled. He had just seen live TV footage of the terrorist attack on the twin towers of World Trade Centre in New York; the terrible carnage that killed over 6,000 people. He described the apocalyptic flames, the second hijacked jet crashing into a tower, the famous New York skyline clouded in smoke and dust.

"It's brilliant," gloated Browning. "I haven't laughed so much in ages. I'm applying for my pilot's licence now."

Index